Lecture Notes in Computer Science   12053

More information about this series at http://www.springer.com/series/7407

William J. Bowman · Ronald Garcia (Eds.)

Trends in Functional Programming

20th International Symposium, TFP 2019
Vancouver, BC, Canada, June 12–14, 2019
Revised Selected Papers

 Springer

Editors
William J. Bowman (iD)
University of British Columbia
Vancouver, BC, Canada

Ronald Garcia
University of British Columbia
Vancouver, BC, Canada

ISSN 0302-9743   ISSN 1611-3349 (electronic)
Lecture Notes in Computer Science
ISBN 978-3-030-47146-0   ISBN 978-3-030-47147-7 (eBook)
https://doi.org/10.1007/978-3-030-47147-7

LNCS Sublibrary: SL1 – Theoretical Computer Science and General Issues

This Springer imprint is published by the registered company Springer Nature Switzerland AG
The registered company address is: Gewerbestrasse 11, 6330 Cham, Switzerland

Preface

This volume contains a selection of the papers presented at TFP 2019: the Symposium on Trends in Function Programming 2019, held June 12–14, 2019, in Vancouver, BC, Canada. TFP is an international forum for researchers with interests in all aspects of functional programming, taking a broad view of current and future trends in the area. It aspires to be a lively environment for presenting the latest research results and other contributions, described in draft papers submitted prior to the symposium. This edition of the symposium is the second to use a new format for selecting articles for publication. In the new format, authors can choose to have their submissions formally reviewed either before or after the symposium. Four full papers were submitted for formal review before the symposium, out of which two were accepted by the Program Committee for presentation and later publication. Each submission was reviewed by at least three reviewers. The Program Committee was asked to either accept or reject the paper as usual, but could also elect to reject a paper and invite it for presentation at TFP. For the remaining six submissions, the Program Committee checked that the drafts were within the scope of TFP and thus worthy of presentation at TFP, and provided a full review to an updated submission after the symposium.

The TFP 2019 program consisted of two keynotes, two other invited talks and seven presentations. The keynote talks were given by Nikhil Swamy (Microsoft Research, USA) on "Structuring the Verification of Imperative Programs with Functional Programming," and Frank Wood (University of British Columbia, Canada) on "Probabilistic Programming." Out of the seven presentations, two full papers were accepted for publication before the symposium as mentioned earlier, whereas a further six full papers were submitted to the formal post-refereeing process. The Program Committee selected four more papers for publication from these, which brings us to the total of six that are included in these proceedings.

We are grateful to everyone at University of British Columbia for their help in preparing and organizing TFP 2019, in particular Lara Hall and Holly Kwan. We also gratefully acknowledge the assistance of the TFP 2019 Program Committee and the TFP Steering Committee for their advice while organizing the symposium.

March 2020

William J. Bowman
Ronald Garcia

Organization

General Chairs

William J. Bowman   University of British Columbia, Canada
Ronald Garcia   University of British Columbia, Canada

Program Committee Chairs

William J. Bowman   University of British Columbia, Canada
Ronald Garcia   University of British Columbia, Canada

Program Committee

Stephanie Balzer	Carnegie Mellon University, USA
Matteo Cimini	University of Massachusetts Lowell, USA
Ryan Culpepper	Northeastern University, USA
Joshua Dunfield	Queen's University, Canada
John Hughes	Chalmers University of Technology, Sweden
Sam Lindley	University of Edinburgh, UK and Imperial College London, UK
Assia Mahboubi	Inria, France
Marco T. Morazan	Seton Hall University, USA
Tom Schrijvers	Katholieke Universiteit Leuven, Belgium
Satnam Singh	Google AI, USA
Scott Smith	Johns Hopkins University, USA
Nicolas Wu	Imperial College London, UK
Viktoria Zsok	Eötvös Loránd University, Hungary

Contents

Quotients by Idempotent Functions
in Cedille

Andrew Marmaduke$^{(\boxtimes)}$, Christopher Jenkins, and Aaron Stump

The University of Iowa, Iowa City, IA 52242, USA
{andrew-marmaduke,christopher-jenkins,aaron-stump}@uiowa.edu

Abstract. We present a simple characterization of *definable quotient types* as being induced by idempotent functions, and an encoding of this in Cedille (a dependently typed programming language) in which both equational constraints *and the packaging* that associates these with elements of the carrier type are irrelevant, facilitating equational reasoning in proofs. We provide several concrete examples of definable quotients using this encoding and give combinators for function lifting (with one variant having zero run-time cost).

Keywords: Quotients · Quotient types · Type theory · Cedille

1 Introduction

Every dependently typed programming language has some built-in notion of *definitional equality* of expressions which is induced by its operational semantics. This notion can then be internalized as an equality type within the language, called *propositional equality*. Propositional equality often enjoys a privileged status, with language and library authors providing support for reasoning with it in the form of, e.g., special rewriting syntax or tactics specifically for it. However, it sometimes occurs that the programmer wishes to consider two expressions of some type A equal up to some arbitrary equivalence relation $\sim$, which will not have the same support as propositional equality. Quotient types provide a solution to this problem by allowing the formation of a new type $A/\sim$ for which the equivalence $a \sim b$ corresponds precisely to propositional equality of the *equivalence classes* $[a]$ and $[b]$ of type $A/\sim$.

As an example, the rational numbers constitute an archetypal application of quotients. First, fractions are defined as a pair of two natural numbers. Next, an equivalence relation is defined between fractions such that a/b is equivalent to c/d if and only if $ad = cb$. The quotient type with respect to this equivalence relation constructs the rational numbers. Alternatively, we can decide whether a/b and c/d are equivalent by comparing *canonical representatives* of their equivalence classes, computed by dividing both numerator and denominator by their greatest common divisor. Observe that this canonical choice operation for rationals is necessarily idempotent. Generalizing, it turns out that rational numbers and all other *definable quotient types* (in the sense of Li [15]) can be characterized by

© Springer Nature Switzerland AG 2020
W. J. Bowman and R. Garcia (Eds.): TFP 2019, LNCS 12053, pp. 1–20, 2020.
https://doi.org/10.1007/978-3-030-47147-7_1

the set of fixpoints of some idempotent function on the carrier type. We call this *quotients by idempotent functions*, and to the best of our knowledge are the first to work with this characterization of definable quotients explicitly.

Of course, definable quotients are, for any suitable characterization of them, definable already in existing proof assistants like Agda or Coq [4,15]. In this work, we argue that certain features of Cedille's type theory makes the encoding of our formulation especially simple, as in particular not only are all required proofs erased (as one expects already in theories with proof irrelevance) but indeed the very *packaging* used to associate terms with their equational constraints is *also* erased during equational reasoning. In summary, our contributions are:

1. a novel and simple characterization of definable quotients by *idempotent functions*;
2. an encoding of this characterization that takes advantage of Cedille's extrinsic typing and notion of erasure to allow every definable quotient to be *definitionally equal to* an element of the carrier type;
3. examples of definable quotients formalized in Cedille (with a code repository available at github.com/cedille/cedille-developments/tree/master/idem-quotients) including:
   - a quotiented identity type (the carrier of which lacks decidable equality);
   - naturals modulo some k;
   - the even and odd subset types of naturals considered as quotient types;
   - finite sets as lists whose elements have decidable equality, whose combination with other definable quotient types highlights the advantages of our encoding;
   - integers as a definable quotient *inductive* type, with constructors compatible with the intended equivalence relation and an induction principle in terms of these;
4. combinators for *lifting* of functions, which for compatible functions can be done such that the lifted function is definitionally equal to the original.

This version of the paper improves upon an earlier draft by more clearly identifying the class of quotient types to which quotients by idempotent functions belong, emphasizing that the advantage of our encoding in Cedille is the disappearance in equations of explicit type coercions between quotient and carrier, focusing on examples of quotients by idempotent functions that contribute to the central argument of the paper, and better contextualizing our contributions in the existing literature on quotient types.

We begin the paper with a brief overview of Cedille's type theory and language features (Sect. 2). Next, we give a general definition of quotients by idempotent functions in Cedille and consider several examples (Sect. 3). Then, we present the satisfied properties of and combinators for our quotients by idempotent functions (Sect. 4). After, we consider the benefits and limitations of our work with respect to the existing literature on quotient types (Sect. 5). Finally, we conclude the paper and reflect on our contributions (Sect. 6).

(a) Equality

$$\frac{FV(t\ t') \subseteq dom(\Gamma)}{\Gamma \vdash \beta\{t'\} : \{t \simeq t\}} \qquad \frac{\Gamma \vdash t : \{t_1 \simeq t_2\} \quad \Gamma \vdash t' : [t_2/x]T}{\Gamma \vdash \rho\ t\ @\ x.T - t' : [t_1/x]T} \qquad \frac{\Gamma \vdash t : \{t_1 \simeq t_2\} \quad \Gamma \vdash t_1 : T}{\Gamma \vdash \varphi\ t - t_1\ \{t_2\} : T}$$

$$|\beta\{t'\}| = |t'|, \qquad\qquad |\rho\ t\ @\ x.T - t'| = |t'|, \qquad\qquad |\varphi\ t - t_1\ \{t_2\}| = |t_2|,$$

(b) Dependent Intersection

$$\frac{\Gamma \vdash t_1 : T_1 \quad \Gamma \vdash t_2 : [t_1/x]T_2 \quad |t_1| = |t_2|}{\Gamma \vdash [t_1, t_2] : \iota\,x{:}T_1.\,T_2} \qquad \frac{\Gamma \vdash t : \iota\,x{:}T_1.\,T_2}{\Gamma \vdash t.1 : T_1} \qquad \frac{\Gamma \vdash t : \iota\,x{:}T_1.\,T_2}{\Gamma \vdash t.2 : [t.1/x]T_2}$$

$$|[t_1, t_2]| = |t_1|, \qquad\qquad |t.1| = |t|, \qquad |t.2| = |t|,$$

(c) Implicit Products

$$\frac{\Gamma, x : T \vdash t' : T' \quad x \notin FV(|t'|)}{\Gamma \vdash \Lambda\,x{:}T.\,t' : \forall\,x{:}T.\,T'} \qquad \frac{\Gamma \vdash t : \forall\,x{:}T'.\,T \quad \Gamma \vdash t' : T'}{\Gamma \vdash t\ \text{-}t' : [t'/x]T}$$

$$|\Lambda\,x{:}T.\,t| = |t|, \qquad\qquad |t\ \text{-}t'| = |t|$$

Fig. 1. Typing and erasure for a fragment of Cedille

2   Background

2.1   CDLE

Cedille's core theory is the *Calculus of Dependent Lambda Eliminations* (CDLE) [21,22]. CDLE is an extension of the impredicative extrinsically-typed Calculus of Constructions [5] with three additional type formers: the *dependent intersections* $\iota\,x{:}T_1.\,T_2$ of Kopylov [14]; the *implicit products* $\forall\,x{:}T_1.\,T_2$ of Miquel [18] (which we may write $T_1 \Rightarrow T_2$ if $x \notin FV(T_2)$); and an equality type $\{t_1 \simeq t_2\}$ of untyped terms. The term language of CDLE is just the untyped λ-calculus, so to make type checking algorithmic Cedille requires users provide some type annotations, and definitional equality of terms is modulo *erasure* of these annotations. Figure 1 gives the term annotations in Cedille associated with these additional type constructs and their erasures. In particular, the erasure of the β axiom and dependent intersections is essential to our encoding of quotients by idempotent functions.

Equality $\{t_1 \simeq t_2\}$ is the type of proofs that t_1 and t_2 are equal, where these two terms are only required to be well-scoped. It is introduced with $\beta\{t'\}$ (for an unrelated t', discussed below) if $|t_1|$ and $|t_2|$ (the *erasures* of t_1 and t_2) are $\beta\eta$-convertible. If t has type $\{t_1 \simeq t_2\}$ it can be eliminated using ρ or φ where $\rho\ t\ @\ x.T - t'$ (which erases to $|t'|$) *rewrites* all occurrences of t_2 in the type $[t_2/x]T$ with t_1 using the guide $@\ x.T$, and $\varphi\ t - t_1\ \{t_2\}$ (which erases to $|t_2|$) *casts* t_2 to the type T assuming that t_1 has type T. For convenience in equational reasoning, Cedille allows the guide to be omitted when the type $[t_1/x]T$ of the

ρ-expression is known contextually, and provides the alternative form $\rho+ \ t - t'$ which normalizes the expected type until it finds occurrences of t_1 to rewrite.

The fact that β may erase to an arbitrary (well-scoped) given term is called the *Kleene trick* [22] as it goes back to Kleene's numeric realizability: any evidence at all may stand as proof for a trivially true equation (in Cedille, if β is written without some desired erasure t' then by default it erases to $\lambda x. x$). In practice, when combined with dependent intersections the Kleene trick enables the formation of a kind of *equational subset type* where elements of a carrier type may also act as proof that some equation concerning them holds, provided the equation is indeed true.

Dependent Intersection $\iota \, x : T_1 . \, T_2$ is the type of terms t which can be seen to have *both* the types T_1 and $[t/x]T_2$. The introduction form $[t_1, t_2]$ is conceptually similar to that of a dependent pair, except that $|t_1|$ must be $\beta\eta$-equivalent to $|t_2|$, thus allowing the erasure of this introduced intersection to simply be $|t_1|$. If t has type $\iota \, x : T_1 . \, T_2$, then the projections $t.1$ and $t.2$ resp. have types T_1 and $[t.1/x]T_2$. Both projections erase to $|t|$.

We provide a simple example of the technique employed in our construction of definable quotients in Cedille: assume we have the type Nat of natural numbers with constructor zero: Nat and function pred : Nat → Nat defined in the usual way. Then, the expression $[\text{zero}, \beta\{\text{zero}\}]$ has type $\iota \, x : \text{Nat.} \, \{x \simeq \text{pred } x\}$ and erases to zero.

Implicit Product $\forall \, x : T_1 . \, T_2$ is the type of functions whose argument x of type T_1 is *erased* and thus not used to compute the result value of type T_2. It is introduced by $\Lambda x. t_2$ (which erases to $|t_2|$), provided that t_2 has type T_2 and further that x *does not occur in the erasure of* t_2. If t has type $\forall \, x : T_1 . \, T_2$ and t_1 has type T_1, then we may form an *erased application* t $-t_1$ (which erases to $|t|$) of type $[t_1/x]T_2$. Our use of implicit products in this paper is necessary for the result described in Sect. 4.1 where it allows a function that is *compatible* with an equivalence relation of some carrier type to be lifted to a function over the (definable) quotient in such a way that the lifted function is *definitionally equal* to the original.

Additional term and type constructs not given in Fig. 1 are summarized here. All types are quantified over with $\forall$ (such as $\forall \, X : \star. \, X \to X$) and within terms abstracted over with Λ (such as $\Lambda X. \lambda x. x$). Term-to-type and type-to-type applications are written with a center-dot (such as $t \cdot T$). Local definitions are written $[x \ = \ t] - t'$, analogous to let $x = t$ in t' in other languages. Cedille also provides a built-in operator ς for symmetry of equality – this could be replaced by a definition using ρ but is provided for convenience.

2.2   Datatypes in Cedille

CDLE lacks a primitive notion of inductive datatype. Firsov et al. [7] show how these may be derived *generically* (in the sense of for any covariant signature functor). As of version 1.1.0, the Cedille tool incorporates this result by allowing users to declare inductive datatypes with usual notation. For example, natural numbers and pairs can be declared with:

```
data Nat : ⋆ =
  | zero : Nat
  | succ : Nat → Nat.
```

```
data Pair (A: ⋆) (B: ⋆) = pair : A → B → Pair.
```

Cedille also has facilities for simple pattern-matching using operator μ', and for combined pattern-matching and recursion with operator μ:

```
fst : ∀ A: ⋆. ∀ B: ⋆. Pair·A·B → A
  = Λ A. Λ B. λ p. μ' p { pair a b → a }.
```

```
add : Nat → Nat → Nat
  = λ m. λ n. μ addN. m { zero → n | succ m' → succ (addN m') }.
```

The operational semantics of μ' is case-branch selection, so for example `fst (pair zero (succ zero))` reduces to `zero`. The operational semantics of μ is combined case-branch selection and fixpoint unrolling. For example, for any m and n of type `Nat`, `add (succ m) n` reduces to `succ` (μ' $addN$. m { `zero` → n | `succ` m' → `succ` ($addN$ m')}).

Declared datatypes automatically come with an induction principle invoked by pattern-matching and recursion with μ (and similarly a non-recursive "proof-by-cases" principle invoked by μ'). An example of this is given below in the proof `addZeroRight` showing `zero` is a right-identity of addition.

```
addZeroRight : Π n: Nat. {add n zero ≃ n}
  = λ n. μ ih. n @(λ x: Nat. {add x zero ≃ x}) {
    | zero → β
    | succ n' → ρ (ih n') @ y. {succ y ≃ succ n'} - β
  }.
```

Here, a guiding type annotation is given explicitly with `@` to help type check each case branch, with the bound variable `x` replaced with the corresponding constructor pattern. In the `zero` case the expected type is {`add zero zero` ≃ `zero`}, which holds by β (the Cedille tool also considers the operational semantics of μ and μ' when checking convertibility of terms in an equation). In the `succ` case the expected type is {`add (succ` n'`) zero` ≃ `succ` n'}. A guide for rewriting is given with `@` where the expected type is first checked to be convertible with {`succ (add` n' `zero)` ≃ `succ` n'}, then the inductive hypothesis `ih` n' is used to perform a rewrite, and finally β is checked against type {`succ` n' ≃ `succ` n'}

Cedille uses a *type-based* approach to termination checking of recursive functions defined with μ [13]. However, this method sometimes requires type coercions be used explicitly on the recursive subdata revealed in case patterns. Most of the recursive functions and proofs in this paper do not require the full power of Cedille's termination checker. Thus, for clarity, we remove these type coercions to de-clutter our presentations and indicate explicitly those functions for which a syntactic guard (as described by Giménez [10]) would be insufficient to ensure termination.

3   Quotient Types by Idempotent Functions

3.1   General Construction

We now present in Cedille quotient types by *idempotent functions*, which we prove in Sect. 5 precisely characterizes *definable* quotients.

```
IdemFn : ⋆ → ⋆ = λ A: ⋆. ι f: A → A. Π a: A. {f (f a) ≃ f a}.
```

```
Quotient : Π A: ⋆. IdemFn·A → ⋆
= λ A: ⋆. λ f: IdemFn·A. ι a: A. {f a ≃ a}.
```

```
qcanon : ∀ A: ⋆. Π f: IdemFn·A. A → Quotient·A f
= Λ A. λ f. λ a. [f.1 a, ρ (f.2 a) - β{f.1 a}].
```

For any carrier A, `IdemFn·A` is the type of functions f over A which also prove themselves idempotent. Thanks to the Kleene trick, this obligation amounts to requiring only *that* they are idempotent. Similarly, `Quotient·A f` (for any type A and f : `IdemFn·A`) is the type of elements of A which are the fixpoints of f, and for any element a of the carrier `qcanon f` maps a to a representative of type `Quotient·A f` by simply applying (the first projection of) f to a and discharging the proof obligation that $\{f (f\ a) \simeq f\ a\}$ by idempotency of f. The intended equivalence relation $a \sim b$ on A then implicitly arises from the propositional equality $\{$`qcanon` $a \simeq$ `qcanon` $b\}$, and need not be given explicitly.

Our motivation for this characterization of definable quotients is its two-fold simplicity, which we reinforce with examples given in the remainder of this section: first, the number of required components is small, being only a carrier type, unary operation, and proof this operation is idempotent; second, the additional term-level structure packing components with these properties is all *erasable*, convenient for equational reasoning within proofs and especially so when these proofs concern multiple quotient types. From this second feature arises in particular the pleasing fact that every element of the quotient type is *definitionally equal* to some element of the carrier type. This can be demonstrated within Cedille by a kind of internalized subtyping relation: the existence of a coercion `qcoerce` from `Quotient·A f` (for every A and f) to A which is definitionally equal to $\lambda x. x$.

```
qcoerce : ∀ A: ⋆. ∀ f: IdemFn·A. Quotient·A f → A
= Λ A. Λ f. λ q. q.1 .
```

```
qcoerceId : {qcoerce ≃ λ q. q} = β.
```

3.2 Typed Equality with UIP

An important property of equality within type theory is whether it validates the principle of *uniqueness of identity proofs* (UIP), which is the statement that any two proofs p_1 and p_2 of $\{t_1 \simeq t_2\}$ (for any t_1 and t_2) are themselves equal. The Kleene trick causes Cedille's built-in equality to be anti-UIP because e.g. both $\beta\{\lambda x.\, \lambda y.\, x\}$ and $\beta\{\lambda x.\, \lambda y.\, y\}$ prove $\{\lambda x.\, x \simeq \lambda x.\, x\}$. However, if UIP is desired then it is possible to construct as a definable quotient an equality type Id that validates UIP. This construction is simple but rather interesting as, unlike other examples we consider, the carrier of this quotient type has *undecidable* equality (it contains divergent λ-expressions). Yet, this does not impede our choosing a canonical representative – for any proof eq we return an equivalent proof which erases to $\lambda x.\, x$.

```
eqRep : ∀ A: ⋆. Π a: A. Π b: A. {a ≃ b} → {a ≃ b}
= Λ A. λ a. λ b. λ eq. ρ eq - β.
```

```
eqRepIdemFn : ∀ A: ⋆. Π a: A. Π b: A. IdemFn·{a ≃ b}
= Λ A. λ a. λ b. [eqRep a b, λ eq. β].
```

We retain typing information by using indices for the quotient type Id.

```
Id : Π A: ⋆. A → A → ⋆
= λ A: ⋆. λ a: A. λ b: A. Quotient·{a ≃ b} (eqRepIdemFn a b).
```

Note that we choose a homogeneous identity type for ease of demonstration, but a heterogeneous or untyped version with UIP is also possible. Finally, we prove that Id validates UIP.

```
UIP : ∀ A: ⋆. Π a: A. Π b: A. Π p: Id·A a b. Π q: Id·A a b.
  Id·(Id·A a b) p q
= Λ A. λ a. λ b. λ p. λ q. [ρ ς p.2 - ρ ς q.2 - β, β].
```

3.3 Natural Numbers Modulo k

The natural numbers modulo k is a family of quotient types where two numbers are equivalent modulo k if their remainders with respect to k are equal. Below, we define the remainder function rem[1] and show with remIdem that it is idempotent. Note that some definitions are omitted (indicated by <..>) in the paper but available in the supplementary code repository[2].

---

[1] The listing of function rem omits necessary type coercions for Cedille to ensure that the recursive call on minus n' k' is well-founded.

[2] github.com/cedille/cedille-developments/tree/master/idem-quotients.

```
rem : Nat → Nat → Nat
= λ n. λ k. μ rec. n {
    | zero → zero
    | succ n' →
      [k' = pred k]
      - if (lt n' k') (succ n') (rec (minus n' k'))
  }.
remIdem : Π n: Nat. Π k: Nat. {rem (rem n k) k ≃ rem n k} = <..>


remIdemFn : Π k: Nat. IdemFn·Nat
= λ k. [λ n. rem n k, λ n. ρ+ (remIdem n k) - β{rem n k}].


Mod : Nat → ⋆ = λ k: Nat. Quotient·Nat (remIdemFn k).
```

In the case of Mod k the idempotent function λn. rem n k canonicalizes the input natural number to a value in the range $[0, k-1]$.

Functions on the natural numbers can be lifted to Mod k either by canonicalizing the output or proving that all outputs of the function are fixpoints of rem. For instance, we can lift natural number addition to Mod k by coercion from Mod k to Nat, followed by addition and canonicalization of the output.

```
    addMod : Π k: Nat. Mod k → Mod k → Mod k
    = λ k. λ n. λ m. qcanon (remIdemFn k) (add n.1 m.1).
```

Li argues that definable quotients aid in reasoning about the quotient type because both setoid and set views of the data are available [15]. We show that facts about the carrier type that are preserved in the quotient type can be easily demonstrated. Here, it is easy to show that addMod is commutative and has an identity element by appealing to the fact that add has these properties.

```
    addModComm : Π k: Nat. Π a: Mod k. Π b: Mod k.
      {addMod k a b ≃ addMod k b a}
    = λ k. λ a. λ b.
      ρ (addComm a.1 b.1) @ x. {rem x k ≃ addMod k b a} - β.


    addModIdLeft : Π k: Nat. Π a: Mod k. {addMod k a zero ≃ a}
    = λ k. λ a. ρ (addZeroRight a.1) @ x. {rem x k ≃ a}
      - ρ (a.2) - β.


    addModIdRight : Π k: Nat. Π a: Mod k. {addMod k zero a ≃ a}
    = λ k. λ a. ρ (a.2) - β.
```

Notice in the proofs addModIdLeft and addModIdRight that we may use zero directly when reasoning about it as an identity element for addMod. This is possible thanks to Cedille's equality being for untyped terms, and sensible because we know that (for all k) qcannon (remIdemFn k) zero is zero *by definition*. Thus, explicit canonicalization of zero is neither required nor desired.

3.4   Even and Odd Natural Numbers

As we have seen, the elements of quotients by idempotent functions in Cedille have (definitionally) equal elements in the carrier type. With this property in mind, we construct the type of even natural numbers and odd natural numbers.

```
toEven : Nat → Nat
= λ n. μ rec. n {
  | zero → zero
  | succ n' → μ' n' {
    | zero → zero
    | succ n'' → succ (succ (rec n''))
    }
  }.
toOdd : Nat → Nat = λ n. succ (toEven n).

toEvenIdem : Π n: Nat. {toEven (toEven n) ≃ toEven n} = <..>
toEvenIdemFn : IdemFn·Nat = <..>

toOddIdem : Π n: Nat. {toOdd (toOdd n) ≃ toOdd n} = <..>
toOddIdemFn : IdemFn·Nat = <..>.

Even : ⋆ = Quotient·Nat toEvenIdemFn.
Odd : ⋆ = Quotient·Nat toOddIdemFn.
```

The idempotent function toEven relates every two consecutive natural numbers, picking the smaller number as the canonical representative. The idempotent function toOdd is similar but chooses the larger number instead. The pair of idempotent functions toEven and toOdd define the same equivalence relation with the only difference being which of the two related numbers are picked. This is in contrast to Mod k where the equivalence relation alone gives a desired computational behavior or algebraic structure. Indeed, the algebraic structure of Mod k is present regardless of the selection of the canonical elements. But for Even and Odd as quotients we are interested in the particular fixpoints of the functions toEven and toOdd.

A fundamental property about even numbers is that addition by two produces an even number. By defining addition by two first on the natural numbers we can lift the function to Even. However, unlike the lifting we did previously we can avoid having to apply toEven on the result and instead prove it is *already* a canonical representative.

```
succSucc : Nat → Nat = λ n. succ (succ n).

evenSSCompat : Π e: Even. {toEven (succSucc e) ≃ succSucc e}
= <..>

evenSuccSucc : Even → Even
= λ e. [succSucc e.1, ρ (evenSSCompat e) - β{succSucc e}].
```

Of course, a similar development can be carried out for odd natural numbers. We call this version of function lifting *compatible*, following Cohen [4]. With compatible lifting the resulting function is definitionally equal to the original function.

A core benefit to our approach is that we can mention elements of the carrier type and the quotient type in equational contexts without any additional type coercions such as projections for dependent records. In a property that decomposes a natural number into an even or odd number we can directly say that the natural number is equal to the corresponding even or odd number (in the return type of evenOrOdd below, Or is the disjoint union type, and the dependent intersections should be read as a kind of existential quantification):

```
evenOrOdd : Π n: Nat. Or·(ι x: Even. {n ≃ x})·(ι x: Odd. {n ≃ x})
= <..>
```

3.5 List as Finite Set

As Cohen argued, quotients are a useful feature in formalizing mathematics [4]. However, they can also be a useful abstraction for computer science. As an example, finite sets are usually defined in terms of trees where an order on the elements is needed. With quotients, we can instead form finite sets as an abstraction over those lists whose elements have decidable equality.

```
EqFn : ⋆ → ⋆ = λ A: ⋆. ι f: A → A → Bool.
   (Π a: A. Π b: A. {f a b ≃ true} ⇒ {a ≃ b}).

distinctCons : ∀ A: ⋆. EqFn·A → A → List·A → List·A
= Λ A. λ eq. λ a. λ l. μ' (find eq a l) {
   | tt → l
   | ff → cons a l
   }.

distinct : ∀ A: ⋆. EqFn·A → List·A → List·A
= Λ A. λ eq. λ l. μ rec. l {
   | nil → nil·A
   | cons a l → distinctCons eq a (rec l)
   }.

distinctIdem : ∀ A: ⋆. Π eq: EqFn·A. Π l: List·A.
   {distinct eq (distinct eq l) ≃ distinct eq l} = <..>
distinctIdemFn : ∀ A: ⋆. Π eq: EqFn·A. IdemFn·(List·A) = <..>

ListSet : Π A: ⋆. EqFn·A → ⋆
= λ A: ⋆. λ eq: EqFn·A. Quotient·(List·A) distinctIdemFn.
```

We need an equality function that decides the equality of terms of the parameter type in order to prove that distinct is idempotent. A quotient of List provides a guarantee about the list that does not alter the underlying structure and does not need to be proven because the list can always be canonicalized. If we allow ourselves an ordering on the elements of A in addition to decidable equality, then we could quotient by a `sort` function to construct a `SortedList` type. Alternatively, we could quotient a tree instead of a list to form a `TreeSet` type.

Throughout the paper, we have highlighted that elements of the quotient type are definitionally equal to certain elements of the carrier type. The advantage of our encoding, and its interaction with Cedille's equality type, is most apparent in the combination of `ListSet` with other definable quotient types. If for example we wished to define a specialized notion of equality between `List·Nat` and `ListSet·Even`, it would be as simple as asking that two terms are equal.

```
EqEvenSet1 : List·Nat → ListSet·Even eqEven → ⋆
  = λ l1: List·Nat. λ l2: ListSet·Even eqEven. {l1 ≃ l2}.
```

However, if we were to use an encoding of definable quotients based on a dependent record or pair type, we would be required to use a homogeneous equality type like `Id` (Sect. 3.2) and explicit coercions between the two sets of quotient and carrier types.

```
EqEvenSet2 : List·Nat → ListSet·Even eqEven → ⋆
  = λ l1: List·Nat. λ l2: ListSet·Even eqEven.
    Id·(List·Nat) l1
      (map (qcoerce -evenIdemFn)
        (qcoerce -(distinctIdemFn eqEven) l2)).
```

With `EqEvenSet1 l1 l2` we know that `l1` and `l2` are (propositionally) equal. An intrinsically typed theory (like Coq or Agda) however must use `EqEvenSet2`, where `qcoerce` would be implemented by record accessors or product projections rather than an identity function. As such, they would remain in proof obligations unless explicitly discharged, meaning for this example we would have to more carefully track coercions for the `ListSet` *and* the `Even` elements when manipulating terms in proofs.

3.6   Quotient Inductive Integers

In prior examples where the carrier type had an induction principle, we would expect that the quotient type constructed from it is also inductive with respect to some canonicity-preserving constructors. Take for example a non-canonical encoding of integers (which we call the pre-integers).

```
data PreInt : ⋆ =
  | pzero : PreInt
  | psucc : PreInt → PreInt
  | ppred : PreInt → PreInt.
```

When phrased as a quotient inductive type, the definition includes the following axioms.

```
spCancel : Π p: PreInt. {psucc (ppred p) ≃ p}
psCancel : Π p: PreInt. {ppred (psucc p) ≃ p}
```

However, these axioms are false because of how type theories like Cedille, Agda, and Coq encode the constructors of `PreInt`. To fix this problem the axioms must be considered as part of the definition of the type. In systems like Cubical Agda the solution is to extend the notion of inductive types to higher inductive types which are allowed to specify path constructors that may depend on previously defined constructors [24]. The underlying semantics of the system then encodes the type appropriately so that all path constructors are satisfied.

With quotient types by idempotent functions we can take a different approach to the problem by defining canonicity-preserving constructors on the type `PreInt`:

```
psucc' : PreInt → PreInt
= λ p. μ' p {
  | pzero → psucc pzero
  | psucc x → psucc (psucc x)
  | ppred x → x
  }.
ppred' : PreInt → PreInt
= λ p. μ' p {
  | pzero → ppred pzero
  | psucc x → x
  | ppred x → ppred (ppred x)
  }.
```

We do not need to define a `pzero'` constructor because it would be definitionally equal to `pzero`. Next, we define the idempotent function which induces the intended equivalence relation by noticing that it should replace every `PreInt` constructor with the corresponding canonicity-preserving version.

```
integer : PreInt → PreInt
= λ p. μ rec. p {
  | pzero → pzero
  | psucc x → psucc' (rec x)
  | ppred x → ppred' (rec x)
  }.
```

When a quotient type is designed with the constructors (`psucc'` and `ppred'`) first and the canonizer (`integer`) second, then the proof that the canonizer is idempotent is equivalent to knowing that the constructors commute with it. To show that `psucc'` and `ppred'` commute with `integer` we need to know that the equational axioms hold. That is, we need to show that the canonical choice for any pre-integer satisfies the cancellation axioms of the canonicity-preserving constructors.

```
EqSP : PreInt → ⋆ = λ p: PreInt. {psucc' (ppred' p) ≃ p}.
eqSP : Π p: PreInt. EqSP (integer p) = <..>

EqPS : PreInt → ⋆ = λ p: PreInt. {ppred' (psucc' p) ≃ p}.
eqPS : Π p: PreInt. EqPS (integer p) = <..>

integerIdem : Π p: PreInt. {integer (integer p) ≃ integer p}
= <..>
integerIdemFn : IdemFn·PreInt = <..>
```

With these lemmas, eqSP and eqPS, the function integer can be shown idempotent without difficulty.

Next, we define the quotient type Int, its corresponding constructors, and prove the cancellation properties.

```
Int : ⋆ = Quotient·PreInt integerIdemFn.

izero : Int = [pzero, β{pzero}].
isucc : Int → Int = <..>
ipred : Int → Int = <..>
sp : Π i: Int. {isucc (ipred i) ≃ i} = <..>
ps : Π i: Int. {ipred (isucc i) ≃ i} = <..>
```

Finally, we can prove an induction principle on Int that references the quotient constructors by induction on the underlying PreInt.

```
induct : ∀ P: Int → ⋆. P izero →
    (Π x: Int. P x → P (isucc x)) →
    (Π y: Int. P y → P (ipred y)) →
    Π i: Int. P i = <..>
```

Furthermore, we can use the induction principle to define addition on the quotient inductive integers as expected.

```
iadd : Int → Int → Int
= λ x. λ y. induct·(λ x: Int. Int) y
    (λ a. λ b. isucc b)
    (λ a. λ b. ipred b)
    x.
```

In contrast to a Cubical Agda definition of quotient inductive integer our construction does not mention a coherence condition about the equational constraints ps and sp. Both the coherence condition and the set truncation condition described by Pinyo and Altenkirch [20] are not true for the equality type of Cedille. However, the type PreInt has a decidable equality. This implies that Int also has a decidable equality because every element can be coerced to an element in PreInt. Thus, construction of quotient inductive types using idempotent functions will always have decidable equalities if the underlying carrier type does. This means that these types, in a Homotopy Type Theory setting, are already sets which is why a coherence condition is not needed. Also, it is important to note that quotient inductive types, as described in Cubical Agda, are more expressive than quotients by idempotent functions. Indeed, we have only the *definable* quotient inductive types.

4 Properties of Quotient Types by Idempotent Functions

In the literature several desired properties of quotient types are listed. Li lists soundness and completeness of the canonicalization function relative to the equivalence relation as requirements [15]. Cohen lists, additionally, a surjection property and lifting properties [4]. First, we briefly demonstrate that some of these properties trivially hold for quotients by idempotent functions. Second, we demonstrate function and property lifting in Sect. 4.1.

In this section we will use abbreviations for the idempotent function, carrier type, and quotient type.

```
import quotient-defs.
module quotient (A: ⋆) (f: IdemFn·A).
Q : ⋆ = Quotient·A f.
canon : A → Q = λ a. qcanon f a.
```

Here, `quotient-defs` contains the definitions found in the beginning of Sect. 3. Now, we define the equivalence relation `Equiv` on `A` that arises from f and show that `canon` is sound and complete (as defined by Li for definable quotients) with respect to it.

```
Equiv : A → A → ⋆ = λ a: A. λ b: A. {f a ≃ f b}.
```

```
sound : Π a: A. Π b: A. Equiv a b → {canon a ≃ canon b}
= λ a. λ b. λ eq. eq.
```

```
complete : Π a: A. Equiv (f.1 a) a
= λ a. ρ (f.2 a) @ x. {x ≃ f a} - β.
```

In Sect. 5 we expand on the equivalence between Li's definable quotients and quotients by idempotent functions. It is also straightforward to show the surjection property of Cohen.

```
surjection : Π q: Q. ι a: A. {q ≃ canon a}
= λ q. [q.1, ρ ς q.2 @ a. {a ≃ canon a} - β{q.1}].
```

Function and property lifting are more interesting in Cedille because `Q` terms have corresponding `A` terms that are definitionally equal.

4.1 Function and Property Lifting

When working with the quotient type `Q`, there may be functions on the carrier type `A` that would be useful to use on `Q`. We have seen this briefly already for both `Mod k` (where addition on `Nat` was lifted) and `Even` (where applying the successor twice on `Nat` was lifted). These two applications are different. Addition on `Nat` was lifted by restricting the input arguments and canonicalizing the output.

Successor twice on `Nat` was lifted by proving that the output returns a canonical element for any canonical input.

We abstract lifting by *canonicalization* to automatically lift any simply typed function on `A` to a simply typed function (with the same shape) on `Q`. This requires that the output of any higher-order inputs are also canonicalized. To accomplish this in Cedille we use an inductive relation `IsSimple`.

```
data IsSimple : (⋆ → ⋆) → ⋆ =
  | base : IsSimple·(λ x: ⋆. x)
  | any : ∀ T: ⋆. IsSimple·(λ x: ⋆. T)
  | arrow : ∀ A: ⋆ → ⋆. ∀ B: ⋆ → ⋆.
    IsSimple·A → IsSimple·B → IsSimple·(λ x: ⋆. A·x → B·x).
```

```
liftByCanon : ∀ F: ⋆ → ⋆.
  IsSimple·F → Pair·(F·A → F·Q)·(F·Q → F·A) = <..>
```

This construction allows for both instances of `A` where it is replaced by `Q` (using the `base` constructor) and also instances of `A` that are not replaced (using the `any` constructor). In the unary case applying `liftByCanon` is definitionally equal to applying `canon` on the output of the operation.

```
liftByCanon1 : (A → A) → Q → Q
= λ op. (fst (liftByCanon (arrow base base))) op.
```

```
liftByCanon1' : (A → A) → Q → Q
= λ op. λ q. canon (op q.1).
```

```
liftByCanon1Eq : Π op: A → A.
  {liftByCanon1 op ≃ liftByCanon1' op}
= λ op. β.
```

Although lifting by canonicalization is very flexible there may be some idempotent functions that are either expensive to compute or would otherwise be unnecessary to re-apply. For example, applying a `filter` function over a `ListSet` would not invalidate the fact that it is a fixpoint of `distinct` but reapplying `distinct` to the output of `filter` will change the complexity from linear to quadratic. This is because `distinct` replaces every `cons` with the `distinct_cons` operation, every application of which destructs and rebuilds (in linear time) the entire list set. To avoid this, an additional compatibility property about the operation to be lifted needs to be proven.

```
Compatible : Π T: ⋆. (T → A) → ⋆
= λ T: ⋆. λ op: T → A. Π t: T. {f (op t) ≃ op t}.
```

```
liftArg : ∀ R: ⋆. Π op: A → R. Q → R
= Λ R. λ op. λ q. op q.1.
```

```
lift : ∀ T: ⋆. Π op: T → A. Compatible·T op ⇒ T → Q
= Λ T. λ op. Λ c. λ t. [op t, ρ (c t) - β{op t}].
```

Knowing that the operation is compatible with the idempotent function is only necessary for lifting the return type of the operation op. Lifting arguments of the function, as long as they are not higher order arguments, is always possible. With liftArg and lift binary functions can be lifted by applying inputs to the operation in the compatibility evidence.

> lift2 : Π op: (A → A → A). (Π a: A. Compatible·A (op a))
> ⇒ Q → Q → Q
> = λ op. Λ c. λ x. liftArg (lift (op x.1) -(c x.1)).

A similar approach is possible for any n-ary function. As expected, compatible lifting will return a definitionally equal operation.

> liftArgId : ∀ R: ⋆. Π op: A → R. {liftArg op ≃ op}
> = Λ T. λ op. β.

> liftId : ∀ T: ⋆. Π op: T → A. {lift op ≃ op}
> = Λ T. λ op. β.

Aside from lifting functions we also wish to lift properties. Given a property on A we lift it to a property on Q by forgetting the fixpoint evidence.

> Lift : (A → ⋆) → Q → ⋆ = λ P: A → ⋆. λ q: Q. P q.1.

> dlift : ∀ P: A → ⋆. (Π a: A. P a) → Π q: Q. Lift·P q
> = Λ P. λ p. λ q. p q.1.

Alternatively, as stated by Hofmann, we have quotient induction where we start with a property on Q and show that it holds for all elements of Q if it holds for the canonical representatives of elements of A.

> qind : ∀ B: Q → ⋆. (Π a: A. B (canon a)) → Π q: Q. B q
> = Λ B. λ c. λ q. ρ ς q.2 - c q.1.

Quotient induction lets us prove, by induction on A, a fact about the quotient type. However, this is not the same as being able to perform induction directly on Q using canonicity-preserving constructors as we showed for quotient inductive integers in Sect. 3.6.

5 Related Work

Quotients have been explored in several existing systems including: Agda, Coq, HOL Light, NuPRL, and others. We survey the existing literature and comment on what is relevant to results presented in this work.

Definable quotients as given by Li [15] are closely related to quotients by idempotent functions. In Li's thesis he formalizes, in Agda, examples of definable quotients and additionally proves that not all quotients of interest are definable. One such example is unordered pairs that lack a total ordering of its components. The type of unordered pairs is also undefinable with an idempotent function. Indeed, the idempotent function must either keep the order of elements or swap the elements and neither choice is fixed without an imposed order.

Li also provides and proves equivalent to definability a notion of *quotients by normalization*. We now show that our formulation of *quotients by idempotent functions* is an equivalent condition to this. The quotient $A/\sim$ of a setoid $(A, \sim)$ is definable by normalization if:

1. there is a function $f : A \to A$;
2. which is *sound*, $\forall a, b : A,\ a \sim b \Rightarrow f(a) = g(b)$;
3. and *complete*, $\forall a : A.\ f(a) \sim a$

and definable by an idempotent function if:

1. there is a function $g : A \to A$;
2. which is *idempotent*, $\forall a : A.\ g(g(a)) = g(a)$;
3. and is *image equivalent*, $\forall a, b : A.\ a \sim b \Leftrightarrow g(a) = g(b)$

Theorem 1. *The two conditions above on setoid $(A, \sim)$ are equivalent.*

Proof. ($\Rightarrow$) Assume a function f which is sound and complete. We wish to provide some function which is idempotent and image equivalent. We pick f: for all $a : A$, we have by completeness that $f(a) \sim a$, and applying soundness to this yields $f(f(a)) = f(a)$, so f is idempotent. For all $a, b : A$, we have already by soundness that $a \sim b \Rightarrow f(a) = f(a)$, and assuming that $f(a) = f(b)$ we have by completeness that $a \sim f(a) = f(b) \sim b$, so f is image equivalent.

($\Leftarrow$) Assume a function g which is idempotent and image equivalent. We wish to provide some function which is sound and complete. Pick g: we have soundness as a direct consequence of image equivalence. For all $a : A$, we have by idempotence that $g(g(a)) = g(a)$, so by image equivalence we have $g(a) \sim a$ showing g is complete.   □

In Coq, Cohen [4] developed two notions of quotient types. The first consists of two functions $pi : Q \to T$ and $repr : T \to Q$ where $\forall x : T.\ pi(repr(x)) = x$; much like as in our presentation, the equivalence relation $x \sim y$ then arises from the equality $repr\ x = repr\ y$. The second notion arises from carrier types T with a *choice structure* which guarantees that, for every equivalence relation, labeled $\sim$, there exists a canonical choice operation $canon : T \to T$ [9]. In translating from the second notion of quotient to the first, Cohen shows that choice structure guarantees that $canon$ is idempotent and defines the quotient type Q as a dependent record containing an element of T and a proof that it is a fixpoint of $canon$. Though this is similar to quotients by idempotent functions, we start with the requirement that the canonical choice operation is idempotent rather than deriving it as a consequence of the seemingly stronger requirement that T has a choice structure.

Moreover, because Coq is an intensional type theory the packaging of the dependent record will not be erased when reasoning about terms of the quotient type Q. Also, the lack of a truly heterogeneous equality type (as opposed to *John Major* equality [17]) in Coq will prevent the direct equational reasoning between carrier and quotient type that is possible in Cedille. This situation is also the same for constructing quotient by idempotent functions in Agda: even using *Prop* or irrelevant record fields so that Q is in a sense a subtype of T, it is not the case that every q of type Q is definitionally equal to some element of type T, and so coercions between these the two must be managed explicitly when performing equational reasoning.

Quotient types in type theory have been studied as early as the 1990s with Hofmann's work on interpreting quotient types in both predicative and impredicative variants of the Calculus of Constructions [11]. Hofmann's work is expanded upon by Veltri who works with impredicative encodings and some additional primitive types to show versions of dependent lifting for quotients [23]. The approach of utilizing normalization is explored in Courtieu's work where he expands the Calculus of Inductive Constructions with type constructors for "normalized types" [6].

Outside of intensional proof assistants like Coq and Agda, Nogin has worked on modular definitions of quotients in the NuPRL system to ease the development burden when using quotients [19]. Prior to Nogin's work NuPRL included quotients as a primitive construct. In modern NuPRL types are identified as partial equivalence relations and quotient types are constructed from this interpretation directly [2]. Quotients are also defined and used in HOL Light and similar systems [12].

In this work we have focused on definable quotient types, but there are several interesting quotients that do not fit into this category. For instance, higher inductive types (of which quotient inductive types are a special case) have been used to model type theory in type theory [1] and finite sets [8]. With the existence of a small core of higher inductive types (one of which is the higher inductive quotient), all set-truncated higher inductive types have been shown to be derivable [25]. Although there are some quotient inductive types that can be modeled as quotients by idempotent functions (such as the quotient inductive integers) it is clear that quotient inductive types are a more expressive formalism.

The presence of non-definable quotients in type theories can have significant consequences. Indeed, Maietti demonstrates that when effective quotients are added to constructive set theory and two universes are postulated that the law of the excluded middle holds for small sets [16]. Likewise, Chicli et al. show in Coq that if quotients of functions spaces are available, where all such quotients have a section mapping, and there is an impredicative universe then the theory is inconsistent [3]. With a theory like Cedille that does not have a universe hierarchy and has impredicative quantification, caution must be used in extending the theory with undefinable quotients (or more generally higher inductive types) as it could make the theory inconsistent.

6   Conclusions

In this work we have described a novel and relatively simple characterization of definable quotient types by idempotent functions, and described an encoding of it within Cedille. We have presented concrete examples of quotient types: an equality type with UIP, naturals modulo k, the even and odd subset of naturals, finite sets (and their combination with even numbers), and a quotiented integer type with an induction principle. We have also developed function lifting operations, showing that in particular compatible functions can be lifted to a definitionally equal function over the quotient type. Moreover, dependent intersection and the Kleene trick in Cedille allow full erasure of the *packaging* of elements of a carrier type with proofs they are fixpoints of some idempotent function, meaning no explicit coercions between the quotient and carrier type are needed for equational reasoning, as would be the case for a similar encoding in other dependently typed languages like Coq and Agda.

We are interested in expanding on this work by investigating what equational constraints for higher inductive types would always guarantee that it is a definable quotient inductive type, and thus derivable within CDLE. Also, in Cedille a notion of (Mendler-style) histomorphism is derivable that allows for more flexibility in recursive definitions [7]. We have shown that induction is possible in terms of the quotient constructors, but we also want to extend this result to histomorphisms on the quotient type.

References

1. Altenkirch, T., Kaposi, A.: Type theory in type theory using quotient inductive types. In: Proceedings of the 43rd Annual ACMSIGPLAN-SIGACT Symposium on Principles of Programming Languages, POPL 2016, vol. 51, pp. 18–29. ACM (2016)
2. Anand, A., Bickford, M., Constable, R.L., Rahli, V.: A type theory with partial equivalence relations as types. In: 20th International Conference on Types for Proofs and Programs (2014)
3. Chicli, L., Pottier, L., Simpson, C.: Mathematical quotients and quotient types in Coq. In: Geuvers, H., Wiedijk, F. (eds.) TYPES 2002. LNCS, vol. 2646, pp. 95–107. Springer, Heidelberg (2003). https://doi.org/10.1007/3-540-39185-1_6
4. Cohen, C.: Pragmatic quotient types in Coq. In: Blazy, S., Paulin-Mohring, C., Pichardie, D. (eds.) ITP 2013. LNCS, vol. 7998, pp. 213–228. Springer, Heidelberg (2013). https://doi.org/10.1007/978-3-642-39634-2_17
5. Coquand, T., Huet, G.: The calculus of constructions. Ph.D. thesis, INRIA (1986)
6. Courtieu, P.: Normalized types. In: Fribourg, L. (ed.) CSL 2001. LNCS, vol. 2142, pp. 554–569. Springer, Heidelberg (2001). https://doi.org/10.1007/3-540-44802-0_39
7. Firsov, D., Blair, R., Stump, A.: Efficient mendler-style lambda-encodings in cedille. In: Avigad, J., Mahboubi, A. (eds.) ITP 2018. LNCS, vol. 10895, pp. 235–252. Springer, Cham (2018). https://doi.org/10.1007/978-3-319-94821-8_14
8. Frumin, D., Geuvers, H., Gondelman, L., Weide, N.V.D.: Finite sets in homotopy type theory. In: Proceedings of the 7th ACM SIGPLAN International Conference on Certified Programs and Proofs, pp. 201–214. ACM (2018)
9. Garillot, F., Gonthier, G., Mahboubi, A., Rideau, L.: Packaging mathematical structures. In: Berghofer, S., Nipkow, T., Urban, C., Wenzel, M. (eds.) TPHOLs 2009. LNCS, vol. 5674, pp. 327–342. Springer, Heidelberg (2009). https://doi.org/10.1007/978-3-642-03359-9_23
10. Giménez, E.: Codifying guarded definitions with recursive schemes. In: Dybjer, P., Nordström, B., Smith, J. (eds.) TYPES 1994. LNCS, vol. 996, pp. 39–59. Springer, Heidelberg (1995). https://doi.org/10.1007/3-540-60579-7_3

11. Hofmann, M.: A simple model for quotient types. In: Dezani-Ciancaglini, M., Plotkin, G. (eds.) TLCA 1995. LNCS, vol. 902, pp. 216–234. Springer, Heidelberg (1995). https://doi.org/10.1007/BFb0014055

12. Homeier, P.V.: A design structure for higher order quotients. In: Hurd, J., Melham, T. (eds.) TPHOLs 2005. LNCS, vol. 3603, pp. 130–146. Springer, Heidelberg (2005). https://doi.org/10.1007/11541868_9

13. Jenkins, C., McDonald, C., Stump, A.: Elaborating inductive datatypes and course-of-values pattern matching to Cedille. CoRR (2019). http://arxiv.org/abs/1903.08233

14. Kopylov, A.: Dependent intersection: a new way of defining records in type theory. In: Proceedings of the 18th Annual IEEE Symposium on Logic in Computer Science, LICS 2003. IEEE Computer Society, Washington, DC (2003)

15. Li, N.: Quotient types in type theory. Ph.D. thesis, University of Nottingham (2015)

16. Maietti, M.E.: About effective quotients in constructive type theory. In: Altenkirch, T., Reus, B., Naraschewski, W. (eds.) TYPES 1998. LNCS, vol. 1657, pp. 166–178. Springer, Heidelberg (1999). https://doi.org/10.1007/3-540-48167-2_12

17. McBride, C.: Elimination with a motive. In: Callaghan, P., Luo, Z., McKinna, J., Pollack, R., Pollack, R. (eds.) TYPES 2000. LNCS, vol. 2277, pp. 197–216. Springer, Heidelberg (2002). https://doi.org/10.1007/3-540-45842-5_13

18. Miquel, A.: The implicit calculus of constructions extending pure type systems with an intersection type binder and subtyping. In: Abramsky, S. (ed.) TLCA 2001. LNCS, vol. 2044, pp. 344–359. Springer, Heidelberg (2001). https://doi.org/10.1007/3-540-45413-6_27

19. Nogin, A.: Quotient types: a modular approach. In: Carreño, V.A., Muñoz, C.A., Tahar, S. (eds.) TPHOLs 2002. LNCS, vol. 2410, pp. 263–280. Springer, Heidelberg (2002). https://doi.org/10.1007/3-540-45685-6_18

20. Pinyo, G., Altenkirch, T.: Integers as a higher inductive type. In: 24th International Conference on Types for Proofs and Programs (2018)

21. Stump, A.: The calculus of dependent lambda eliminations. J. Funct. Program. **27**, e14 (2017)

22. Stump, A.: Syntax and semantics of Cedille (2018). https://arxiv.org/abs/1806.04709

23. Veltri, N.: Two set-based implementations of quotients in type theory. In: Proceedings of the 14th Symposium on Programming Languages and Software Tools, pp. 194–205 (2015)

24. Vezzosi, A., Mörtberg, A., Abel, A.: Cubical agda: a dependently typed programming language with univalence and higher inductive types, vol. 3, p. 87. ACM (2019)

25. van der Weide, N., Geuvers, H.: The construction of set-truncated higher inductive types. In: Thirty-Fifth Conference on the Mathematical Foundations of Programming Semantics (2019)

Early Experience in Teaching
the Basics of Functional Language Design
with a Language Type Checker

Matteo Cimini[(✉)]

University of Massachusetts Lowell, Lowell, MA 01854, USA
`matteo_cimini@uml.edu`

Abstract. In this paper we set forth the thesis that a language type checker can be an effective tool in teaching language design principles of functional languages. We have used *TypeSoundnessCertifier*, a tool for type checking languages and certifying their soundness, in the context of a graduate course in programming languages. In this paper we offer details on how the course took place, and we report on some data gathered during evaluations. Although the work reported in this paper is not statistically significant, we share our experience to show the type of studies that we are conducting, and to inspire similar and larger studies towards gathering evidence for, or against, our thesis.

Keywords: Language design · Teaching · Functional languages

1 Background

In this paper, we share our experience in teaching one instance of a course in programming languages. The name of the course is *Design of Programming Languages*. The course has been a semester long graduate level course. The first half of the course covered programming languages theory, and two key learning outcomes of this part are:

1 Understanding basic methods and tools of programming languages theory. This includes that students must be able to read and write grammars and semantics of language definitions.
2 Using such tools in the design of toy functional languages that are type sound.

What Basic Methods and Tools? Much emphasis has been allocated in exposing students to the theory and practice of defining programming languages the way they are typically shared within the research community. Although there are many approaches to the formal semantics of programming languages, and there is no consensus as to which approach is the best, the approach with small step operational semantics seems to be one of the most widespread. We have then used this approach, also adopted in standard textbooks [10,11].

© Springer Nature Switzerland AG 2020
W. J. Bowman and R. Garcia (Eds.): TFP 2019, LNCS 12053, pp. 21–37, 2020.
https://doi.org/10.1007/978-3-030-47147-7_2

Types $T ::= \text{Int} \mid T \to T \mid \text{List } T$
Expressions $e ::= x \mid \lambda x : T.e \mid e\,e \mid \text{nil} \mid \text{cons } e\,e$
              $\mid \text{head } e \mid \text{tail } e \mid \text{error}$
Value $v ::= \lambda x.e \mid \text{nil} \mid \text{cons } v\,v$
Errors $er ::= \text{error}$
Contexts $E ::= E\,e \mid v\,E \mid \text{cons } E\,e \mid \text{cons } v\,E$
              $\mid \text{head } E \mid \text{tail } E$

Type System $\boxed{\Gamma \vdash e : T}$

$$
\frac{\Gamma, x : T_1 \vdash e : T_2}{\Gamma \vdash \lambda x : T_1.e : T_1 \to T_2} \; (\text{T-LAMBDA})
\qquad
\frac{\Gamma \vdash e_1 : T_1 \to T_2 \qquad \Gamma \vdash e_2 : T_1}{\Gamma \vdash e_1\,e_2 : T_2} \; (\text{T-APP})
$$

$$
\frac{}{\Gamma \vdash \text{nil} : \text{List } T} \; (\text{T-NIL})
\qquad
\frac{\Gamma \vdash e_1 : T \qquad \Gamma \vdash e_2 : \text{List } T}{\Gamma \vdash \text{cons } e_1\,e_2 : \text{List } T} \; (\text{T-CONS})
$$

$$
\frac{\Gamma \vdash e : \text{List } T}{\Gamma \vdash \text{head } e : T} \; (\text{T-HEAD})
\qquad
\frac{\Gamma \vdash e : \text{List } T}{\Gamma \vdash \text{tail } e : \text{List } T} \; (\text{T-TAIL})
\qquad
\frac{}{\Gamma \vdash \text{error} : T} \; (\text{T-ERROR})
$$

Dynamic Semantics $\boxed{e \longrightarrow e}$

$$
(\lambda x : T.e)\, v \longrightarrow e[v/x] \qquad\qquad (\text{BETA})
$$
$$
\text{head nil} \longrightarrow \text{error} \qquad\qquad (\text{R-HEAD-NIL})
$$
$$
\text{head (cons } v_1\,v_2) \longrightarrow v_1 \qquad\qquad (\text{R-HEAD-CONS})
$$
$$
\text{tail nil} \longrightarrow \text{error} \qquad\qquad (\text{R-TAIL-NIL})
$$
$$
\text{tail (cons } v_1\,v_2) \longrightarrow v_2 \qquad\qquad (\text{R-TAIL-CONS})
$$

$$
\frac{e \longrightarrow e'}{E[e] \longrightarrow E[e']} \; (\text{CTX})
\qquad\qquad
E[er] \longrightarrow er \;\; (\text{ERR-CTX})
$$

Fig. 1. A simply typed lambda-calculus with lists.

To make an example of a language defined with this approach, Fig. 1 shows the definition of a simply typed lambda-calculus with lists (Int only serves as a base type). The language definition includes a BNF grammar for the syntax of the language. With the grammar, language designers declare types and expressions. Next, language designers decide which expressions constitute *values*. These are the possible results of successful computations. Similarly, the language designer may define which expressions constitute *errors*, which are possible outcomes of computations when something goes wrong. The syntactic category *evaluation contexts* declares within which context we allow reduction to take place.

A language definition also includes inference rules that are used to populate relations that are of interest for the language at hand. These are inductive definitions, typically. Archetypical examples of such relations are a typing judgement, with shape $\Gamma \vdash e : T$ in the particular example of Fig. 1, and a reduction relation, with shape $e \longrightarrow e$ in Fig. 1. Inference rules are a convenient medium to formally define relations.

Learning outcome **1** prescribes that students be fluent in understanding language definitions like that of Fig. 1, and like those found, for example, in the first chapters of Pierce's TAPL book [11]. Students are also called to be able to model languages of comparable difficulty on their own.

Type Soundness. One of the most important properties for modern programming languages is type soundness. This property ensures that the type system at hand faithfully predicts the shapes of values that will be encountered at run-time. In other words, expressions that, at compile-time, are classified of a certain type will indeed yield a value of that type at run-time, if evaluated.

Two aspects that are key, at least in the context of languages such as that of Fig. 1, to achieve type soundness are *progress*, that is (roughly), all behavior is specified, and *type preservation*, that is, in a computational step $e \longrightarrow e'$ we have that e and e' have the same type.

The focus of this paper is on the learning outcome **2**, in which type soundness is central: Students must not only be able to define languages, but be also able to devise languages that are type sound and amenable to standard proofs.

1.1   TypeSoundnessCertifier

A distinctive feature of the course is the use of a software tool called *TypeSoundnessCertifier* [6]. *TypeSoundnessCertifier* is a tool for type checking language definitions and certifying their soundness. The tool is based on theoretical results by Cimini, Miller and Siek that have been described in a preprint paper on the arXiv [7]. The tool and its theoretical underpinning are *not* contributions of this present paper. We here simply report on our experience in using the tool. To this aim, we review some features of the tool as reported in Cimini et al. [7].

TypeSoundnessCertifier makes use of a domain-specific language to define the grammar, typing rules and operational semantics of languages. Figure 2 shows the language definition in *TypeSoundnessCertifier* for the simply typed lambda-calculus with lists (as in Fig. 1, int serves just as base type).   This definition describes a grammar (lines 1–9)[1], a type system (lines 11–20), and a dynamic semantics (lines 22–26), and does so with, essentially, a textual representation of the syntax that is typically used in operational semantics[2]. Perhaps, the biggest

---

[1] A constraint of our system is that it works with closed terms as values, therefore a variable x cannot be declared as a value.

[2] This is not a novelty. The Ott language, for example, achieved the same effect previously.

```
1   Expression E ::= x | (abs T (x)E) | (app E E) | emptyList
2                   | (cons E E) | (head E) | (tail E)
3                   | error
4   Type T ::= int | (arrow T T) | (list T)
5   Value V ::= (abs T (x)E) | emptyList | (cons V V)
6   Error ::= error
7   Context C ::= [] | (app C E) | (app V C)
8                   | (cons C E) | (cons V C)
9                   | (head C) | (tail C)
10
11  Gamma |- (abs T1 (x)E) : (arrow T1 T2) <==
12                                  Gamma , x : T1 |- E : T2.
13  Gamma |- emptyList : (list T).
14  Gamma |- (cons E1 E2) : (list T) <==
15              Gamma |- E1 : T /\ Gamma |- E2 : (list T).
16  Gamma |- (app E1 E2) : T2 <==
17          Gamma |- E1 : (arrow T1 T2) /\ Gamma |- E2 : T1.
18  Gamma |- (head E) : T <== Gamma |- E : (list T).
19  Gamma |- (tail E) : (list T) <== Gamma |- E : (list T).
20  Gamma |- error : T.
21
22  (app (abs T (x)E) V) --> E[V/x].
23  (head emptyList) --> error.
24  (head (cons V1 V2)) --> V1.
25  (tail emptyList) --> error.
26  (tail (cons V1 V2)) --> V2.
```

Fig. 2. Example of language definition in *TypeSoundnessCertifier*. Binding is limited to unary lexical scoping [5], which is sufficient in the scope of our course. We express binding with syntax such as (x)E, that is, x is bound in E. This is similar to the directive (+ bind x in e +) in the Ott tool [15]. E[V/x] represents the capture-avoiding substitution.

departure is that grammar variables are always capitalized and the horizontal line of an inference rule

$$\frac{premises}{conclusion}$$

is replaced with an inverse implication <== that can be read *"provided that"*. Students that have been exposed to operational semantics would likely find no difficulties in connecting the syntax of the tool with what they know.

Type Systems for Language Design Principles. A relevant feature of *TypeSoundnessCertifier* is that the tool type checks language definitions and makes sure that the components of the language (value declarations, typing rules, reduction semantics rules, etc.) are all in order so that type soundness automatically holds.

Previous approaches to type checking languages are based on intrinsic typing [2,3,13,14]. In that approach, soundness is achieved indirectly by leveraging on the good properties of a host meta type theory. For example, if you can make your language definition type check within a logic with exhaustive pattern-matching that is strongly normalizing then the progress theorem, which is one aspect of type soundness, holds for you. The unique feature of *TypeSoundnessCertifier* is that, unlike the intrinsic typing approach, is based on a type system that explicitly models language design principles and invariants of the (object) language being defined. Some examples of design principles that *TypeSoundnessCertifier* enforces on the object language are:

– Classification of the operators of the language in *introduction forms* (such as the abstraction in the simply typed lambda-calculus), *elimination forms* (such as application), *derived operators* (such as `let` and `letrec` in ML-like languages), *errors* and *error handlers* (such as `try` in languages with exceptions).
– Elimination forms of a type manipulate values of that type. That is, for the beta-reduction rule (`app` (`abs T (x)E`) `V`) $\longrightarrow$ E[V/x] *TypeSoundnessCertifier* detects that `app` has been classified as an elimination form of type `arrow`. Then it checks that the principal argument (in Harper's terminology [10]), which is highlighted, is a value and that is built with an introduction form of the type `arrow`. In this case, `abs` is an introduction form of `arrow` indeed. Furthermore, *TypeSoundnessCertifier* detects that (`abs T (x)E`) is indeed declared in the grammar of values.
– If an operational semantics rule requires the argument of an operator to be a value, then that argument must be an evaluation context. For example, in the beta-reduction rule (`app (abs T (x)E) V`) $\longrightarrow$ E[`V` /x] the second argument is a value `V`, hence the tool checks that an evaluation context such as (`cons V C`) exists. Without such evaluation context, the expression that is equivalent to the lambda-calculus term $((\lambda x.x)\ ((\lambda x.x)\ 3))$ would be stuck, jeopardizing type soundness.
– Each elimination form of a type T must have a reduction rule defined for *each* of the values of the type T. To make an example, this invariant prescribes that we do not forget to define the behavior of the `head` list operation for the empty list, and that we give a reduction rule such that (`head emptyList`) $\longrightarrow$ `error` or otherwise our programs may get stuck, jeopardizing type soundness.

These are only few of the language design principles that *TypeSoundnessCertifier* enforces. The interested reader is invited to refer to the archived paper of Cimini, Miller and Siek [7], which makes these principles explicit, and formulates them in the context of a formal type system over language definitions.

Informative Error Messages. One of the features of the *TypeSoundnessCertifier* tool that we highlight here is its ability of pinpointing design mistakes that hinder type soundness[3]. A few illustrative examples are:

- Suppose that we deleted the rule at line 23 of the code in Fig. 2, *TypeSoundnessCertifier* would print the error message *"Operator **head** is elimination form for the type **list** but does not have a reduction rule for handling one of the values of type **list**: value **emptyList"**.
- Suppose we deleted the context declaration (app C E) at line 7, *TypeSoundnessCertifier* would print the error message *"The principal argument of the elimination form **app** is not declared as evaluation context, hence some programs may get stuck"*
- Suppose we omit to type check the second argument of cons at line 15, *TypeSoundnessCertifier* would print this typing rule saying *"This typing rule does not assign a type to expression **E2"**
- Suppose we replaced line 24 with (head (cons V1 V2)) $\longrightarrow$ V2 , i.e. now the head operation returns the rest of the list, then *TypeSoundnessCertifier* would print the error message *"Reduction rule of **head** for handling a value **cons** is not type preserving"*.
- Were we to change context declaration (cons C E) to (cons C V) at line 8, *TypeSoundnessCertifier* would reject the definition and print the error message *"Evaluation contexts have cyclic dependencies, hence some programs may get stuck"*. (The reader can verify that with evaluation contexts cons $E\ v$ | cons $v\ E$ the expression (cons $((\lambda x.x)$ 3) $((\lambda x.x)$ emptyList)) is stuck. The first argument will not be evaluated until the second is a value, but the second will not start evaluating until the first becomes a value.)

1.2   Our Thesis on Teaching with Language Type Checkers

Thanks to the explicit modeling of language design principles with a type system, the *TypeSoundnessCertifier* tool has a high-level view on the language being analyzed and can report design mistakes using the same vocabulary of language designers. Because of this, we believe that *TypeSoundnessCertifier* can be an effective tool for teaching functional language design to those students that are engaging in a programming languages course and are exposed to programming languages theory, including its vocabulary. Furthermore, the tool can be used to collect statistics on the frequency of design mistakes that students may make during their language modeling exercises. These statistics may inform instructors towards best practices in teaching.

---

[3] For those language definitions that *TypeSoundnessCertifier* type check as type sound, the tool also produces a machine-checked proof in the Abella theorem prover [1,4], hence the name of the tool. However, we are not concerned with this aspect of the tool.

Scope of our Teaching Experience and Objectives of This Paper. Our long-term goal is to demonstrate that the claim above be true. However, the teaching experience that we report on here is rather restricted in scope, and lacking in statistical significance. We therefore leave the claim as an open thesis yet to be substantiated. Below, we make the scope of our teaching experience clear.

Functional languages: We focus on functional languages only. In particular, we have restricted ourselves to an operational semantics relation with shape $e \longrightarrow e$, that is, the computation is a rewrite of an expression into another expression.

Basic designs: We have restricted ourselves to language design patterns of the like of those that have been pointed out in the previous section. These are certainly not enough to guarantee type soundness for modern functional languages features such as modules, type classes, macros, and other complex features. They are enough, however, to define simple functional languages.

Early experience: Finally, we stress that we report on an early experience. This paper is based, indeed, on only one instance of a course. Furthermore, the study had only 11 student participants in total.

In this paper, we make the following contributions.

- We set forth the thesis that a language type checker can be an effective tool for teaching the basics of functional language design. This paper does not substantiate this claim, doing so is part of our ongoing work.
- We give details about the course we have taught for the benefit of instructors that would like to replicate/adapt this teaching experience (Sect. 2), possibly contributing to gathering evidence for, or against, our thesis.
- We share some simple statistics and our impressions about them, but we make sure that it be clear that no conclusion can be drawn from our experience. More, and more extended experiments should be conducted (Sect. 3).

2   The Details of the Course

The course is a graduate level course in CS and has been divided into two parts: Programming languages theory and advanced features[4]. Only the first part is relevant to this paper, and we shall give some details as to what it comprised: in class, outside of the class, and during the evaluation.

2.1   In Class

The part on programming languages theory has been addressed in the first half of the course (7 weeks, lectures amounted to around 3 hours per week). We have adopted the Pierce's TAPL textbook [11], of which we have covered the typical chapters on the simply typed lambda-calculi with common datatypes, and the chapters on languages with references, and subtyping.

---

[4] Advanced features included monads, gradual typing [16,17], and data race freedom in the Rust type system, to name a few.

A Note on Teaching Strategy. It is hard to point out what worked and what did not in only one iteration of the course. In our opinion, the following elements have been fitting choices for the course. The first is that we have devoted a whole week to the proof of type soundness of a toy functional languages with few operators such as functions, booleans and if-then-else, lists and pairs. This part has covered the proof in great details. The second is that we have demonstrated the *TypeSoundnessCertifier* tool in class over a number of examples from TAPL. The third is that we aimed at connecting the dots between

- (i) language design,
- (ii) the tool
- (iii) how programs can go wrong, and
- (iv) the proof of type soundness.

We have given four examples of language design principles in Sect. 1.1, which we have then taught in class. For example, let us consider the beta-reduction rule $(\lambda x.e\ v) \longrightarrow e[v/x]$ and the fact that it fires only so long as the argument is a value. (i) A language design principle that applies is that an evaluation context such as $(v\ E)$ must exist. Then, it is beneficial to (ii) show that *TypeSoundness-Certifier* rejects the language when that context is missing. It is also beneficial to (iii) show an example of program that gets stuck in that situation, such as $(\lambda x.x\ (\text{head}\ [1]))$. Finally, it is instructive to (iv) show where in the proof of type soundness we reach a point where we cannot complete the proof.

2.2   Outside of the Class

Students have been encouraged to download the tool and practice using it outside of the class. *TypeSoundnessCertifier* has a repository of examples that includes a number of language definitions that are automatically checked as type sound [6]. Students have been invited to browse and reason over these examples. To encourage practice, the instructor invited the students to model three operations with *TypeSoundnessCertifier*. The three operations have an increasing level of difficulty:

- `length` e, as in: `length` $[4,5,7] \longrightarrow^* 3$.
- `reverseRange` e, as in: `reverseRange` $3 \longrightarrow^* [3,2,1]$. (A reversed range is easier than range, as it does not need a helper function).
- `map`, the typical operator in functional programming languages.

Solving these tasks was encouraged but not mandatory. Future instances of the course may make those tasks, or comparable tasks, mandatory.

Length, ReverseRange, and Map. To solve these three tasks, students were called to write three language definitions from scratch in *TypeSoundnessCertifier*, one for each of the operators above, and have the tool type check the definitions as type sound. In each of the tasks, students were asked to give the syntax for expressions, values, types, and evaluation contexts, as well as modeling appropriate typing rules and reduction semantics rules.

To give the reader an idea on how difficult the requested tasks are, and what aspects they would exercise, we give solutions below.

length: A possible language definition for length includes natural numbers and is the following.

```
1   Expression E ::= zero | (succ E) | emptyList
2                    | (cons E E) | (length E)
3   Type T ::= int | (list T)
4   Value V ::= zero | (succ V) | emptyList
5                  | (cons V1 V2)
6   Context C ::= [] | (succ C) | (cons C E)
7                  | (cons V C) | (length C)
8
9   Gamma |- zero : int.
10  Gamma |- (succ E) : int <== Gamma |- E : int.
11  Gamma |- emptyList : (list T).
12  Gamma |- (cons E1 E2) : (list T) <==
13                  Gamma |- E1 : T /\ Gamma |- E2 : (list
                        T).
14  Gamma |- (length E) : int <== Gamma |- E : (list T).
15
16  (length emptyList) --> zero.
17  (length (cons V1 V2)) --> (succ (length V2)).
```

An interesting aspect of this solution is that the recursive call to length appears as argument of succ at line 17. This means that reductions must be performed within the context of succ. To provide a solution, the student must have a good grasp on evaluation contexts and how they work.

reverseRange: A possible solution is below.

```
1   Expression E ::= zero | (succ E) | emptyList
2                    | (cons E E) | (reverseRange E)
3   Type T ::= int | (list T)
4   Value V ::= zero | (succ V) | emptyList
5                  | (cons V1 V2)
6   Context C ::= [] | (succ C) | (cons C E)
7                  | (cons V C) | (reverseRange C)
8
9   Gamma |- zero : int.
10  Gamma |- (succ E) : int <== Gamma |- E : int.
11  Gamma |- emptyList : (list T).
12  Gamma |- (cons E1 E2) : (list T) <==
13                  Gamma |- E1 : T /\ Gamma |- E2 : (list T).
14  Gamma |- (reverseRange E) : (list int) <==
15                                      Gamma |- E : int.
16
17  (reverseRange zero) --> emptyList.
18  (reverseRange (succ V))
19                  --> (cons (succ V) (reverseRange V)).
```

Similarly to `length`, lines 18–19 prescribe that reduction occurs in the context of `cons`. An aspect that is more difficult in `reverseRange` than in `length` is making this reduction rule correctly typed, and such that the type of the right-hand side of `-->` is the same as that of the left-hand side. In `length`, the task is easier because `succ` has only one argument while `cons` has two arguments. Students would have to think a little more about types in solving the task for `reverseRange`.

<u>map</u>: A possible formulation of `map` is the following.

```
Expression E ::= x | (abs T (x)E) | (app E E) | zero
               | (succ E) | emptyList | (cons E E)
               | (map E E)
Type T ::= int | (arrow T T) | (list T)
Value V ::= (abs T (x)E) | zero | (succ V) | emptyList
          | (cons V1 V2)
Context C ::= [] | (succ C) | (cons C E) | (cons V C)
            | (app C E) | (app V C) | (map C E)
            | (map V C)


Gamma |- zero : int.
Gamma |- (succ E) : int <== Gamma |- E : int.
Gamma |- emptyList : (list T).
Gamma |- (cons E1 E2) : (list T)
                    <== Gamma |- E1 : T
                    /\ Gamma |- E2 : (list T).
Gamma |- (abs T1 (x)E) : (arrow T1 T2)
                    <== Gamma, x : T1 |- E : T2.
Gamma |- (app E1 E2) : T2
                    <== Gamma |- E1 : (arrow T1 T2)
                    /\ Gamma |- E2 : T1.
Gamma |- (map E1 E2) : (list T2)
                    <== Gamma |- E1 : (list T1)
                    /\ Gamma |- E2 : (arrow T1 T2).

(app (abs T (x)E) V) --> E[V/x].
(map emptyList V) -->  emptyList.
(map (cons V1 V2) V3)
                --> (cons (app V3 V1)  (map V2 V3)).
```

This task exercises the two aspects mentioned previously, but at a greater level of difficulty.

2.3   The Evaluation

Each student arranged an appointment to meet with the instructor at the instructor's office. Students have been evaluated in the context of this meeting. This appointment was individual for each student. The student used a laptop with *TypeSoundnessCertifier* installed. The instructor assigned the student with the task of modeling a simple language with *TypeSoundnessCertifier*.

All students have been assigned the same language, which we here call **filterOpt**, and whose details are given below. The student did know that this part of the evaluation would consist of modeling a language but did not know what specific language would be assigned prior to the meeting. The student had 20 min to complete the task. The task was completed successfully when **filterOpt** was modeled and *TypeSoundnessCertifier* said that it was a type sound language definition. During language modeling, students could invoke *TypeSoundnessCertifier* as many times as they pleased. The number of failed attempts and the nature of the mistakes reported by the tool did not affect the grade. The grade was assigned based on how close the language definition of the student was to the requested solution after 20 min. Roughly speaking, this time limit did not count the time that was not spent in using modeling skills or interacting with the tool to realize such skills. For example, if students did not remember something of the tool syntax, they may have spent time fixing parser errors, or asked the instructor about it. This time did not count. The rational for this is that the focus of the instructor was exclusively on evaluating the language modeling skills of students, not their memorization skills w.r.t. the domain-specific language at hand. In replicating/adapting this teaching experience, other instructors may have a different take on this aspect.

*The **filterOpt** (Toy) Language.* The student was provided with an existing language definition that included functions, booleans, if-then-else and lists. The task was to extend this language definition with

- option types (with operators `none`, `some` e, `get` e), and
- an operator called `filterOpt`, a variant of the filter operation of functional programming. `filterOpt` l f takes a list l of elements of type T, and a function f from T to booleans, and creates a list in which every element v of l is (`some` v), if $f(v)$ is true, or `none`, if $f(v)$ is false[5].

To model a type sound language, the student was called to update the syntax for expressions, values, types, and evaluation contexts, as well as adding appropriate typing rules and reduction semantics rules. To give the reader an intuition of how difficult the requested task is, below we show a possible solution of it in *TypeSoundnessCertifier*. (We show only the relevant part and omit the rest using dots . . .).

```
Expression E ::= ... | none | (some E) | (get E)
                         | (filterOpt E E)
Type T ::= ... | (option T)
Value V ::= ... | none | (some V)
Error ::= error
Context C ::= ... | (some C) | (get C)
                         | (filterOpt C E) | (filterOpt V C)
```

---

[5] Since a solution for the ordinary filter operation is comparable to that of `map`, and `map` has been given as exercise (see Sect. 2.2), we preferred to make the exam more difficult with `filterOpt`.

```
Gamma |- none : (option T).
Gamma |- (some E) : (option T) <== Gamma |- E : T.
Gamma |- (get E) : T <== Gamma |- E : (option T).
Gamma |- (filterOpt E1 E2) : (list (option T)) <==
    Gamma |- E1 : (list T) /\ Gamma |- E2 : (arrow T
        bool).
Gamma |- error : T.

(get none) --> error.
(get (some V)) --> V.
(filterOpt emptyList V) -->  emptyList.
(filterOpt (cons V1 V2) V3)
            --> (cons
                (if (app V3 V1) (some V1) none)
                (filterOpt V2 V3)
              ).
```

3   Report on Our Experience

The course had 11 students participants. We have kept note of the mistakes that *TypeSoundnessCertifier* has reported during evaluations. Below, we share some data about these evaluations, and our impressions about them. It is important to notice that the total number of evaluations (11) is largely insufficient, and we cannot draw general conclusions from our data.

3.1   Students' Mistakes

– Missing evaluation contexts: 5 out of 11 students forgot to declare some evaluation contexts. Our impression is that, for future experiments, this aspect should be monitored: If future data supports the conclusion that this mistake is frequent, it may be appropriate to adjust the teaching style towards allocating more emphasis to evaluation contexts.
– Reduction rules failed type preservation: 4 out of 11 students failed in defining a type preserving reduction rule. Again, we should monitor this aspect and see if future experiments support a conclusion that this is a frequent mistake. In this case, different instructors may have a different view on this aspect. On one hand, type errors in the modeling of a reduction rule may be seen much like type errors in programming. Overall, we are hardly worried if our students do not write a perfectly well-typed program at first attempt.

On the other hand, it is to say that, at least in our setting, reduction rules are typically a one line effort involving a few expressions whose types must match. It is, therefore, legitimate for some instructors to think that type errors on simple reduction rules may not be equivalent to type errors on, say, a program with 30 lines of code that a student attempts to type check. For simple languages, these errors may be the mirror of a deeper misunderstanding or poor training in how types and typing work. Therefore, in that case instructors may decide to adjust their teaching style in class and include more examples, exercises and homework on this aspect.

This particular author leans towards the latter view, but understands that other instructors may not, hence both views have been critically mentioned.

– Missing value declarations: 3 out of 11 students forgot to declare a value in the grammar of values. In the future, we would like to monitor this aspect. In language design, having a clear idea of the values of the language at hand is paramount, and determining values should be one of the first actions of language designers. If future data supports the conclusion that missing value declarations is frequent, it may entail some confusion on the end of students. Instructors may want to allocate more emphasis on the role of values.

3.2   Overall Experience in Using TypeSoundnessCertifier

Ultimately, 6 out of 11 students completed the task successfully:

– 1 student succeeded at the 6th attempt,
– 1 student succeeded at the 4th attempt,
– 3 students succeeded at the 3rd attempt,
– 1 student succeeded at first attempt, i.e., no errors.

When students failed their attempts, they received a feedback from *TypeSoundnessCertifier* in the form of an error message. In that case, they returned to the language definition, and tried to fix it. On average, students who completed the task invoked the tool 3.333 times before succeeding. If we excluded the student with exceptional performance as outlier (no errors), students invoked the tool 3.8 times on average before succeeding. That some students did not complete the task is not uncommon, as it may not be the case that all students score perfectly at a course exam.

At the end of the course, we have given a survey to participants but unfortunately it did not receive a large participation: 6 students out of 11 have participated. The survey comprised statements to assess whether the tool was helpful in modeling languages and helped achieve the expected learning outcome. Students assigned a grade to the statem'ents amongst

– Strongly Agree (SA)
– Somewhat Agree (SWA)
– Neither Agree nor Disagree (Neith)
– Somewhat Disagree (SWD)
– Strongly Disagree (SD)
– N/A or do not remember (NA)

Figure 3 shows how many participants selected a grade per each statement. The low participation makes it impossible to draw any conclusion at this time. We show the survey as an example of the studies that we are conducting in the context of this project.

	SA	SWA	Neith	SWD	SD	NA
TypeSoundnessCertifier helped me model languages correctly	**3**	**3**				
I have a better understanding on how to model languages thanks to the TypeSoundnessCertifier tool	**3**	**2**	**1**			
I modeled languages with confidence for trusting that the TypeSoundnessCertifier tool would catch my mistakes	**2**	**4**				
Feedback from the TypeSoundnessCertifier tool helped me do better during the evaluation	**2**	**3**	**1**			

Fig. 3. Results from the survey. (No conclusion can be drawn from this figure.) Here, the term *languages* refer to those languages that are in the scope described in this paper and not, generally, *any* language.

4   Related and Future Work

Related Work. There are various syllabi on programming languages theory that have a marked focus on exposing students to the meta-theoretic properties of programming languages. Many syllabi are based on PLT Redex [9], Software Foundations [12], TAPL [11], and PFPL [10], among others.

We are not aware of any course that accompanies (a part of) those syllabi with the use of a language type checker that is capable of pinpointing design mistakes that hinder type soundness.

Future Work. In the future, we would like to replicate our course experience several times, and report on our extended findings to the community. We especially would like to conduct large studies that collect statistics on the frequency of language design mistakes. These statistics may be precious to inform best practices to teachers. Outside of academic courses, ideal venues for conducting our studies at a larger scale would be in the context of conference tutorials and summer schools, but we have no specific plans in this regard at the time of writing.

The setting of our course evaluation was such to impose a time constraint (20 min). This may have influenced students in the way they have used the tool during their evaluations. Some may have decided to frequently invoke the tool and incrementally obtain the correct solution based on the tools' feedback, while some others may have decided to write a first attempt of the whole solution as quickly as possible. In future studies, especially in those that are not in the context of an academic course evaluation, we would like to relax the time constraint, as well as remove the dependency of the users' outcome to an academic grade. We also would like to ask users, after having used the tool, whether they have employed a strategy intentionally. Measures such as these may constitute the basis for classifying user experiences much more precisely.

We would like to expand the course to make subtyping a relevant part of the evaluation. *TypeSoundnessCertifier* handles subtyping (see [6]) but this feature was not part of the language **filterOpt**. *TypeSoundnessCertifier* checks only standard shapes of subtyping. In particular, inference rules that define subtyping can be axioms (such as Int <: Float) or have recursive calls on arguments. Moreover, such recursive calls can only be of covariant, contravariant and invariant shapes. Of course, these are restricted shapes that do not nearly exhaust the kind of subtyping relations that language designers may want to adopt. It would be interesting to extend the tool to more liberal shapes, and incorporate such feature in the context of our course.

Similarly, Cimini, Miller and Siek have plans on extending their results to languages with stores, and on upgrading *TypeSoundnessCertifier* accordingly. In this instance of the course, languages with stores (and also subtyping) have been covered with lectures based on TAPL, with no use of an auxiliary language type checker, but as soon as that feature is captured by *TypeSoundnessCertifier* we believe it would be possible to create a semester-long course syllabus based on the tool. We also plan on extending the tool to cover properties other than type soundness. This may entail that we first establish the language design principles that facilitate or are necessary to satisfy a property, and formulate a type checker over languages accordingly.

When a reduction rule is not type preserving it may not always be the fault of the rule for being ill-designed. As an example, below the reduction rule on the left is correct but the typing rule on the right is mistaken (tail should return List T).

$$\text{tail} \ (\text{cons} \ v_1 \ v_2) \longrightarrow v_2 \qquad \frac{\Gamma \vdash e : \text{List} \ T}{\Gamma \vdash \text{tail} \ e : \boxed{T}}$$

The current take of *TypeSoundnessCertifier* is to firmly trust the type system. In this case, *TypeSoundnessCertifier* blames the reduction rule for not respecting types. It would be interesting to explore an extension of the tool in which the reversed perspective is available, i.e., the tool firmly trusts the reduction rule and blames typing rules. Users could choose which perspective to adopt before running the tool, or may ask the tool to provide the feedback from both perspectives.

We plan to explore the usefulness of the error messages of *TypeSoundness-Certifier*. Examples of our messages have been shown in Sect. 1.1. In Fig. 3 the fourth statement, which is about the feedback from the tool, had a generally positive response but ranked the lowest. (It is to notice that the number of responses was small). Can we find a way to report better messages to users? A direction that we would like to explore is to provide a human-readable counter-example that witnesses the design mistake. In this regard, it would be beneficial if counter-examples also suggested a solution. A challenge here is that there may be several errors in a language definition and we need to establish which ones to provide a counter-example for. Identifying a suitable error is important as there may be an error that is at the root of several errors. We believe that error reporting in this context can be a challenging research problem.

We would like to empower *TypeSoundnessCertifier* with automatic grading capabilities in the style of Automata Tutor [8]. The challenges in such an endeavor is in accommodating the different viewpoints that different instructors might have on how mistakes should affect the grade. For example, some instructors may find mistakes on type preservation unacceptable and decide to detract substantial points for that kind of mistakes. Simultaneously, they may consider missing evaluation contexts as a harmless oversight and detract a small amount of points for that. Other instructors may have the opposite viewpoint w.r.t. these mistakes. To accommodate these scenarios, we envision *TypeSoundnessCertifier* to load a table that associates a weight to each type of mistake from an external configuration file.

5   Conclusions

Our thesis is that a language type checker can be an effective tool in teaching functional language design. We have used *TypeSoundnessCertifier* in the context of an instance of a course in programming languages. The work here reported is not statistically significant, and we leave the claim as an open question. Nonetheless, we have offered details on how our course took place, and reported on some data gathered during our evaluations. This paper shows the type of studies that we are, and we will be, conducting in the future to obtain evidence for, or against, our thesis. We offer these details also to inspire our colleagues to engage in similar studies. The fact that 6 out of 11 students could complete a language design task through the feedback of the tool is encouraging. It was certainly a joy to see students try their language definitions against the tool, receive feedback, fix accordingly, and ultimately succeed.

Acknowledgements. We thank Dale Miller and Jeremy Siek for their comments on Sect. 1.1. We are thankful to our anonymous reviewers for their suggestions, which improved this paper. Also, we thank the students who participated to the study being reported.

References

1. Abella Development Team. http://abella-prover.org
2. Altenkirch, T., Reus, B.: Monadic presentations of lambda terms using generalized inductive types. In: Flum, J., Rodriguez-Artalejo, M. (eds.) CSL 1999. LNCS, vol. 1683, pp. 453–468. Springer, Heidelberg (1999). https://doi.org/10.1007/3-540-48168-0_32. http://dl.acm.org/citation.cfm?id=647849.737066
3. Augustsson, L., Carlsson, M.: An exercise in dependent types: a well-typed interpreter. In: Workshop on Dependent Types in Programming, Gothenburg (1999)
4. Baelde, D., Chaudhuri, K., Gacek, A., Miller, D., Nadathur, G., Tiu, A., Wang, Y.: Abella: a system for reasoning about relational specifications. J. Formaliz. Reason. **7**(2), 1–89 (2014). https://doi.org/10.6092/issn.1972-5787/4650

5. Cheney, J.: Toward a general theory of names: binding and scope. In: Proceedings of the 3rd ACM SIGPLAN Workshop on Mechanized Reasoning About Languages with Variable Binding, MERLIN 2005, pp. 33–40. ACM, New York (2005). http://doi.acm.org/10.1145/1088454.1088459

6. Cimini, M.: TypeSoundnessCertifier (2015). https://github.com/mcimini/TypeSoundnessCertifier

7. Cimini, M., Miller, D., Siek, J.G.: Well-typed languages are sound. CoRR abs/1611.05105 (2016). http://arxiv.org/abs/1611.05105

8. D'Antoni, L., Weavery, M., Weinert, A., Alur, R.: Automata tutor and what we learned from building an online teaching tool. Bull. EATCS **117** (2015). http://eatcs.org/beatcs/index.php/beatcs/article/view/365

9. Felleisen, M., Findler, R.B., Flatt, M.: Semantics Engineering with PLT Redex. The MIT Press, London (2009)

10. Harper, R.: Practical Foundations for Programming Languages. Cambridge University Press, New York (2012)

11. Pierce, B.C.: Types and Programming Languages. MIT Press, Cambridge (2002)

12. Pierce, B.C., et al.: Software Foundations. Electronic textbook (2014). www.cis.upenn.edu/~bcpierce/sf

13. Poulsen, C.B., Rouvoet, A., Tolmach, A., Krebbers, R., Visser, E.: Intrinsically-typed definitional interpreters for imperative languages **2**(POPL), 16:1–16:34 (2018). https://doi.org/10.1145/3158104

14. Reynolds, J.C.: The meaning of types - from intrinsic to extrinsic semantics (2000)

15. Sewell, P., et al.: Ott: effective tool support for the working semanticist. In: Proceedings of the 12th ACM SIGPLAN International Conference on Functional Programming, ICFP 2007, Freiburg, Germany, 1–3 October 2007, pp. 1–12 (2007). https://doi.org/10.1145/1291151.1291155

16. Siek, J.G., Taha, W.: Gradual typing for functional languages. In: Scheme and Functional Programming Workshop, pp. 81–92, September 2006

17. Tobin-Hochstadt, S., Felleisen, M.: Interlanguage migration: from scripts to programs. In: Companion to the 21st ACM SIGPLAN Symposium on Object-Oriented Programming Systems, Languages, and Applications, OOPSLA 2006, pp. 964–974. ACM, New York (2006). https://doi.org/10.1145/1176617.1176755, http://doi.acm.org/10.1145/1176617.1176755

Verifying Selective CPS Transformation for Shift and Reset

Chiaki Ishio$^{(\boxtimes)}$ and Kenichi Asai$^{(\boxtimes)}$

Ochanomizu University, Tokyo, Japan
{ishio.chiaki,asai}@is.ocha.ac.jp

Abstract. A selective CPS transformation enables us to execute a program with delimited control operators, shift and reset, in a standard functional language without support for control operators. The selective CPS transformation dispatches not only on the structure of the input term but also its purity: it transforms only those parts that actually involve control effects. As such, the selective CPS transformation consists of many rules, each for one possible combination of the purity of subterms, making its verification tedious and error-prone. In this paper, we first formalize a monomorphic version of the selective CPS transformation in the Agda proof assistant. We use intrinsically typed term and context representations together with parameterized higher-order abstract syntax (PHOAS) to represent binding structures. We then prove the correctness of the transformation, i.e., the equality of terms is preserved by the CPS transformation. Through the formalization, we confirmed that all the rules of the selective CPS transformation in the previous work are correct, but found that one lemma on the behavior of shift was not precise.

Keywords: Selective CPS Transformation · Shift/Reset · Agda · PHOAS

1 Introduction

A continuation represents the rest of the computation that remains to be done in a program. Although programmers are usually not so aware of continuations in their program, every program has its own continuation. For example, even in a simple arithmetic expression $1 + 2 * 3$, we first evaluate the multiplication $2 * 3$. At this point, the continuation takes the result of the multiplication, and adds 1 to the result. The idea of continuations has been applied in many ways, such as let-insertion in partial evaluation [13], non-deterministic programming [7], and representing monads [10].

To express continuations explicitly in a program, we can use control operators. For instance, shift/reset [7] is a pair of delimited control operators, where shift captures the continuation that is delimited by reset. Although control operators enable us to manipulate continuations easily, not so many programming languages support control operators.

© Springer Nature Switzerland AG 2020
W. J. Bowman and R. Garcia (Eds.): TFP 2019, LNCS 12053, pp. 38–57, 2020.
https://doi.org/10.1007/978-3-030-47147-7_3

Another way to express continuations in a program is to transform the program into continuation-passing style (CPS). Even if the programming language does not support any control operators, we can transform the source program that includes control operators into the output program that handles continuations explicitly without control operators. In this way, it is possible to implement control operators in a programming language that has no support for control operators.

In a proper CPS program, every function in a program carries an additional argument that represents the current continuation. This is what the standard CPS transformation produces; it translates the whole input program into CPS, no matter if the input program uses any control operators or not. However, this approach has its weakness. Because all the functions in the output program of the standard CPS transformation carry a continuation, the output program has the new cost that might affect its performance.

Instead, the selective CPS transformation detects the expressions that require the CPS transformation, runs the CPS transformation for those parts only, and leaves the rest of the program as is. This approach reduces the cost of carrying the continuation around the program. For example, Kim et al. [12] translated ML programs with exception handlers both in the standard and selective CPS transformation, and showed that the performance of the output program of the selective CPS transformation was better than the standard version. As such, Rompf et al. [17] used the selective CPS transformation to efficiently implement shift and reset in Scala.

The target transformation in this paper is the selective CPS transformation for shift and reset [2]. It uses two annotations, *impure* and *pure*, to show whether the program triggers any control effects or not. For example, since the program that includes shift operator may use continuations in a non-standard way, it is automatically annotated as impure. The impure parts of the program are transformed into CPS, while the pure parts are kept as they are.

This paper verifies the monomorphic version of the selective CPS transformation for call-by-value lambda calculus extended with shift and reset [2], using the proof assistant Agda [16]. We show that the transformation preserves the relation between two terms: if term e_1 is reduced to e_2, the translated term $[\![e_1]\!]$ is equal to $[\![e_2]\!]$. Since the definition of our selective CPS transformation has evolved from Danvy and Filinski's standard CPS transformation [8], the overall structure of those proofs are similar to each other.

However, the proof for the selective CPS transformation contains two main difficulties. One is the greater number of cases to analyse. This is because we put impure/pure annotations at every subexpression in the source program. For example, in the definition of the selective CPS transfromation, the translation rule for the function application $[\![e_1 @ e_2]\!]$ is divided into nine cases: one case for when the surrounding context is pure so that the application must also be completely pure, and eight cases for when the surrounding context is impure in which the body of the function e_1, the argument e_2, and the application (@) are either impure or pure.

The other difficulty is that the evaluation contexts become more complex because of the annotations. In our proof, we often need to compare the same two evaluation contexts consisting of the same expression but with different annotations for their holes (Sect. 2.4).

To handle these two complexities, it is highly desirable to implement the source language and the necessary definitions as simple as possible. Representing name binding using de Bruijn index is an option, but we choose parameterized higher-order abstract syntax (PHOAS) [4]. For necessary definitions such as substitution and reduction, we use relational representations. Also, we use intrinsically typed term representations so that only well-typed terms are definable [1]. These implementing strategies are useful in alleviating the tediousness for both proof writers and readers.

Through the proof formalization in Agda, we confirm that the definition of the selective CPS transformation [2] is correct. However, we find that one crucial lemma that characterizes the behavior of the `shift` operator was not precise. In this paper, we show the precise version of the lemma as "shift lemma".

The contributions of this paper are summarized as follows:

- We prove the correctness of the selective CPS transformation for call-by-value lambda calculus with `shift` and `reset`, using Agda.
- We find that one lemma in the previous work was not precise. We present the precise version of it.
- We provide a non-trivial case study of taking advantage of PHOAS and intrinsically typed representations in formalization.

The rest of the paper is organized as follows. After introducing source terms in Sect. 2, we formalize the selective CPS transformation in Sect. 3. The correctness and necessary lemmas are shown in Sect. 4. Related work is discussed in Sect. 5 and the paper concludes in Sect. 6.

The formalized proof in Agda is available at:
http://pllab.is.ocha.ac.jp/~asai/papers/tfp19.agda

2   Direct-Style Terms

In Fig. 1, we introduce the source language of the selective CPS transformation. We call terms in the source language *direct-style terms*. We first show how we formalize purity annotations, types, and terms, followed by substitution, contexts, and reduction rules.

2.1   Purity Annotations, Types, and Terms

Purity annotations are either i (impure) or p (pure). Impure expressions possibly capture continuations and trigger control effects, while pure expressions never do. For example, an expression that includes `shift` is impure, while numbers and variables are basically pure. The two annotations satisfy the inequality relation $p < i$, meaning that pure terms can be lifted to impure terms.

$$a ::= \mathsf{p} \mid \mathsf{i} \qquad\qquad \text{purity annotations}$$
$$\tau ::= \mathsf{Nat} \mid \tau_2 \to \tau_1 @\mathrm{cps}[\tau_3, \tau_4, a] \qquad\qquad \text{types}$$

$$\Gamma ::= \cdot \mid \Gamma, x : \tau \qquad\qquad \text{type environments}$$

$$v ::= n \mid x \mid \lambda^a x.\, A_1 \qquad\qquad \text{values}$$
$$e ::= v \mid A_1 @^a A_2 \mid S^a c.\, A_1 \mid \langle A_1 \rangle \qquad\qquad \text{terms}$$
$$A ::= e^a \qquad\qquad \text{annotated terms}$$

Fig. 1. Purity annotations, types, and terms

A type is either a base type Nat or an arrow type $\tau_2 \to \tau_1 @\mathrm{cps}[\tau_3, \tau_4, a]$. The arrow type is a function type from τ_2 to τ_1, but the application of the function changes the answer type (the type of the surrounding delimited context) from τ_3 to τ_4. The annotation a indicates the purity of the function. When it is pure, the function does not use any control effects when applied. In that case, the types τ_3 and τ_4 must be equal. When a is impure, the function possibly triggers control effects. In that case, the answer type may change.

Direct-style terms are represented as annotated terms, where all the subterms are decorated with purity annotations. A value is either a natural number n, a variable x, or an abstraction $\lambda^a x.\, A_1$. The purity annotation a here specifies the purity of the body of the function observed from outside: even if the top-most annotation of A_1 is p, it can be lifted to i because of the type inference. A term is either a value, an application, a $\mathtt{shift}$ construct, or a reset expression. The purity annotation a in an application indicates if the execution of the function would trigger control effects. In the same way as an abstraction, a in $(S^a c.\, A_1)$ indicates if the continuation c would be treated as either impure or pure.

Although the definition in Fig. 1 uses a named representation of variables for readability, we employ PHOAS by Chlipala [4] in the Agda formalization. That is, an abstraction and a $\mathtt{shift}$ construct are formalized using a binder in the metalanguage (i.e., Agda) and a variable is formalized as a constructor applied to a variable parameterized in the metalanguage. We do not go into the details of PHOAS, however, since PHOAS works naturally for most cases.[1] We will explain explicitly when the PHOAS is used in a non-trivial way.

Figure 2 shows the (monomorphic) typing rules for terms [2].[2] We can read the judgement $\Gamma \vdash e^a : \tau_1 @\mathrm{cps}[\tau_2, \tau_3, a]$ as: in a type environment Γ, an annotated term e^a has type τ_1 and the execution of e^a changes the answer type from τ_2 to τ_3. The typing rules are the same as the standard ones [6] except for the purity annotations. In addition to an inequality constraint of the form $a_1 \leq a_2$ on purity annotations, the typing rules include a constraint of the form

---

[1] PHOAS prevents us from case splitting on the body of an abstraction and a $\mathtt{shift}$ construct until they are applied. It is not a problem for formalizing and verifying CPS transformations.

[2] We do not consider let-polymorphism in this paper. See [19] for the formalization of a (non-selective) CPS transformation of lambda calculus (without control operators) extended with let-polymorphism.

$$\boxed{\Gamma \vdash e^a : \tau_1 \,@\mathrm{cps}[\tau_2, \tau_3, a]}$$

$$\frac{x : \tau_1 \in \Gamma}{\Gamma \vdash x^\mathsf{p} : \tau_1 \,@\mathrm{cps}[\tau_2, \tau_2, \mathsf{p}]} \;(\text{Var}) \qquad \frac{}{\Gamma \vdash n^\mathsf{p} : \mathsf{Nat}\,@\mathrm{cps}[\tau_1, \tau_1, \mathsf{p}]} \;(\text{Nat})$$

$$\frac{\Gamma, x : \tau_2 \vdash e_1{}^{a_1} : \tau_1 \,@\mathrm{cps}[\tau_3, \tau_4, a_1] \quad a_1 \le a_2 \quad \tau_3 \ne \tau_4 \Rightarrow a_1 = \mathsf{i}}{\Gamma \vdash (\lambda^{a_2} x. e_1{}^{a_1})^\mathsf{p} : (\tau_2 \to \tau_1 @\mathrm{cps}[\tau_3, \tau_4, a_2])\,@\mathrm{cps}[\tau_5, \tau_5, \mathsf{p}]} \;(\text{Fun})$$

$$\frac{a_1 \le a \quad a_2 \le a \quad a_3 \le a \quad \tau_5 \ne \tau_6 \Rightarrow a_1 = \mathsf{i} \quad \tau_4 \ne \tau_5 \Rightarrow a_2 = \mathsf{i} \quad \tau_3 \ne \tau_4 \Rightarrow a_3 = \mathsf{i}}{\Gamma \vdash e_1{}^{a_1} : (\tau_2 \to \tau_1 @\mathrm{cps}[\tau_3, \tau_4, a_3])\,@\mathrm{cps}[\tau_5, \tau_6, a_1] \quad \Gamma \vdash e_2{}^{a_2} : \tau_2 \,@\mathrm{cps}[\tau_4, \tau_5, a_2]}{\Gamma \vdash (e_1{}^{a_1} @^{a_3} e_2{}^{a_2})^a : \tau_1 \,@\mathrm{cps}[\tau_3, \tau_6, a]} \;(\text{App})$$

$$\frac{\Gamma, c : (\tau_3 \to \tau_4 @\mathrm{cps}[\alpha, \alpha, a_2]) \vdash e_1{}^{a_1} : \tau_1 \,@\mathrm{cps}[\tau_1, \tau_2, a_1] \quad \tau_1 \ne \tau_2 \Rightarrow a_1 = \mathsf{i}}{\Gamma \vdash (S^{a_2} c. e_1{}^{a_1})^\mathsf{i} : \tau_3 \,@\mathrm{cps}[\tau_4, \tau_2, \mathsf{i}]} \;(\text{Shift})$$

$$\frac{\Gamma \vdash e_1{}^{a_1} : \tau_1 \,@\mathrm{cps}[\tau_1, \tau_2, a_1] \quad \tau_1 \ne \tau_2 \Rightarrow a_1 = \mathsf{i}}{\Gamma \vdash \langle e_1{}^{a_1} \rangle^\mathsf{p} : \tau_2 \,@\mathrm{cps}[\tau_3, \tau_3, \mathsf{p}]} \;(\text{Reset})$$

Fig. 2. Typing rules

$\tau_1 \ne \tau_2 \Rightarrow a_1 = \mathsf{i}$. It ensures the well-formedness of types: if τ_1 and τ_2 differ, the annotation a_1 must be i, or, if the annotation a_1 is p, τ_1 and τ_2 must be equal.

In the Agda formalization, we use an intrinsically typed representation where the typing rules are incorporated into the definition of terms. Although we show a grammar of terms in Fig. 1, the actual definition of terms is given by Fig. 2.

2.2   Substitution Relation

Figure 3 shows the substitution relation for direct-style terms. It has the form $e^a[v^\mathsf{p}/y] = e'^a$, meaning that e^a possibly has a free variable y, and substituting v^p for y in e^a results in e'^a. The use of the same annotation a indicates that the substitution does not change the purity of the term. Since we have to mention a free variable y to define the substitution relation, it is defined using the higher-order representation [4]. Namely, y in e^a is bound at the metalanguage (Agda).

When a variable y^p is the one to be replaced (S-Var=), we immediately replace it with v^p. Otherwise, we leave the variable as is (S-Var $\ne$). The rule (S-Fun) utilizes PHOAS. The body $e_1{}^{a_1}$ of an abstraction $\lambda^{a_2} x. e_1{}^{a_1}$ may contain free occurrences of variable x. In the premise of (S-Fun), the variable x is bound in the metalanguage: we require that $e_1{}^{a_1}[v^\mathsf{p}/y] = e_1'{}^{a_1}$ holds for any x. The same technique is used in (S-Shift).

Chlipala shows that substitution can be implemented both as a relation and a function in PHOAS [5]. In our implementation, we define substitution as a relation, not as a function, following our previous work [19]. Although defining substitution by a function in PHOAS is neat, the relational definition appears to work better in combination with other program transformations.

Since the substitution relation is typed, it automatically proves that the substitution preserves types.

$$\boxed{e^a[v^{\mathsf{p}}/y] = e'^a} \qquad \overline{y^{\mathsf{p}}[v^{\mathsf{p}}/y] = v^{\mathsf{p}}} \ (\text{S-Var=}) \qquad \overline{x^{\mathsf{p}}[v^{\mathsf{p}}/y] = x^{\mathsf{p}}} \ (\text{S-Var}\neq)$$

$$\frac{}{n^{\mathsf{p}}[v^{\mathsf{p}}/y] = n^{\mathsf{p}}} \ (\text{S-Nat}) \qquad \frac{\forall x.\,(e_1{}^{a_1}[v^{\mathsf{p}}/y] = e_1'{}^{a_1})}{(\lambda^{a_2}x.\,e_1{}^{a_1})^{\mathsf{p}}[v^{\mathsf{p}}/y] = (\lambda^{a_2}x.\,e_1'{}^{a_1})^{\mathsf{p}}} \ (\text{S-Fun})$$

$$\frac{e_1{}^{a_1}[v^{\mathsf{p}}/y] = e_1'{}^{a_1} \qquad e_2{}^{a_2}[v^{\mathsf{p}}/y] = e_2'{}^{a_2}}{(e_1{}^{a_1}\ @^{a_3}\ e_2{}^{a_2})^a[v^{\mathsf{p}}/y] = (e_1'{}^{a_1}\ @^{a_3}\ e_2'{}^{a_2})^a} \ (\text{S-App})$$

$$\frac{\forall c.\,(e_1{}^{a_1}[v^{\mathsf{p}}/y] = e_1'{}^{a_1})}{(\mathcal{S}^{a_2}c.\,e_1{}^{a_1})^{\mathsf{i}}[v^{\mathsf{p}}/y] = (\mathcal{S}^{a_2}c.\,e_1'{}^{a_1})^{\mathsf{i}}} \ (\text{S-Shift}) \qquad \frac{e_1{}^{a_1}[v^{\mathsf{p}}/y] = e_1'{}^{a_1}}{\langle e_1{}^{a_1}\rangle^{\mathsf{p}}[v^{\mathsf{p}}/y] = \langle e_1'{}^{a_1}\rangle^{\mathsf{p}}} \ (\text{S-Reset})$$

Fig. 3. Substitution relation for direct-style terms

2.3   Frames and Evaluation Contexts

This section presents frames and evaluation contexts to be used for defining the reduction rules in Sect. 2.5. Frames enforce call-by-value, left-to-right evaluation order. Each frame has one hole. A redex in the hole will be evaluated next. Many layers of frames constitute an evaluation context. Both frames and evaluation context are standard except that they are decorated with types and purity annotations.

Figure 4 shows the definition of frames. In addition to the standard frames enforcing left-to-right evaluation, we have another frame used only in a reset construct. As in terms, frames are also decorated with purity annotations. In particular, the superscript a_0 of F^{a_0} and $F_p^{a_0}$ describes the purity annotation of the hole of the frames.

The type of frames, represented by σ_{f}, consists of types of the hole and the frame. The type in the bracket, $\tau_1@\mathrm{cps}[\tau_2, \tau_3, a_1]$, is the type of a term to be plugged into the hole, whereas the type after the bracket, $\tau_4@\mathrm{cps}[\tau_5, \tau_6, a_2]$, is the type of the whole term when the hole is plugged with a term.

We have two kinds of frames, a standard frame F^{a_0} and a *pure* frame $F_p^{a_0}$, which excludes the reset frame.[3] Pure frames are necessary to define a reduction rule for the **shift** construct, where we capture the context up to the nearest surrounding reset construct.

The typing rules for frames (also in Fig. 4) are derived from those for terms. The rules $(F\text{-App}_1)$ and $(F_p\text{-App}_1)$ are for when the function part of an application is being evaluated. Thus, the type of the function in (App) in Fig. 2 is

---

[3] Following Kameyama and Hasegawa [11], the word 'pure' in a pure frame (and a pure context to be introduced soon) is used to mean "no surrounding reset constructs", not whether control effects are used or not.

placed in the bracket, while the type of the whole application is placed after the bracket. The purity annotation a_1 of the hole $[\,]^{a_1}$ means that the hole should receive a term with annotation a_1. The argument and other constraints are all inherited from (APP).

$$\sigma_f \quad ::= [\tau_1@\mathrm{cps}[\tau_2,\tau_3,a_1]]_f\ \tau_4@\mathrm{cps}[\tau_5,\tau_6,a_2] \qquad\qquad \text{frame types}$$
$$F^{a_0} ::= ([\,]^{a_0}@^{a_3}e_2{}^{a_2})^a \mid (v_1{}^{\mathrm{p}}@^{a_3}[\,]^{a_0})^a \mid \langle[\,]^{a_0}\rangle^{\mathrm{p}}\ (a_i \le a \text{ for all } i)\ \text{frames}$$
$$F_p^{a_0} ::= ([\,]^{a_0}@^{a_3}e_2{}^{a_2})^a \mid (v_1{}^{\mathrm{p}}@^{a_3}[\,]^{a_0})^a \qquad\quad (a_i \le a \text{ for all } i)\ \text{pure frames}$$

$$\boxed{\Gamma \vdash F^{a_0} : \sigma_f} \quad \boxed{\Gamma \vdash F_p^{a_0} : \sigma_f}$$

$$\frac{\begin{array}{c} a_1 \le a \quad a_2 \le a \quad a_3 \le a \\ \tau_5 \ne \tau_6 \Rightarrow a_1 = \mathsf{i} \quad \tau_4 \ne \tau_5 \Rightarrow a_2 = \mathsf{i} \quad \tau_3 \ne \tau_4 \Rightarrow a_3 = \mathsf{i} \\ \Gamma \vdash e_2{}^{a_2} : \tau_2@\mathrm{cps}[\tau_4,\tau_5,a_2] \end{array}}{\Gamma \vdash ([\,]^{a_1}@^{a_3}e_2{}^{a_2})^a : [(\tau_2 \to \tau_1@\mathrm{cps}[\tau_3,\tau_4,a_3])@\mathrm{cps}[\tau_5,\tau_6,a_1]]_f\ \tau_1@\mathrm{cps}[\tau_3,\tau_6,a]} \quad \begin{array}{c}(F\text{-}\mathrm{APP}_1)\\(F_p\text{-}\mathrm{APP}_1)\end{array}$$

$$\frac{\begin{array}{c} a_2 \le a \quad a_3 \le a \quad \tau_4 \ne \tau_5 \Rightarrow a_2 = \mathsf{i} \quad \tau_3 \ne \tau_4 \Rightarrow a_3 = \mathsf{i} \\ \Gamma \vdash v_1 : (\tau_2 \to \tau_1@\mathrm{cps}[\tau_3,\tau_4,a_3])@\mathrm{cps}[\tau_5,\tau_5,\mathrm{p}] \end{array}}{\Gamma \vdash (v_1{}^{\mathrm{p}}@^{a_3}[\,]^{a_2})^a : [\tau_2@\mathrm{cps}[\tau_4,\tau_5,a_2]]_f\ \tau_1@\mathrm{cps}[\tau_3,\tau_5,a]} \quad (F\text{-}\mathrm{APP}_2,\ F_p\text{-}\mathrm{APP}_2)$$

$$\frac{\tau_1 \ne \tau_2 \Rightarrow a_1 = \mathsf{i}}{\Gamma \vdash \langle[\,]^{a_1}\rangle^{\mathrm{p}} : [\tau_1@\mathrm{cps}[\tau_1,\tau_2,a_1]]_f\ \tau_2@\mathrm{cps}[\tau_3,\tau_3,\mathrm{p}]} \quad (F\text{-}\mathrm{RESET})$$

Fig. 4. Frames and pure frames for direct-style terms

$$\sigma_c \quad ::= [\tau_1@\mathrm{cps}[\tau_2,\tau_3,a_1]]_c\ \tau_4@\mathrm{cps}[\tau_5,\tau_6,a_2] \quad \text{context types}$$
$$E_p^{a_0} ::= [\,]^{a_0} \mid F_p^{a_1} \circ E_p^{a_0} \qquad\qquad \text{pure evaluation contexts}$$

$$\boxed{\Gamma \vdash E_p^{a_0} : \sigma_c} \qquad \frac{\tau_2 \ne \tau_3 \Rightarrow a = \mathsf{i}}{\Gamma \vdash [\,]^a : [\tau_1@\mathrm{cps}[\tau_2,\tau_3,a]]_c\ \tau_1@\mathrm{cps}[\tau_2,\tau_3,a]} \quad (E_p\text{-}\mathrm{HOLE})$$

$$\frac{\begin{array}{c} \Gamma \vdash F_p^{a_2} : [\tau_4@\mathrm{cps}[\tau_5,\tau_3,a_2]]_f\ \tau_6@\mathrm{cps}[\tau_7,\tau_3,a_3] \\ \Gamma \vdash E_p^{a_1} : [\tau_1@\mathrm{cps}[\tau_2,\tau_3,a_1]]_c\ \tau_4@\mathrm{cps}[\tau_5,\tau_3,a_2] \end{array}}{\Gamma \vdash F_p^{a_2} \circ E_p^{a_1} : [\tau_1@\mathrm{cps}[\tau_2,\tau_3,a_1]]_c\ \tau_6@\mathrm{cps}[\tau_7,\tau_3,a_3]} \quad (E_p\text{-}\mathrm{FRAME})$$

Fig. 5. Pure evaluation contexts for direct-style terms

The rules $(F\text{-}\mathrm{APP}_2)$ and $(F_p\text{-}\mathrm{APP}_2)$ are similar except that the function part is already known to be a value v_1. Since the value is pure ($a_1 = \mathrm{p}$), the answer types τ_5 and τ_6 in (APP) is unified and the corresponding constraints are removed. The rule $(F\text{-}\mathrm{RESET})$ is derived from (RESET) in a similar way.

Next, we define pure evaluation contexts $E_p^{a_0}$ in Fig. 5. A pure evaluation context consists of a sequence of pure frames, whose type is expressed as σ_c.

Similarly to frames, the hole of a context has type $\tau_1@\mathrm{cps}[\tau_2, \tau_3, a_1]$, while the return type of the context is $\tau_4@\mathrm{cps}[\tau_5, \tau_6, a_2]$.

For the empty evaluation context, the type of the term to be plugged into the hole, $\tau_1@\mathrm{cps}[\tau_2, \tau_3, a_1]$, becomes the type of the entire evaluation context; see (E_p-HOLE). In the rule (E_p-FRAME), we add a new pure frame $F_p^{a_2}$ on top of a pure evaluation context $E_p^{a_0}$. Since the hole of the evaluation context $E_p^{a_0}$ becomes the hole of the entire evaluation context, the type and the annotation of the hole becomes the type and the annotation of the hole of $E_p^{a_0}$. Also, the type of the whole evaluation context is updated by the application of $F_p^{a_2}$.

$$\boxed{F_p^{a_1} \cong_f F_p^{a_1'}}$$

$$\frac{}{([\,]^{a_1}@^{a_3}e_2{}^{a_2})^a \cong_f ([\,]^{a_1'}@^{a_3}e_2{}^{a_2})^a}\ (\cong_f\text{-APP}_1)$$

$$\frac{}{(v_1{}^p@^{a_3}[\,]^{a_1})^a \cong_f (v_1{}^p@^{a_3}[\,]^{a_1'})^a}\ (\cong_f\text{-APP}_2)$$

$$\boxed{F^{a_1} \cong_f F^{a_1'}}\quad \text{The two rules above and:}\quad \frac{}{\langle[\,]^{a_1}\rangle^p \cong_f \langle[\,]^{a_1'}\rangle^p}\ (\cong_f\text{-RESET})$$

$$\boxed{E_p^{a_1} \cong_c E_p^{a_1'}}\quad \frac{}{[\,]^{a_1} \cong_c [\,]^{a_1'}}\ (\cong_c\text{-HOLE})\quad \frac{F_p^{a_2} \cong_f F_p^{a_2'}\quad E_p^{a_1} \cong_c E_p^{a_1'}}{(F_p^{a_2}\circ E_p^{a_1}) \cong_c (F_p^{a_2'}\circ E_p^{a_1'})}\ (\cong_c\text{-FRAME})$$

Fig. 6. Relation between frames and contexts with impure/pure holes

Defining (pure) frames and (pure) evaluation contexts in a typeful manner is non-trivial. Once they are defined, we can also define functions to plug a term into a frame and an evaluation context in a typeful manner.

2.4 Frames and Contexts with Impure/Pure Holes

In Sect. 2.3, we formalized the frames and the evaluation contexts. To define the reduction relation using them, we need a relation between the same evaluation contexts with different purity annotations for their holes. In this section, we define such relations before we move on to the reduction rules. See Fig. 6.

Two pure evaluation contexts $E_p^{a_1}$ and $E_p^{a_1'}$ are equal, written $E_p^{a_1} \cong_c E_p^{a_1'}$, if they are identical except that the purity of the hole is a_1 for the former and a_1' for the latter. We start with the minimal case ($\cong_c$-HOLE). When both holes receive terms that have the same type but different purity annotations, we regard those holes as equal. We can extend it with a recursive rule ($\cong_c$-FRAME). If the two contexts are equal ($E_p^{a_1} \cong_c E_p^{a_1'}$), the equality is maintained when we add the same frames on top of the contexts. The purity of the holes of the newly added frames, $F_p^{a_2}$ and $F_p^{a_2'}$, can be different, because even if $E_p^{a_1}$ and $E_p^{a_1'}$ are the same except for the purity of their holes, discrepancy between a_1 and a_1' can propagate to the purity of $E_p^{a_1}$ and $E_p^{a_1'}$, and hence the holes of $F_p^{a_2}$ and $F_p^{a_2'}$.

Similarly to evaluation contexts, two pure frames $F_p^{a_1}$ and $F_p^{a_1'}$ are equal, written $F_p^{a_1} \cong_f F_p^{a_1'}$, if they are identical except that the purity of the hole is a_1 for the former and a_1' for the latter. The same is true for the standard frames F^{a_1} and $F^{a_1'}$, including the case of the reset construct.

2.5   Reduction Relation

We are now ready to define a reduction relation for the direct-style terms in Fig. 7. Our implementation employs the equality relation between pure contexts defined in the previous section, as well as the substitution relation in Sect. 2.2.

The rule (R-BETA) is the standard β_v-reduction in the lambda calculus, except for the purity annotations and the constraint. If we have a substitution relation between $e_1{}^{a_1}$ and $e_1'{}^{a_1'}$ and the annotations satisfy the relation $a_1 \le a_3 \le a$, we can perform β_v-reduction. The rule (R-FRAME) reduces a term within the two frames F^{a_1} and $F^{a_1'}$ that satisfy the equality relation ($F^{a_1} \cong_f F^{a_1'}$). This is the first instance where we use the same frames with different purity annotations. Repeated use of (R-FRAME) allows us to reduce a term within an arbitrary evaluation context. The rule (R-RESET) returns a value v_1 when the body of a reset expression is already a value v_1.

$$\boxed{e^a \rightsquigarrow e'^{a'}}$$

$$\frac{a_1 \le a_3 \le a \quad e_1{}^{a_1}[v_2{}^p/y] = e_1'{}^{a_1}}{((\lambda^{a_3} x.\, e_1{}^{a_1})^p\, @^{a_3}\, v_2{}^p)^a \rightsquigarrow e_1'{}^{a_1}} \text{ (R-BETA)}$$

$$\frac{F^{a_1} \cong_f F^{a_1'} \quad e_1{}^{a_1} \rightsquigarrow e_1'{}^{a_1'}}{F^{a_1}[e_1{}^{a_1}] \rightsquigarrow F^{a_1'}[e_1'{}^{a_1'}]} \text{ (R-FRAME)} \qquad \frac{}{\langle v_1{}^p \rangle^p \rightsquigarrow v_1{}^p} \text{ (R-RESET)}$$

$$\frac{a_1 \le a_3 \le a_4 \quad E_p^i \cong_c E_p^p}{\langle (E_p^i[(S^{a_2} c.\, e_1{}^{a_1})^i])^i \rangle^p \rightsquigarrow \langle ((\lambda^{a_3} c.\, e_1{}^{a_1})^p\, @^{a_3}\, (\lambda^{a_2} x.\, \langle (E_p^p[x^p])^{a_5} \rangle^p)^p)^{a_4} \rangle^p} \text{ (R-SHIFT)}$$

Fig. 7. Reduction rules

Finally, the rule (R-SHIFT) shows how we execute the **shift** construct. The expression $\langle (E_p^i[(S^{a_2} c.\, e_1{}^{a_1})^i])^i \rangle^p$ is executed in the following way: when a **shift** construct appears in a pure evaluation context E_p^i within a reset construct, it captures the current delimited context E_p^i, reifies it to a function $\lambda^{a_2} x.\, \langle (E_p^p[x^p])^{a_5} \rangle^p$, binds it to the variable c, and executes the body $e_1{}^{a_1}$. Note that before the reduction, the context is plugged with an impure term $(S^{a_2} c.\, e_1{}^{a_1})^i$, while after the reduction, it is plugged with a pure term x^p. Since we keep track of the type of the hole of contexts, we cannot use an identical context to both of them. This is the second and crucial case where we need the equality relation for pure contexts we introduced in Sect. 2.4. We use two pure contexts, E_p^i and E_p^p, that are equal except for the purity of their holes ($E_p^i \cong_c E_p^p$). Before the reduction, the pure context has the form E_p^i. After the reduction, it becomes E_p^p.

Since we employ PHOAS, the reader might think that we could avoid this complication by making contexts higher order: we define a function that, given the purity of a plugged term, returns a suitable context. In fact, we can define the reduction rule for the shift construct this way. However, we will later have to prove a lemma on the behavior of the shift construct by induction on the structure of pure evaluation contexts. At that point, the higher-order method fails: we cannot dispatch on the structure of pure evaluation contexts since they are higher order. This is why we define the equality on pure contexts. Biernacki and Polesiuk [3] define a similar relation between typed contexts.

Because terms are defined in a typeful manner in the Agda formalization, the definition of the reduction relation also serves as a proof of the preservation property, i.e., the reduction preserves types.[4]

$$
\begin{aligned}
\tau &:= \mathsf{Nat} \mid \tau_1 \to \tau_2 & \text{CPS types} \\
v &:= n \mid x \mid \underline{\lambda} x.\, e & \text{CPS values} \\
e &:= v \mid e_1 \,\underline{@}\, e_2 \mid \underline{\mathsf{let}}\, x = e_1 \,\underline{\mathsf{in}}\, e_2 & \text{CPS terms}
\end{aligned}
$$

Fig. 8. CPS types, CPS values, and CPS terms

$$
\boxed{e[v/y] = e'} \qquad \frac{}{y[v/y] = v} \ (\text{Scps-Var=}) \qquad \frac{}{x[v/y] = x} \ (\text{Scps-Var}\neq)
$$

$$
\frac{}{n[v/y] = n} \ (\text{Scps-Nat}) \qquad \frac{\forall x.\, (e_1[v/y] = e_1')}{(\underline{\lambda} x.\, e_1)[v/y] = (\underline{\lambda} x.\, e_1')} \ (\text{Scps-Fun})
$$

$$
\frac{e_1[v/y] = e_1' \qquad e_2[v/y] = e_2'}{(e_1 \,\underline{@}\, e_2)[v/y] = (e_1' \,\underline{@}\, e_2')} \ (\text{Scps-App})
$$

Fig. 9. Substitution relation for CPS terms

3   Selective CPS Transformation

In this section, we introduce the selective CPS transformation. Direct-style terms in the previous section are transformed into CPS terms, which is the standard lambda calculus free from any purity annotations or answer types. We call them CPS terms because they are the target of the selective CPS transformation. Since direct-style terms include control operators and the CPS transformation is selective, the target of the CPS transformation is not in proper CPS; it may contain nested applications.

---

[4] On the other hand, it looks difficult to prove the progress property in this formalization, because the relational definition of substitution prohibits us from extracting the result of substitution (reduct) from the higher-order representation of a redex. This is not a problem since we do not need the progress property.

3.1 CPS Terms

Figure 8 shows the definition of CPS terms. We distinguish CPS terms from direct-style ones by representing them without any annotations. Also, we use underlines to express syntactic constructors in CPS terms.

A CPS type is either a base type Nat or the function type $\tau_1 \to \tau_2$ without any answer types or purity annotations. CPS values and CPS terms are defined in accordance with the simply-typed lambda calculus. For readability, we introduce the $\underline{\text{let}}$ construct, which is an abbreviation for a function application:

$$\underline{\text{let}}\, x = e_1 \,\underline{\text{in}}\, e_2 \;\equiv\; (\underline{\lambda} x.\, e_2)\,\underline{@}\, e_1.$$

We define a substitution relation for CPS terms in Fig. 9. Similarly to the direct-style terms, it employs PHOAS. In particular, the rule (SCPS-FUN) specifies that the substitution relation for the body of the abstraction should hold for any choice of x in the metalanguage.

$$
\begin{aligned}
\llbracket n^{\mathsf{p}} \rrbracket_{\mathsf{p}} &= n \\
\llbracket x^{\mathsf{p}} \rrbracket_{\mathsf{p}} &= x \\
\llbracket (\lambda^{\mathsf{p}} x.\, e_1{}^{\mathsf{p}})^{\mathsf{p}} \rrbracket_{\mathsf{p}} &= \underline{\lambda} x.\, \llbracket e_1{}^{\mathsf{p}} \rrbracket_{\mathsf{p}} \\
\llbracket (\lambda^{\mathsf{i}} x.\, e_1{}^{\mathsf{p}})^{\mathsf{p}} \rrbracket_{\mathsf{p}} &= \underline{\lambda} x.\, \underline{\lambda} k.\, k \,\underline{@}\, \llbracket e_1{}^{\mathsf{p}} \rrbracket_{\mathsf{p}} \\
\llbracket (\lambda^{\mathsf{i}} x.\, e_1{}^{\mathsf{i}})^{\mathsf{p}} \rrbracket_{\mathsf{p}} &= \underline{\lambda} x.\, \underline{\lambda} k.\, \llbracket e_1{}^{\mathsf{i}} \rrbracket_{\mathsf{i}} \,\underline{@}\, (\underline{\lambda} v.\, k \,\underline{@}\, v) \\
\llbracket (e_1{}^{\mathsf{p}} \,@^{\mathsf{p}}\, e_2{}^{\mathsf{p}})^{\mathsf{p}} \rrbracket_{\mathsf{p}} &= \llbracket e_1{}^{\mathsf{p}} \rrbracket_{\mathsf{p}} \,\underline{@}\, \llbracket e_2{}^{\mathsf{p}} \rrbracket_{\mathsf{p}} \\
\llbracket \langle e_1{}^{\mathsf{p}} \rangle^{\mathsf{p}} \rrbracket_{\mathsf{p}} &= \llbracket e_1{}^{\mathsf{p}} \rrbracket_{\mathsf{p}} \\
\llbracket \langle e_1{}^{\mathsf{i}} \rangle^{\mathsf{p}} \rrbracket_{\mathsf{p}} &= \llbracket e_1{}^{\mathsf{i}} \rrbracket_{\mathsf{i}} \,\underline{@}\, (\underline{\lambda} v.\, v) \\[4pt]
\llbracket (e_1{}^{\mathsf{p}} \,@^{\mathsf{p}}\, e_2{}^{\mathsf{p}})^{\mathsf{i}} \rrbracket_{\mathsf{i}} &= \underline{\lambda} \kappa.\, (\underline{\lambda} v.\, \kappa \,\overline{@}\, v) \,\underline{@}\, (\llbracket e_1{}^{\mathsf{p}} \rrbracket_{\mathsf{p}} \,\underline{@}\, \llbracket e_2{}^{\mathsf{p}} \rrbracket_{\mathsf{p}}) \\
\llbracket (e_1{}^{\mathsf{p}} \,@^{\mathsf{p}}\, e_2{}^{\mathsf{i}})^{\mathsf{i}} \rrbracket_{\mathsf{i}} &= \underline{\lambda} \kappa.\, (\underline{\lambda} v_1.\, \llbracket e_2{}^{\mathsf{i}} \rrbracket_{\mathsf{i}} \,\underline{@}\, (\underline{\lambda} v_2.\, (\underline{\lambda} v.\, \kappa \,\overline{@}\, v) \,\underline{@}\, (v_1 \,\underline{@}\, v_2))) \,\underline{@}\, \llbracket e_1{}^{\mathsf{p}} \rrbracket_{\mathsf{p}} \\
\llbracket (e_1{}^{\mathsf{i}} \,@^{\mathsf{p}}\, e_2{}^{\mathsf{p}})^{\mathsf{i}} \rrbracket_{\mathsf{i}} &= \underline{\lambda} \kappa.\, \llbracket e_1{}^{\mathsf{i}} \rrbracket_{\mathsf{i}} \,\underline{@}\, (\underline{\lambda} v_1.\, (\underline{\lambda} v.\, \kappa \,\overline{@}\, v) \,\underline{@}\, (v_1 \,\underline{@}\, \llbracket e_2{}^{\mathsf{p}} \rrbracket_{\mathsf{p}})) \\
\llbracket (e_1{}^{\mathsf{i}} \,@^{\mathsf{p}}\, e_2{}^{\mathsf{i}})^{\mathsf{i}} \rrbracket_{\mathsf{i}} &= \underline{\lambda} \kappa.\, \llbracket e_1{}^{\mathsf{i}} \rrbracket_{\mathsf{i}} \,\underline{@}\, (\underline{\lambda} v_1.\, \llbracket e_2{}^{\mathsf{i}} \rrbracket_{\mathsf{i}} \,\underline{@}\, (\underline{\lambda} v_2.\, (\underline{\lambda} v.\, \kappa \,\overline{@}\, v) \,\underline{@}\, (v_1 \,\underline{@}\, v_2))) \\
\llbracket (e_1{}^{\mathsf{p}} \,@^{\mathsf{i}}\, e_2{}^{\mathsf{p}})^{\mathsf{i}} \rrbracket_{\mathsf{i}} &= \underline{\lambda} \kappa.\, (\llbracket e_1{}^{\mathsf{p}} \rrbracket_{\mathsf{p}} \,\underline{@}\, \llbracket e_2{}^{\mathsf{p}} \rrbracket_{\mathsf{p}}) \,\underline{@}\, (\underline{\lambda} v.\, \kappa \,\overline{@}\, v) \\
\llbracket (e_1{}^{\mathsf{p}} \,@^{\mathsf{i}}\, e_2{}^{\mathsf{i}})^{\mathsf{i}} \rrbracket_{\mathsf{i}} &= \underline{\lambda} \kappa.\, (\underline{\lambda} v_1.\, \llbracket e_2{}^{\mathsf{i}} \rrbracket_{\mathsf{i}} \,\underline{@}\, (\underline{\lambda} v_2.\, (v_1 \,\underline{@}\, v_2) \,\underline{@}\, (\underline{\lambda} v.\, \kappa \,\overline{@}\, v))) \,\underline{@}\, \llbracket e_1{}^{\mathsf{p}} \rrbracket_{\mathsf{p}} \\
\llbracket (e_1{}^{\mathsf{i}} \,@^{\mathsf{i}}\, e_2{}^{\mathsf{p}})^{\mathsf{i}} \rrbracket_{\mathsf{i}} &= \underline{\lambda} \kappa.\, \llbracket e_1{}^{\mathsf{i}} \rrbracket_{\mathsf{i}} \,\underline{@}\, (\underline{\lambda} v_1.\, (v_1 \,\underline{@}\, \llbracket e_2{}^{\mathsf{p}} \rrbracket_{\mathsf{p}}) \,\underline{@}\, (\underline{\lambda} v.\, \kappa \,\overline{@}\, v)) \\
\llbracket (e_1{}^{\mathsf{i}} \,@^{\mathsf{i}}\, e_2{}^{\mathsf{i}})^{\mathsf{i}} \rrbracket_{\mathsf{i}} &= \underline{\lambda} \kappa.\, \llbracket e_1{}^{\mathsf{i}} \rrbracket_{\mathsf{i}} \,\underline{@}\, (\underline{\lambda} v_1.\, \llbracket e_2{}^{\mathsf{i}} \rrbracket_{\mathsf{i}} \,\underline{@}\, (\underline{\lambda} v_2.\, (v_1 \,\underline{@}\, v_2) \,\underline{@}\, (\underline{\lambda} v.\, \kappa \,\overline{@}\, v))) \\
\llbracket (S^{\mathsf{p}} c.\, e_1{}^{\mathsf{p}})^{\mathsf{i}} \rrbracket_{\mathsf{i}} &= \underline{\lambda} \kappa.\, \underline{\text{let}}\, x = \underline{\lambda} v.\, \kappa \,\overline{@}\, v \,\underline{\text{in}}\, \llbracket e_1{}^{\mathsf{p}} \rrbracket_{\mathsf{p}} \\
\llbracket (S^{\mathsf{p}} c.\, e_1{}^{\mathsf{i}})^{\mathsf{i}} \rrbracket_{\mathsf{i}} &= \underline{\lambda} \kappa.\, \underline{\text{let}}\, x = \underline{\lambda} v.\, \kappa \,\overline{@}\, v \,\underline{\text{in}}\, \llbracket e_1{}^{\mathsf{i}} \rrbracket_{\mathsf{i}} \,\underline{@}\, (\underline{\lambda} v.\, v) \\
\llbracket (S^{\mathsf{i}} c.\, e_1{}^{\mathsf{p}})^{\mathsf{i}} \rrbracket_{\mathsf{i}} &= \underline{\lambda} \kappa.\, \underline{\text{let}}\, x = \underline{\lambda} v.\, \underline{\lambda} k'.\, k' \,\underline{@}\, (\kappa \,\overline{@}\, v) \,\underline{\text{in}}\, \llbracket e_1{}^{\mathsf{p}} \rrbracket_{\mathsf{p}} \\
\llbracket (S^{\mathsf{i}} c.\, e_1{}^{\mathsf{i}})^{\mathsf{i}} \rrbracket_{\mathsf{i}} &= \underline{\lambda} \kappa.\, \underline{\text{let}}\, x = \underline{\lambda} v.\, \underline{\lambda} k'.\, k' \,\underline{@}\, (\kappa \,\overline{@}\, v) \,\underline{\text{in}}\, \llbracket e_1{}^{\mathsf{i}} \rrbracket_{\mathsf{i}} \,\underline{@}\, (\underline{\lambda} v.\, v)
\end{aligned}
$$

Fig. 10. Selective CPS transformation from direct-style terms to two-level CPS terms

We also have the standard equality relation for the CPS terms, written as $\sim$, consisting of β_v-equality and equality in arbitrary contexts, as well as reflexivity, symmetry, and transitivity. On top of these, we use two rules that are known to hold in the call-by-value lambda calculus [11]. One is β_Ω-rule:

$$(\underline{\lambda} x.\, E[x]) \,\underline{@}\, e \sim E[e] \quad \text{if } x \text{ does not occur free in } E$$

where E is a call-by-value, left-to-right, evaluation context. The other is an instance of β_{lift}-rule:

$$(\underline{\text{let }} x = e_1 \underline{\text{ in }} e_2)\, \underline{@}\, v \sim \underline{\text{let }} x = e_1 \underline{\text{ in }} (e_2\, \underline{@}\, v) \quad \text{if } x \text{ does not occur free in } v$$

We use an equality relation rather than a reduction relation for CPS terms, because only the equality is known to be preserved in the presence of control operators [2]. It is still an open problem whether it is possible to define a reduction-preserving CPS transformation for programs with control operators.

3.2   Selective CPS Transformation

Figure 10 shows the one-pass selective CPS transformation. The definition is taken from our previous work [2] as is, except that the $\underline{\text{let}}$ construct here is interpreted as monomorphic rather than polymorphic.

Given a direct-style term, this selective CPS transformation produces two-level terms with overlines and underlines. Following Danvy and Filinski [8], we call overlined constructs *static* and underlined ones *dynamic*. Among the obtained two-level term, the static parts (administrative β-redexes) are reduced to produce the final result that consists of only dynamic parts. This style of the CPS transformation is called "two-pass", because a two-level term is first produced and the static parts are reduced afterwards. However, it is possible to remove administrative β-redexes by implementing static terms in metalanguage level and reducing them at the transformation time. In our implementation, the static lambda abstraction ($\overline{\lambda}$) is written in Agda's lambda abstraction, while the dynamic lambda abstraction ($\underline{\lambda}$) is written using the lambda abstraction construct in CPS values shown in Fig. 8. The CPS transformation that uses these two-level terms is called "one-pass", because it reduces the administrative β-redexes during the CPS transformation.

The selective CPS transformation in Fig. 10 consists of two kinds of transformations: one for pure terms and the other for impure terms. When e_1 is pure, we leave the term in direct style, since it means that no control effects are used in e_1 and it is not necessary to transform it into CPS. Thus, $[\![e_1{}^\mathsf{p}]\!]_\mathsf{p}$ is basically an identity function, returning e_1 with annotations removed but transforms impure parts hidden under an abstraction. When e_1 is impure, on the other hand, $[\![e_1{}^\mathsf{i}]\!]_\mathsf{i}$ receives a static continuation κ at transformation time and returns an appropriate result according to the purity of the subterms of e_1.

At first, the many cases of the selective CPS transformation for impure terms are a bit overwhelming, but if we look at the last cases of an application and a `shift` construct, we find that they are exactly the familiar definition of the non-selective CPS transformation. All the other rules are their simplification, turning the pure parts back into direct style. See [2] for more details.

4   Correctness of the Transformation

In this section, we prove the correctness of the selective CPS transformation. We begin with a few definitions and necessary lemmas.

4.1　Schematic

A continuation κ is said to be *schematic*, if κ does not manipulate nor destroy the syntactic structure of the value it receives [8]. The theorem we prove (Theorem 1) requires this property.

Definition 1 (schematic). *Assume that y does not occur free in κ. A static continuation κ is schematic, if it satisfies $(\kappa \overline{@} y)[v/y] = \kappa \overline{@} v$, for any CPS value v.*

To understand what a schematic continuation is, it is instructive to see when a continuation is not schematic. A continuation κ_0 is not schematic if it returns 1 when applied to a CPS-term variable, and returns 2 otherwise, as can be seen:

$$(\kappa_0 \overline{@} y)[v/y] = 1[v/y] = 1 \neq 2 = \kappa_0 \overline{@} v.$$

We want to regard $(\kappa_0 \overline{@} y)[v/y]$ and $\kappa_0 \overline{@} v$ are equal, because substituting v for y in $(\kappa_0 \overline{@} y)$ appears to yield $(\kappa_0 \overline{@} v)$. This is not the case as shown above, however. Note that when we write $(\kappa_0 \overline{@} y)[v/y]$, the static application happens *before* the substitution is performed. The continuation κ_0 is not schematic because it behaves differently according to the syntactic structure of its argument. We exclude such ill-behaved continuations.

4.2　Substitution Lemma

Throughout the proof in Sect. 4.5, we need a substitution lemma whenever we substitute a direct-style value over the selective CPS transformation.

To show the substitution lemma, we first define a substitution relation for static continuations.

Definition 2 (substitution on continuation). *We write $\kappa_1[v/y] = \kappa_2$, if for any v_1 and v_1' such that $v_1[v/y] = v_1'$, we have $(\kappa_1 \overline{@} v_1)[v/y] = \kappa_2 \overline{@} v_1'$.*

Substitution on static continuations is defined by substitution on continuations applied to values in the same substitution relation.

Since we have two transformations, one for pure terms and the other for impure terms, the substitution lemma is divided into two parts. Furthermore, we have two subcases for the impure case, one for substituting both a term and a continuation (corresponding to standard function application) and the other for substituting a continuation only (corresponding to a continuation application).

Lemma 1 (substitution).

(1) If $\Gamma, y : \tau \vdash e_1^\mathsf{p} : \tau_1 \,@\mathrm{cps}[\tau_2, \tau_2, \mathsf{p}]$, $\Gamma \vdash e_2^\mathsf{p} : \tau_1 \,@\mathrm{cps}[\tau_2, \tau_2, \mathsf{p}]$, $\Gamma \vdash v^\mathsf{p} : \tau \,@\mathrm{cps}[\alpha, \alpha, \mathsf{p}]$, and $e_1^\mathsf{p}[v^\mathsf{p}/y] = e_2^\mathsf{p}$, then we have $[\![e_1^\mathsf{p}]\!]_\mathsf{p}[[\![v^\mathsf{p}]\!]_\mathsf{p}/y] = [\![e_2^\mathsf{p}]\!]_\mathsf{p}$.

(2) If $\Gamma, y : \tau \vdash e_1^\mathsf{i} : \tau_1 \,@\mathrm{cps}[\tau_2, \tau_3, \mathsf{i}]$, $\Gamma \vdash e_2^\mathsf{i} : \tau_1 \,@\mathrm{cps}[\tau_2, \tau_3, \mathsf{i}]$, $\Gamma \vdash v^\mathsf{p} : \tau \,@\mathrm{cps}[\alpha, \alpha, \mathsf{p}]$, $e_1^\mathsf{i}[v^\mathsf{p}/y] = e_2^\mathsf{i}$, and $\kappa_1[[\![v^\mathsf{p}]\!]_\mathsf{p}/y] = \kappa_2$, then we have $([\![e_1^\mathsf{i}]\!]_\mathsf{i} \overline{@} \kappa_1)[[\![v^\mathsf{p}]\!]_\mathsf{p}/y] = ([\![e_2^\mathsf{i}]\!]_\mathsf{i} \overline{@} \kappa_2)$.

(3) If $\Gamma \vdash e_1{}^i : \tau_1 @\mathrm{cps}[\tau_2, \tau_3, i]$, $\kappa_1[v/y] = \kappa_2$, and y does not appear in $e_1{}^i$, then we have $(\llbracket e_1{}^i \rrbracket_i \, \overline{@} \, \kappa_1)[v/y] = (\llbracket e_1{}^i \rrbracket_i \, \overline{@} \, \kappa_2)$.

The statements (1) and (2) in the substitution lemma can be proved by mutual induction on the derivation of $e_1{}^a[v^p/y] = e_2{}^a$ and case analysis on $e_1{}^a$. Essentially, we have nine cases for the statement (1) (two cases for a variable, $\llbracket x^p \rrbracket_p$ and $\llbracket y^p \rrbracket_p$, and one case for all the other cases of $\llbracket e^p \rrbracket_p$) and twelve cases for the statement (2) (one case for all the cases of $\llbracket e^i \rrbracket_i$).

The statement (3) is proved independently by induction on the structure of impure terms $e_1{}^i$, with twelve cases, one for all the cases of $\llbracket e^i \rrbracket_i$.

4.3   Continuation Reduction Lemma

We also need a lemma to replace continuations of the impure CPS transformation.

Lemma 2 (continuation reduction). *If $\Gamma \vdash e_1{}^i : \tau_1 @\mathrm{cps}[\tau_2, \tau_3, i]$, κ_1 and κ_2 are schematic, and $\kappa_1 \, \overline{@} \, \llbracket v^p \rrbracket_p \sim \kappa_2 \, \overline{@} \, \llbracket v^p \rrbracket_p$ for any v^p, then we have $\llbracket e_1{}^i \rrbracket_i \, \overline{@} \, \kappa_1 \sim \llbracket e_1{}^i \rrbracket_i \, \overline{@} \, \kappa_2$.*

We prove this lemma by induction on the structure of $e_1{}^i$. When $e_1{}^i$ has the form of (App), we examine all the possible purity annotations a_1, a_2, and a_3, which makes up to eight cases. It is also possible for $e_1{}^i$ to have the form of (Shift), and we have four cases for all the combinations of the purity annotations in (Shift).

4.4   Shift Lemma

Before proving the main theorem, we need to characterize the behavior of the `shift` construct. It extracts the `shift` construct out of the surrounding pure evaluation context and enables us to reason about the `shift` construct separately.[5]

Lemma 3 (shift lemma). *If $\Gamma \vdash E_p^i : [\tau_1 @\mathrm{cps}[\tau_2, \tau_3, i]]_c \, \tau_4 @\mathrm{cps}[\tau_5, \tau_3, i]$, $\Gamma \vdash E_p^p : [\tau_1 @\mathrm{cps}[\tau_2, \tau_2, p]]_c \, \tau_4 @\mathrm{cps}[\tau_5, \tau_2, a]$, $E_p^i \cong_c E_p^p$, $\Gamma \vdash e_1 : \tau @\mathrm{cps}[\tau, \tau_3, a_1]$, and κ is schematic, then we have*

$$\llbracket (E_p^i[S^{a_2} c. e_1{}^{a_1}])^i \rrbracket_i \, \overline{@} \, \kappa \sim \llbracket ((\lambda^{a_3} x. (E_p^p[x])^a)^p @^{a_3} (S^{a_2} c. e_1{}^{a_1})^i)^i \rrbracket_i \, \overline{@} \, \kappa$$

The shift lemma can be proved by induction on the structure of pure contexts, i.e., on the derivation of $E_p^i \cong_c E_p^p$. When both contexts are holes (i.e., $[]^i \cong_c []^p$), we deduce that $a = p$ from the second premise and $(E_p^p\text{-Hole})$. We could then

---

[5] We conjecture that the same lemma holds not only for a `shift` construct but also for an arbitrary expression. We have not formalized the general case yet, however.

dispatch on the remaining purity annotations, a_1, a_2, and a_3, which yields eight cases in total.

When both contexts have at least one pure frame, we split into two cases according to the structure of the top pure frame. By careful analysis, possibly sharing the proofs as much as possible, we have ten cases for APP_1 and six cases for APP_2.

Once the statement of the shift lemma is fixed, it is not too hard to prove the lemma, except for the many tedious cases (around 4900 lines in Agda). We could prove the inductive cases by first applying the induction hypothesis and then using various reduction rules. The rules to use are often clear from the goals. However, it was not at all trivial to find the right statement of the lemma. For example, the expression $E_p^{\mathrm{i}}[S^{a_2}c.\,e_1{}^{a_1}]$ is always surrounded by a reset construct whenever we use this lemma. However, placing a reset construct around it would make the induction hypothesis too weak to prove the lemma. The definition of the equality between two pure evaluation contexts is subtle, as well as the types (answer types in particular) and purity annotations of E_p^{i} and E_p^{p}. Basically, we started from the most general types and collected necessary constraints; but we needed to try many variations before reaching the current statement.

In the previous work [2], we presented the shift lemma as follows.

$$[\![(E_p^{\mathrm{i}}[(S^{a_2}c.\,e_1{}^{a_1})^{\mathrm{i}}])^{\mathrm{i}}]\!]_{\mathrm{i}}\,\overline{@}\,\kappa \sim [\![(S^{a_2}c.\,e_1{}^{a_1})^{\mathrm{i}}]\!]_{\mathrm{i}}\,\overline{@}\,(\overline{\lambda}x.\,[\![E_p^{\mathrm{p}}[x^{\mathrm{p}}]]\!]_{\mathrm{i}}\,\overline{@}\,\kappa)$$

When we tried to formalize this lemma in Agda, we found that the statement did not even type check. The static continuation $(\overline{\lambda}x.\,[\![E_p^{\mathrm{p}}[x^{\mathrm{p}}]]\!]_{\mathrm{i}}\,\overline{@}\,\kappa)$ receives a CPS value in x, but when it is plugged into the pure context E_p^{p}, it has to be a direct-style term since $E_p^{\mathrm{p}}[x^{\mathrm{p}}]$ is an argument to $[\![\cdot]\!]_{\mathrm{i}}$. The present shift lemma avoids this problem by keeping the whole lambda abstraction $(\lambda^{a_3}x.\,E_p^{\mathrm{p}}[x]^a)$ in direct style. If we expand the right-hand side of the shift lemma for the case $a = a_3 = \mathrm{i}$, we have:

$$[\![((\lambda^{\mathrm{i}}x.\,(E_p^{\mathrm{p}}[x])^{\mathrm{i}})^{\mathrm{p}}\,@^{\mathrm{i}}\,(S^{a_2}c.\,e_1{}^{a_1})^{\mathrm{i}})^{\mathrm{i}}]\!]_{\mathrm{i}}\,\overline{@}\,\kappa$$
$$\equiv (\underline{\lambda}v_1.\,[\![(S^{a_2}c.\,e_1{}^{a_1})^{\mathrm{i}}]\!]_{\mathrm{i}}\,\overline{@}\,(\overline{\lambda}v_2.\,(v_1\,\underline{@}\,v_2)\,\underline{@}\,(\underline{\lambda}v.\,\kappa\,\overline{@}\,v)))\,\underline{@}\,[\![(\lambda^{\mathrm{i}}x.\,(E_p^{\mathrm{p}}[x])^{\mathrm{i}})^{\mathrm{p}}]\!]_{\mathrm{p}}$$
$$\sim [\![(S^{a_2}c.\,e_1{}^{a_1})^{\mathrm{i}}]\!]_{\mathrm{i}}\,\overline{@}\,(\overline{\lambda}v_2.\,([\![(\lambda^{\mathrm{i}}x.\,(E_p^{\mathrm{p}}[x])^{\mathrm{i}})^{\mathrm{p}}]\!]_{\mathrm{p}}\,\underline{@}\,v_2)\,\underline{@}\,(\underline{\lambda}v.\,\kappa\,\overline{@}\,v))$$
$$\equiv [\![(S^{a_2}c.\,e_1{}^{a_1})^{\mathrm{i}}]\!]_{\mathrm{i}}\,\overline{@}\,(\overline{\lambda}v_2.\,((\underline{\lambda}x.\,\underline{\lambda}k.\,[\![(E_p^{\mathrm{p}}[x])^{\mathrm{i}}]\!]_{\mathrm{i}}\,\overline{@}\,(\overline{\lambda}v.\,k\,\underline{@}\,v))\,\underline{@}\,v_2)\,\underline{@}\,(\underline{\lambda}v.\,\kappa\,\overline{@}\,v))$$

It seems if we could further perform two β_{v}-reductions in the static continuation, we would obtain the previous shift lemma. It is not possible, however, since we cannot substitute an arbitrary CPS value v_2 into a direct-style variable x. To substitute x, we first need to transform v_2 back to direct style.

Besides, we observe that the previous lemma covered only the case $a = a_3 = \mathrm{i}$.

4.5   Proof of the Correctness of the CPS Transformation

We now prove the main theorem: the correctness of our selective CPS transformation. It states that whenever a direct-style term is reduced to another term, their translations are equal in the target language. We have three cases depending on the annotation of the reduction: either $e_1{}^{\mathrm{p}} \rightsquigarrow e_2{}^{\mathrm{p}}$, $e_1{}^{\mathrm{i}} \rightsquigarrow e_2{}^{\mathrm{p}}$, or $e_1{}^{\mathrm{i}} \rightsquigarrow e_2{}^{\mathrm{i}}$.

Theorem 1 (correctness).

(1) *If* $\Gamma \vdash e_1{}^{\mathsf{p}} : \tau_1 \,@\mathrm{cps}[\tau_2, \tau_2, \mathsf{p}]$ *and* $e_1{}^{\mathsf{p}} \rightsquigarrow e_2{}^{\mathsf{p}}$, *then* $[\![e_1{}^{\mathsf{p}}]\!]_{\mathsf{p}} \sim [\![e_2{}^{\mathsf{p}}]\!]_{\mathsf{p}}$.

(2) *If* $\Gamma \vdash e_1{}^{\mathsf{i}} : \tau_1 \,@\mathrm{cps}[\tau_2, \tau_2, \mathsf{i}]$ *and* $e_1{}^{\mathsf{i}} \rightsquigarrow e_2{}^{\mathsf{p}}$,
   then $[\![e_1{}^{\mathsf{i}}]\!]_{\mathsf{i}} \,\overline{@}\, \kappa \sim (\lambda v.\, \kappa \,\overline{@}\, v) \,\underline{@}\, [\![e_2{}^{\mathsf{p}}]\!]_{\mathsf{p}}$.

(3) *If* $\Gamma \vdash e_1{}^{\mathsf{i}} : \tau_1 \,@\mathrm{cps}[\tau_2, \tau_3, \mathsf{i}]$, $e_1{}^{\mathsf{i}} \rightsquigarrow e_2{}^{\mathsf{i}}$, *and* κ *is schematic,*
   then $[\![e_1{}^{\mathsf{i}}]\!]_{\mathsf{i}} \,\overline{@}\, \kappa \sim [\![e_2{}^{\mathsf{i}}]\!]_{\mathsf{i}} \,\overline{@}\, \kappa$.

The proof is by induction on the derivation of the reduction relation $e_1{}^{a_1} \rightsquigarrow e_2{}^{a_2}$. The statement (2) is the easiest to prove. Since the only possible reduction of the form $e_1{}^{\mathsf{i}} \rightsquigarrow e_2{}^{\mathsf{p}}$ is (R-BETA), we simply consider this case (two cases according to the purity of the body of the applied function). We need no condition on κ in this case. Note that (R-SHIFT) does not apply here, because the redex is a reset construct, which is pure.

To prove the statement (3), we also consider the case for (R-FRAME) in addition to (R-BETA). The case for (R-FRAME) is long (but routine) because we have to consider all the possible combinations of purity for each case of frames. The case for (R-BETA) is similar to the statement (2), but we additionally need a condition on κ to be schematic. This can be understood by the fact that an application to a static continuation happens in all the cases of $[\![(e_1{}^{a_1} \,@^{a_3}\, e_2{}^{a_2})^a]\!]_{\mathsf{i}}$. Without κ being schematic, we cannot perform the substitution incurred by (R-BETA).

The statement (1) is the most difficult to prove. In addition to (R-BETA) and (R-FRAME), we need to consider (R-RESET) and (R-SHIFT). Among them, the cases for (R-BETA) and (R-RESET) are simple. The case for (R-FRAME) requires many subcases, but all are straightforward. The hard part is the case for (R-SHIFT). In (R-SHIFT), we have five purity annotations, a_1, a_2, a_3, a_4, and a_5. Among them, a_1, a_3, and a_4 should satisfy $a_1 \le a_3 \le a_4$, and we have four possible patterns:

$$(a_1, a_3, a_4) \in \{(\mathsf{p}, \mathsf{p}, \mathsf{p}), (\mathsf{p}, \mathsf{p}, \mathsf{i}), (\mathsf{p}, \mathsf{i}, \mathsf{i}), (\mathsf{i}, \mathsf{i}, \mathsf{i})\}.$$

Also we have arbitrary annotations a_2 and a_5. Since the result of the selective CPS transformation differs for each case, we have to split over all the possible cases for those purity annotations. Thus, we have sixteen cases for (R-SHIFT), each being quite complex.

We pick out one of the most complicated cases from (R-SHIFT) in Fig. 11, where $a_1 = \mathsf{p}$ and $a_2 = a_3 = a_4 = a_5 = \mathsf{i}$. The goal is to show that the expressions (1) and (16) are equal in the target language. At the beginning of the figure, the expression (1) is equivalent to the next expression (2) by the definition of the selective CPS transformation. We represent the evaluation in the metalanguage (i.e., definitional equality) by connecting the expressions with $\equiv$. We then use the shift lemma to extract the $\mathtt{shift}$ construct out of its context, which is reduced to the expression (4).

We then perform a series of β_v-reduction forward from (5) to (8). In (4), substituting the variable v_1 with $(\lambda x.\, \underline{\lambda} k.\, ([\![(E_p^{\mathsf{p}}[x^{\mathsf{p}}])^{\mathsf{i}}]\!]_{\mathsf{i}} \,\overline{@}\, (\overline{\lambda} v.\, k \,\underline{@}\, v)))$ generates (5).

$$(1) \quad [\![\langle (E_p^i [(S^i c. e_1{}^p)^i])^i \rangle^i]\!]_p^p$$

$$(2) \quad \equiv [\![(E_p^i [(S^i c. e_1{}^p)^i])^i]\!]_i \, \overline{@} \, (\overline{\lambda} v. \, v)$$

$$(3) \quad \sim [\![((\lambda^i x. (E_p^p [x^p])^i)^p \, @^i \, (S^i c. e_1{}^p)^i)^i]\!]_i \overline{@} \, (\overline{\lambda} v. \, v) \qquad\qquad \text{Lemma 3}$$

$$(4) \quad \equiv (\underline{\lambda} v_1. \, \underline{\text{let}} \, x = (\lambda x. \, \underline{\lambda} k'. \, k' \, \underline{@} \, ((v_1 \, \underline{@} \, x) \, \underline{@} \, (\underline{\lambda} v. \, v))) \, \underline{\text{in}} \, [\![e_1{}^p]\!]_p)$$
$$\underline{@} \, (\lambda x. \, \underline{\lambda} k. \, ([\![(E_p^p [x^p])^i]\!]_i \, \overline{@} \, (\overline{\lambda} v. \, k \, \underline{@} \, v)))$$

$$(5) \quad \sim \, \underline{\text{let}} \, x = \underline{\lambda} x. \, \underline{\lambda} k'. \, k' \, \underline{@} \, (((\underline{\lambda} x. \, \underline{\lambda} k. \, ([\![(E_p^p [x^p])^i]\!]_i \, \overline{@} \, (\overline{\lambda} v. \, k \, \underline{@} \, v))) \, \underline{@} \, x) \, \underline{@} \, (\underline{\lambda} v. \, v)) \, \underline{\text{in}} \, [\![e_1{}^p]\!]_p$$
$$\beta_v$$

$$(6) \quad \sim \, \underline{\text{let}} \, x = \underline{\lambda} x. \, \underline{\lambda} k'. \, k' \, \underline{@} \, ((\underline{\lambda} k. \, ([\![(E_p^p [x^p])^i]\!]_i \, \overline{@} \, (\overline{\lambda} v. \, k \, \underline{@} \, v))) \, \underline{@} \, (\underline{\lambda} v. \, v)) \, \underline{\text{in}} \, [\![e_1{}^p]\!]_p$$
$$\text{Lemma 1 (2)}, \beta_v$$

$$(7) \quad \sim \, \underline{\text{let}} \, x = \underline{\lambda} x. \, \underline{\lambda} k'. \, k' \, \underline{@} \, ([\![(E_p^p [x^p])^i]\!]_i \, \overline{@} \, (\overline{\lambda} v. \, (\underline{\lambda} v. \, v) \, \underline{@} \, v)) \, \underline{\text{in}} \, [\![e_1{}^p]\!]_p \quad \text{Lemma 1 (3)}, \beta_v$$

$$(8) \quad \sim \, \underline{\text{let}} \, x = \underline{\lambda} x. \, \underline{\lambda} k'. \, k' \, \underline{@} \, ([\![(E_p^p [x^p])^i]\!]_i \, \overline{@} \, (\overline{\lambda} v. \, v)) \, \underline{\text{in}} \, [\![e_1{}^p]\!]_p \qquad \text{Lemma 2}, \beta_v$$

$$(9) \quad \sim \, \underline{\text{let}} \, x = \underline{\lambda} x. \, \underline{\lambda} k'. \, k' \, \underline{@} \, ([\![(E_p^p [x^p])^i]\!]_i \, \overline{@} \, (\overline{\lambda} v. \, v)) \, \underline{\text{in}} \, ((\underline{\lambda} v. \, v) \, \underline{@} \, [\![e_1{}^p]\!]_p) \qquad\qquad \beta_\Omega$$

$$(10) \quad \sim \, \underline{\text{let}} \, x = \underline{\lambda} x. \, \underline{\lambda} k'. \, k' \, \underline{@} \, ([\![(E_p^p [x^p])^i]\!]_i \, \overline{@} \, (\overline{\lambda} v. \, v)) \, \underline{\text{in}} \, ((\underline{\lambda} y. \, (y \, \underline{@} \, [\![e_1{}^p]\!]_p)) \, \underline{@} \, (\underline{\lambda} v. \, v)) \qquad\qquad \beta_v$$

$$(11) \quad \sim \, (\underline{\text{let}} \, x = \underline{\lambda} x. \, \underline{\lambda} k'. \, k' \, \underline{@} \, ([\![(E_p^p [x^p])^i]\!]_i \, \overline{@} \, (\overline{\lambda} v. \, v)) \, \underline{\text{in}} \, (\underline{\lambda} y. \, y \, \underline{@} \, [\![e_1{}^p]\!]_p)) \, \underline{@} \, (\underline{\lambda} v. \, v) \qquad \beta_{lift}$$

$$(12) \quad \equiv ((\underline{\lambda} x. \, \underline{\lambda} y. \, y \, \underline{@} \, [\![e_1{}^p]\!]_p) \, \underline{@} \, (\underline{\lambda} x. \, \underline{\lambda} k'. \, k' \, \underline{@} \, ([\![(E_p^p [x^p])^i]\!]_i \, \overline{@} \, (\overline{\lambda} v. \, v)))) \, \underline{@} \, (\underline{\lambda} v. \, v)$$

$$(13) \quad \equiv ([\![(\lambda^i x. \, e_1{}^p)^p]\!]_p \, \underline{@} \, [\![(\lambda^i x. \, \langle (E_p^p [x^p])^i \rangle^p)^p]\!]_p) \, \underline{@} \, (\underline{\lambda} v. \, v)$$

$$(14) \quad \equiv (\overline{\lambda} \kappa. \, ([\![(\lambda^i x. \, e_1{}^p)^p]\!]_p \, \underline{@} \, [\![(\lambda^i x. \, \langle (E_p^p [x^p])^i \rangle^p)^p]\!]_p) \, \underline{@} \, (\underline{\lambda} v. \, \kappa \, \overline{@} \, v)) \, \overline{@} \, (\overline{\lambda} v. \, v)$$

$$(15) \quad \equiv [\![((\lambda^i x. \, e_1{}^p)^p \, @^i \, (\lambda^i x. \, \langle (E_p^p [x^p])^i \rangle^p)^p)^i]\!]_i \, \overline{@} \, (\overline{\lambda} v. \, v)$$

$$(16) \quad \equiv [\![\langle ((\lambda^i x. \, e_1{}^p)^p \, @^i \, (\lambda^i x. \, \langle (E_p^p [x^p])^i \rangle^p)^p)^i \rangle^i]\!]_p$$

Fig. 11. An extract of the proof of correctness of the CPS transformation

We use Lemma 1 on (5) and (6). In (5), we choose Lemma 1 (2), because we substitute the variable x^p in the body of the impure transformation $[\![(E_p^p [x^p])^i]\!]_i$. In (6), on the other hand, we apply Lemma 1 (3), because substitution is necessary only in the continuation part of the impure transformation; PHOAS representation ensures that the variable k does not appear in $[\![(E_p^p [x^p])^i]\!]_i$. In (7), we perform the standard β_v-reduction on $(\overline{\lambda} v. \, (\underline{\lambda} v. \, v) \, \underline{@} \, v)$. It requires Lemma 2 because the reduction happens in the continuation passed to the impure transformation. Without the lemma, we do not know how the continuation is used in $[\![(E_p^p [x^p])^i]\!]_i$ and thus if we can perform β_v-reduction before the static application.

At this point, we jump to the goal (16) and perform reduction backward. We successively expand the outermost reset (15), an application (14), followed by static reduction (13), and two abstractions (12). Looking at the goal expression (8), we rewrite (12) to use a let expression (11). In (11), the body of the let expression $(\underline{\lambda} y. \, y \, \underline{@} \, [\![e_1{}^p]\!]_p)$ eventually receive the argument $(\overline{\lambda} v. \, (\underline{\lambda} v. \, v) \, \underline{@} \, v)$. We use β_{lift} to reorder the let expression and the application to obtain (10). We then perform the standard β_v-reduction in the body of the let-expression in (10). Finally, we reduce the application $((\underline{\lambda} v. \, v) \, \underline{@} \, [\![e_1{}^p]\!]_p)$ in (9) to obtain (8). This is not the standard β_v-reduction, since $e_1{}^p$ in $[\![e_1{}^p]\!]_p$ could have the form (APP) or (SHIFT) and may not be a CPS value. Instead, we use β_Ω with an empty evaluation context.

4.6   Notes on Agda Formalization

Regarding the formalization, we have discussed the advantages of PHOAS, intrinsically typed representations, and the relational representations so far. Other than those techniques, we also rely on equational reasoning. As used in the Agda standard library, we implemented an equational reasoning module for reduction relation. When using this module, there are mainly three parts to fill in: the current expression $\mathcal{E}$, the expected transformation rule f, and the evaluated expression $f(\mathcal{E})$. However, because Agda can automatically generate $f(\mathcal{E})$ from f and $\mathcal{E}$ by solving constraints, and because the initial $\mathcal{E}$ is given, we only need to work manually on f. This turned out to be useful, especially when the size of $\mathcal{E}$ and $f(\mathcal{E})$ is large.

Even with the equational reasoning, however, the overall proof process is quite tedious. Because Agda does not have a strong automated proof search engine as in Coq, we had to fill in all the rules manually, even when what we have to do was clear from the shape of the expression. Our experience suggests that if we prove the same theorem in Coq using automated proof search, we would obtain much smaller proof. The current proof script in Agda has around 7800 lines in total. It consists of:

- source/target term and the selective CPS transformation (700 lines),
- necessary lemmas including shift lemma (5200 lines), and
- the main proof (Theorem 1) (1900 lines).

After the proof is finished, we reexamined the structure of the proof and rearranged it in a nicer form as presented in this paper. Despite its length, we believe the proof is clear enough to say that it reflects the simple manual proof of the correctness of the standard non-selective CPS transformation, yet highlights what we need for the selective CPS transformation.

5   Related Work

As far as we are aware, Biernacki and Polesiuk's work [3] is the only one that formalized the selective CPS transformation using a proof assistant. They formalize a selective CPS transformation for a calculus with $\mathtt{shift}_0$ and $\mathtt{reset}_0$ and show the coherence of effect subtyping in Coq. They also use a typed representation for contexts in a similar way as we did. Although we handle similar delimited control operators, the semantics as well as the selective CPS transformation of $\mathtt{shift}_0$ and $\mathtt{reset}_0$ [14] are quite different from those of $\mathtt{shift}$ and $\mathtt{reset}$. The overall structure of the proof is also different: they use step-indexed logical relations whereas we use more basic equality relation.

As for non-selective CPS transformations, many researchers have formalized various flavors of calculi in various languages: in Isabelle/HOL with a complete formalization of α-equivalence [15], in Twelf in a relational form [18], and in Coq using two sets of de Bruijn indices [9].

Our work is directly based on Chlipala's work [4] using PHOAS, formalizing the simply-typed lambda calculus and System F in Coq. We also follow Chlipala in employing the relational presentation of substitution. Our work is a nontrivial case study showing the effectiveness of these techniques in formalizing CPS transformations.

As another case study, we have previously applied Chlipala's technique in formalizing a CPS transformation for the lambda calculus extended with let-polymorphism [19]. The current work is different from the previous one in that we target a selective CPS transformation rather than the non-selective one and we handle delimited control operators rather than let-polymorphism. Ultimately, we plan to incorporate both delimited control operators and let-polymorphism, but it is still left as future work.

6   Conclusion

In this paper, we have formalized and proved the correctness of the selective CPS transformation for `shift` and `reset` in Agda. We investigated and implemented every definition in the previous work, and found that the selective CPS transformation is correct, but one lemma was not precise. We provided the precise version of the lemma as "shift lemma". We used PHOAS and intrinsically typed term and context representation, which worked smoothly in formalizing CPS transformations in a typeful manner. For evaluation contexts, we introduced a relation between two evaluation contexts with different purity annotations.

Our future work includes proof automation and an extension to let-polymorphism. Through the formalization, we found that each step of the proof is simple, but the whole proof script became quite long. We are currently working on automating the proof using Agda's reflection API. We hope to reduce the amount of work for completing the proof by using the mechanism that is similar to tactics in Coq. Another direction for future work would be to merge the current work with our previous work on the correctness of a CPS transformation for a let-polymorphic language [19]. Although the proof in this paper is not short, its overall structure is clear enough. We hope to merge the two results into one, resulting in the full formalization of the calculus presented in [2].

Acknowledgements. We would like to thank Youyou Cong and anonymous reviewers for valuable comments and feedbacks. This work was partly supported by JSPS KAKENHI under Grant No. JP18H03218.

References

1. Altenkirch, T., Reus, B.: Monadic presentations of lambda terms using generalized inductive types. In: Flum, J., Rodriguez-Artalejo, M. (eds.) CSL 1999. LNCS, vol. 1683, pp. 453–468. Springer, Heidelberg (1999). https://doi.org/10.1007/3-540-48168-0_32
2. Asai, K., Uehara, C.: Selective CPS transformation for shift and reset. In: Proceedings of the ACM SIGPLAN Workshop on Partial Evaluation and Program Manipulation (PEPM 2018), pp. 40–52 (2018)

3. Biernacki, D., Polesiuk, P.: Logical relations for coherence of effect subtyping. Log. Methods Comput. Sci. **14**(1), 1–28 (2018)
4. Chlipala, A.: Parametric higher-order abstract syntax for mechanized semantics. In: Proceedings of the ACM SIGPLAN International Conference on Functional Programming (ICFP 2008), pp. 143–156, September 2008
5. Chlipala, A.: Certified Programming with Dependent Types. MIT Press, Cambridge (2013)
6. Danvy, O., Filinski, A.: A functional abstraction of typed contexts. Technical report 89/12, DIKU, University of Copenhagen, July 1989
7. Danvy, O., Filinski, A.: Abstracting control. In: Proceedings of the ACM Conference on LISP and Functional Programming (LFP 1990), pp. 151–160 (1990)
8. Danvy, O., Filinski, A.: Representing control: a study of the CPS transformation. Math. Struct. Comput. Sci. **2**(4), 361–391 (1992)
9. Dargaye, Z., Leroy, X.: Mechanized verification of CPS transformations. In: Dershowitz, N., Voronkov, A. (eds.) LPAR 2007. LNCS (LNAI), vol. 4790, pp. 211–225. Springer, Heidelberg (2007). https://doi.org/10.1007/978-3-540-75560-9_17
10. Filinski, A.: Representing monads. In: Proceedings of the 21st ACM SIGPLAN-SIGACT Symposium on Principles of Programming Languages, pp. 446–457. ACM (1994)
11. Kameyama, Y., Hasegawa, M.: A sound and complete axiomatization of delimited continuations. In: Proceedings of the Eighth ACM SIGPLAN International Conference on Functional Programming (ICFP 2003), pp. 177–188 (2003)
12. Kim, J., Yi, K., Danvy, O.: Assessing the overhead of ML exceptions by selective CPS transformation. In: Proceedings of the 1998 ACM SIGPLAN Workshop on ML, pp. 103–114 (1998)
13. Lawall, J.L., Danvy, O.: Continuation-based partial evaluation. In: Proceedings of the 1994 ACM Conference on LISP and Functional Programming (LFP 1994), pp. 227–238 (1994)
14. Materzok, M., Biernacki, D.: Subtyping delimited continuations. In: Proceedings of the ACM SIGPLAN International Conference on Functional Programming (ICFP 2011), pp. 81–93, September 2011
15. Minamide, Y., Okuma, K.: Verifying CPS transformations in Isabelle/HOL. In: Proceedings of the 2003 ACM SIGPLAN Workshop on Mechanized Reasoning about Languages with Variable Binding (MERLIN 2003), pp. 1–8 (2003)
16. Norell, U.: Towards a practical programming language based on dependent type theory. Ph.D. thesis, Chalmers University of Technology, SE-412 96, Göteborg, Sweden, September 2007
17. Rompf, T., Maier, I., Odersky, M.: Implementing first-class polymorphic delimited continuations by a type-directed selective CPS-transform. In: Proceedings of the 2009 ACM SIGPLAN International Conference on Functional Programming (ICFP 2009), pp. 317–328. ACM (2009)
18. Tian, Y.H.: Mechanically verifying correctness of CPS compilation. In: Proceeding of the Twelfth Computing: The Australasian Theory Symposium (CATS 2006), vol. 51, pp. 41–51 (2006)
19. Yamada, U., Asai, K.: Certifying CPS transformation of let-polymorphic calculus using PHOAS. In: Proceedings of the 16th Asian Symposium on Programming Languages and Systems (APLAS 2018), pp. 375–393 (2018)

How to Specify It!
A Guide to Writing Properties of Pure Functions

John Hughes[(⊠)]

Chalmers University of Technology and Quviq AB, Göteborg, Sweden
`rjmh@chalmers.se`

Abstract. Property-based testing tools test software against a *specification*, rather than a set of examples. This tutorial paper presents five generic approaches to writing such specifications (for purely functional code). We discuss the costs, benefits, and bug-finding power of each approach, with reference to a simple example with eight buggy variants. The lessons learned should help the reader to develop effective property-based tests in the future.

1 Introduction

Property-based testing (PBT) is an approach to testing software by defining general properties that ought to hold of the code, and using (usually randomly) generated test cases to test that they do, while reporting minimized failing tests if they don't. Pioneered by QuickCheck[1] in Haskell [9], the method is now supported by a variety of tools in many programming languages, and is increasingly popular in practice. Searching for "property-based testing" on Youtube finds many videos on the topic—most of the top 100 recorded at developer conferences and meetings, where (mostly) other people than this author present ideas, tools and methods for PBT, or applications that make use of it. Clearly, property-based testing is an idea whose time has come. But equally clearly, it is also poorly understood, requiring explanation over and over again!

We have found that many developers trying property-based testing for the first time find it difficult to identify *properties to write*—and find the simple examples in tutorials difficult to generalize. This is known as the *oracle problem* [3], and it is common to all approaches that use test case generation.

In this paper, therefore, we take a simple—but non-trivial—example of a purely functional data structure, and present five different approaches to writing properties (invariants, postconditions, metamorphic properties and the preservation of equivalence, inductive properties, and model-based properties). We show the necessity of testing the random generators and shrinkers that property-based testing depends on. We discuss the pitfalls to keep in mind for each kind of property, and we compare and contrast their effectiveness, with the help of eight buggy implementations. We hope that the concrete advice presented here will

---

[1] http://hackage.haskell.org/package/QuickCheck.

© Springer Nature Switzerland AG 2020
W. J. Bowman and R. Garcia (Eds.): TFP 2019, LNCS 12053, pp. 58–83, 2020.
https://doi.org/10.1007/978-3-030-47147-7_4

enable readers to side-step the "where do I start?" question, navigate the zoo of different kinds of property, and quickly derive the benefits that property-based testing has to offer.

2   A Primer in Property-Based Testing

Property-based testing is an approach to random testing pioneered by QuickCheck[2] in Haskell [9], in which universally quantified properties are evaluated as tests in randomly generated cases, and failing tests are simplified by a search for similar, smaller cases. There is no precise definition of the term, however: indeed, MacIver writes[3]

> 'Historically the definition of property-based testing has been "The thing that QuickCheck does".'

The basic idea has been reimplemented many times—Wikipedia in 2019 lists more than 50 implementations, in 36 different programming languages[4], of all programming paradigms. Among contemporary PBT tools are, for example, ScalaCheck [19] for the JVM, FsCheck[5] for .NET, Quviq QuickCheck [2,16] and Proper [17,20] for the BEAM, Hypothesis[6] for Python, PrologCheck [1] for Prolog, and SmallCheck [23]; SmartCheck [21] and LeanCheck [4] for Haskell, among many others. These implementations vary in quality and features, but the ideas in this paper—while presented using Haskell QuickCheck—should be relevant to a user of any of them.

Suppose, then, that we need to test the *reverse* function on lists. Any developer will be able to write a unit test such as the following:

$$test\_Reverse = reverse\ [1, 2, 3] == [3, 2, 1]$$

Here the ($==$) operator is an equality comparison for use in tests, which displays a message including the compared values if the comparison is *False*.

This test is written in the same form as most test cases worldwide: we apply the function under test (*reverse*) to known arguments ($[1, 2, 3]$), and then compare the result to a known expected value ($[3, 2, 1]$). Developers are practiced in coming up with these examples, and predicting expected results. But what happens when we try to write a property instead?

$$prop\_Reverse :: [Int] \rightarrow Property$$
$$prop\_Reverse\ xs = reverse\ xs == ???$$

---

[2] http://hackage.haskell.org/package/QuickCheck.
[3] https://hypothesis.works/articles/what-is-property-based-testing/.
[4] https://en.wikipedia.org/wiki/QuickCheck.
[5] https://fscheck.github.io/FsCheck/.
[6] https://pypi.org/project/hypothesis/.

The property is parameterised on *xs*, which will be randomly generated by QuickCheck; we state a monomorphic type signature explicitly, even though the *reverse* function is polymorphic, to tell QuickCheck what type of test data to generate. The result type is *Property*, not *Bool*, because this is what (==) returns—*Property*s are not pure booleans, because they can generate diagnostic output, among other things.

The property can clearly test *reverse* in a much wider range of cases than the unit test—*any* randomly generated list, rather than just the list $[1, 2, 3]$—which is a great advantage. But the question is: *what is the expected result?* That is, what should we replace ??? by in the definition above? Since the argument to *reverse* is not known in advance, we cannot precompute the expected result. We could write test code to *predict* it, as in

$$prop\_Reverse :: [Int] \to Property$$
$$prop\_Reverse \ xs = reverse \ xs == predictRev \ xs$$

but *predictRev is not easier to write than reverse*—it is *exactly the same function!*

This is the most obvious approach to writing properties—to replicate the implementation in the test code—and it is deeply unsatisfying. It is both an *expensive* approach, because the replica of the implementation may be as complex as the implementation under test, and of *low value*, because there is a grave risk that misconceptions in the implementation will be replicated in the test code. "Expensive" and "low value" is an unfortunate combination of characteristics for a software testing method!

"Avoid replicating your code in your tests."

We can finesse this problem by rewriting the property so that it does not refer to an expected result, instead checking some *property* of the result. For example, *reverse* is its own inverse:

$$prop\_Reverse :: [Int] \to Property$$
$$prop\_Reverse \ xs = reverse \ (reverse \ xs) == xs$$

Now we can pass the property to QuickCheck, to run a series of random tests (by default 100):

```
*Examples> quickCheck prop_Reverse
+++ OK, passed 100 tests.
```

We have met our goal of testing *reverse* on 100 random lists, but this property is not very strong—if we had accidentally defined

$$reverse \ xs = xs$$

then it would still pass (whereas the unit test above would report a bug).

We can define another property that this *buggy* implementation of *reverse* passes, but the correct definition fails:

$$prop\_Wrong :: [\,Int\,] \rightarrow Property$$
$$prop\_Wrong \; xs = reverse \; xs === xs$$

Since *reverse* is actually correctly implemented, this allows us to show what happens when a property fails:

```
*Examples> quickCheck prop_Wrong
*** Failed! Falsified (after 5 tests and 3 shrinks):
[0,1]
[1,0] /= [0,1]
```

Here the first line after the failure message shows the value of *xs* for which the test failed ($[0, 1]$), while the second line is the message generated by ($===$), telling us that the result of *reverse* (that is, $[1, 0]$) was not the expected value ($[0, 1]$).

Interestingly, the counterexample QuickCheck reports for this property is almost always $[0, 1]$, and occasionally $[1, 0]$. These are not the random counterexamples that QuickCheck finds first; they are the result of *shrinking* the random counterexamples via a systematic greedy search for a simpler failing test. Shrinking lists tries to remove elements, and numbers shrink towards zero; the reason we see these two counterexamples is that *xs* must contain at least two different elements to falsify the property, and 0 and 1 are the smallest pair of different integers. Shrinking is one of the most useful features of property-based testing, resulting in counterexamples which are usually easy to debug, because *every part* of the counterexample is relevant to the failure.

Now we have seen the benefits of property-based testing—random generation of very many test cases, and shrinking of counterexamples to minimal failing tests—and the major pitfall: the temptation to replicate the implementation in the tests, incurring high costs for little benefit. In the remainder of this paper, we present systematic ways to define properties *without* falling into this trap. We will (largely) ignore the question of how to generate *effective* test cases—that are good at reaching buggy behaviour in the implementation under test—even though this is an active research topic in its own right (see, for example, the field of *concolic testing* [12, 24]). While generating good test cases is important, in the absence of good properties, they are of little value.

3   Our Running Example: Binary Search Trees

The code we shall develop properties for is an implementation of finite maps (from keys to values) as binary search trees. The definition of the tree type is shown in Fig. 1; a tree is either a *Leaf*, or a *Branch* containing a left subtree, a key, a value, and a right subtree. The operations we will test are those that create trees (*nil*, *insert*, *delete* and *union*), and that *find* the value associated with a key in the tree. We will also use auxiliary operations: *toList*, which returns a sorted list of the key-value pairs in the tree, and *keys* which is defined in terms of it. The implementation itself is standard, and is not included here.

Before writing properties of binary search trees, we must define a *generator* and a *shrinker* for this type. We use the definitions in Fig. 2, which generate

```
data BST k v = Leaf | Branch (BST k v) k v (BST k v)
  deriving (Eq, Show, Generic)

-- the operations under test
find   :: Ord k ⇒ k → BST k v → Maybe v
nil    :: BST k v
insert :: Ord k ⇒ k → v → BST k v → BST k v
delete :: Ord k ⇒ k       → BST k v → BST k v
union  :: Ord k ⇒ BST k v → BST k v → BST k v

-- auxiliary operations
toList :: BST k v → [(k, v)]
keys   :: BST k v → [k]
```

Fig. 1. The API under test: binary search trees.

```
instance (Ord k, Arbitrary k, Arbitrary v) ⇒ Arbitrary (BST k v) where
  arbitrary = do
    kvs ← arbitrary
    return $ foldr (uncurry insert) nil (kvs :: [(k, v)])
  shrink = genericShrink
```

Fig. 2. Generating and shrinking binary search trees.

trees by creating a random list of keys and values and inserting them into the empty tree, and shrink trees using a generic method provided by QuickCheck. The type restriction in the definition of *arbitrary* is needed to fix *kvs* to be a list, because *foldr* is overloaded to work over any *Foldable* collection. We shall revisit both these definitions later, but they will do for now.

We need to *fix an instance type* for testing; for the time being, we choose to let both keys and values be integers, and define

```
type Key = Int
type Val = Int
type Tree = BST Int Int
```

Int is usually an acceptably good choice as an instance for testing polymorphic properties, although we will return to this choice later. In the rest of this article *we omit type signatures on properties* for brevity, although in reality they must be given, to tell QuickCheck to use the types above.

4   Approaches to Writing Properties

4.1   Validity Testing

"Every operation should return valid results."

Many data-structures need to satisfy invariant properties, above and beyond being well-typed, and binary search trees are no exception: the keys in the tree

$$prop\_NilValid = valid\ (nil :: Tree)$$
$$prop\_InsertValid\ k\ v\ t = valid\ (insert\ k\ v\ t)$$
$$prop\_DeleteValid\ k\ t = valid\ (delete\ k\ t)$$
$$prop\_UnionValid\ t\ t' = valid\ (union\ t\ t')$$

Fig. 3. Validity properties.

should be ordered. In this section, we shall see how to write properties that check that this invariant is preserved by each operation.

We can capture the invariant by the following function:

$$valid\ Leaf = True$$
$$valid\ (Branch\ l\ k\ \_v\ r) =$$
$$valid\ l \wedge valid\ r \wedge$$
$$all\ (<k)\ (keys\ l) \wedge all\ (>k)\ (keys\ r)$$

That is, all the *keys* in a left subtree must be less than the key in the node, and all the *keys* in the right subtree must be greater.

This definition is obviously correct, but it is an inefficient implementation of the validity checking function; it is quadratic in the size of the tree in the worst case. A more efficient implementation would exploit the validity of the left and right subtrees, and compare only the *last* key in the left subtree, and the *first* key in the right subtree, against the key in a *Branch* node. But the equivalence of these two definitions depends on reasoning, and we prefer to *avoid reasoning that is not checked by tests*—if it turns out to be wrong, or is invalidated by later changes to the code, then tests using the more efficient definition might fail to detect some bugs. Testing that two definitions are equivalent would require testing a property such as

$$prop\_ValidEquivalent\ t = valid\ t == fastValid\ t$$

and to do so, we would need a generator that can produce *both valid and invalid trees*, so this is not a straightforward extension. We prefer, therefore, to use the obvious-but-inefficient definition, at least initially. The trees we are generating are relatively small, so quadratic complexity is not a problem.

"Test your tests."

Now it is straightforward to define properties that check that every operation that constructs a tree, constructs a valid one (see Fig. 3). However, these properties, by themselves, do not provide good testing for validity. To see why, let us plant a bug in *insert*, so that it creates duplicate entries when inserting a key that is already present (bug (2) in Sect. 5). *prop_InsertValid* fails as it should, but so do *prop_DeleteValid* and *prop_UnionValid*:

```
=== prop_InsertValid from BSTSpec.hs:19 ===
*** Failed! Falsified (after 6 tests and 8 shrinks):
0
```

```
0
Branch Leaf 0 0 Leaf

=== prop_DeleteValid from BSTSpec.hs:22 ===
*** Failed! Falsified (after 8 tests and 7 shrinks):
0
Branch Leaf 1 0 (Branch Leaf 0 0 Leaf)

=== prop_UnionValid from BSTSpec.hs:25 ===
*** Failed! Falsified (after 7 tests and 9 shrinks):
Branch Leaf 0 0 (Branch Leaf 0 0 Leaf)
Leaf
```

Thus, at first sight, there is nothing to indicate that the bug is in *insert*; all of *insert*, *delete* and *union* can return invalid trees! However, *delete* and *union* are *given* invalid trees as inputs in the tests above, and we cannot expect them to return valid trees in this case, so these reported failures are "false positives."

The problem here is that the *generator* for trees is producing invalid ones (because it is defined in terms of *insert*). We could add a precondition to each property, requiring the tree to be valid, as in:

$$prop\_DeleteValid \ k \ t = valid \ t \implies valid \ (delete \ k \ t)$$

which would discard invalid test cases (not satisfying the precondition) without running them, and thus make the properties pass. This is potentially inefficient (we might spend much of our testing time discarding test cases), but it is also really just applying a sticking plaster: what we *want* is that all generated trees should be valid! We can test this by defining an additional property:

$$prop\_ArbitraryValid \ t = valid \ t$$

which at first sight seems to be testing that *all* trees are valid, but in fact tests that *all trees generated by the Arbitrary instance* are valid. If this property fails, then it is the generator that needs to be fixed—there is no point in looking at failures of other properties, as they are likely caused by the failing generator.

Usually the generator for a type *is* intended to fulfill its invariant, but—as in this case—is defined independently. A property such as *prop_ArbitraryValid* is essential to check that these definitions are mutually consistent.

It is also possible for the *shrink* function to violate a datatype invariant. For this reason, we should also write a property requiring all the smaller test cases returned by *shrink* to be valid:

$$prop\_ShrinkValid \ t = all \ valid \ (shrink \ t)$$

Unfortunately, with the definitions given so far, this property fails:

```
=== prop_ShrinkValid from BSTSpec.hs:28 ===
*** Failed! Falsified (after 6 tests and 8 shrinks):
Branch (Branch Leaf 0 0 Leaf) 0 1 Leaf
```

Inspection reveals that this argument to *shrink* is *already* invalid—and so it is no surprise that *shrink* might include invalid trees in its result. The problem here is that, even though QuickCheck initially found a *valid* tree with an invalid shrink, *it shrunk the test case before reporting it using the invalid shrink function*, resulting in an invalid tree with invalid shrinks. What we want to see, when debugging, is a *valid* tree with an invalid shrink; to ensure that this is what QuickCheck reports, we must add a *valid t* $\implies$ precondition to this property. This precondition should always hold for a randomly generated test (provided *arbitrary* is correct), but prevents such a test case being shrunk to an invalid case when the property fails; thus, we avoid the potential inefficiency discussed on page 7, whereby preconditions cause many randomly generated tests to be discarded.

We can also reexpress the check in a slightly different, but equivalent form, so that when a failing test is reported we see both the valid original tree, and the invalid tree that it is shrunk to:

$$prop\_ShrinkValid\ t = valid\ t \implies filter\ (not \circ valid)\ (shrink\ t) == [\ ]$$

With these changes the failing test is easy to interpret:

```
=== prop_ShrinkValid from BSTSpec.hs:28 ===
*** Failed! Falsified (after 7 tests and 8 shrinks):
Branch (Branch Leaf 0 0 Leaf) 1 0 Leaf
[Branch (Branch Leaf 0 0 Leaf) 0 0 Leaf] /= []
```

We see that shrinking the key 1 to 0 invalidated the invariant.

We must thus redefine shrinking for the *BST* type to enforce the invariant. There are various ways of doing so, but perhaps the simplest is to continue to use *genericShrink*, but discard smaller trees where the invariant is broken:

$$shrink = filter\ valid \circ genericShrink$$

This section illustrates well the importance of *testing our tests*; it is vital to test generators and shrinkers *independently* of the operations under test, because a bug in either can result in many very-hard-to-debug failures in other properties.

> **Summary:** *Validity testing consists of defining a function to check the invariants of your datatypes, writing properties to test that your generators and shrinkers only produce valid results, and writing a property for each function under test that performs a single random call, and checks that the return value is valid.*

Validity properties are important to test, whenever a datatype has an invariant, but they are far from sufficient by themselves. Consider this: *if every function returning a BST were defined to return nil in every case*, then all the properties written so far would pass. *insert* could be defined to delete the key instead, or *union* could be defined to implement set difference—as long as the invariant is preserved, the properties will still pass. Thus, we must move on to properties that better capture the *intended behaviour* of each operation.

4.2   Postconditions

"Postconditions relate return values to arguments of a single call."

A *postcondition* is a property that should be *True* after a call, or (equivalently, for a pure function) *True* of its result. Thus, we can define properties by asking ourselves "What should be *True* after calling f?". For example, after calling *insert*, then we should be able to *find* the key just inserted, and any previously inserted keys with unchanged values.

$$prop\_InsertPost\ k\ v\ t\ k' =$$
$$find\ k'\ (insert\ k\ v\ t) \Longequiv \textbf{if}\ k \equiv k'\ \textbf{then}\ Just\ v\ \textbf{else}\ find\ k'\ t$$

One may wonder whether it is best to parameterize this property on *two different* keys, or just on one: after all, for the type chosen, independently generated keys k and k' are equal in only around 3.3% of cases, so most test effort is devoted to checking the **else**-branch in the property, namely that *other* keys than the one inserted are preserved. However, using the *same* key for k and k' would weaken the property drastically—for example, an implementation of *insert* that discarded the original tree entirely would still pass. Moreover, nothing hinders us from defining and testing a specialized property:

$$prop\_InsertPostSameKey\ k\ v\ t = prop\_InsertPost\ k\ v\ t\ k$$

Testing this property devotes *all* test effort to the case of finding a newly inserted key, but does not require us to replicate the code in the more general postcondition.

We can write similar postconditions for *delete* and *union*; writing the property for *union* forces us to specify that *union* is left-biased (since union of finite maps cannot be commutative).

$$prop\_UnionPost\ t\ t'\ k = find\ k\ (union\ t\ t') \Longequiv (find\ k\ t <|> find\ k\ t')$$

(where ($<|>$) is the operation that chooses one of two *Maybe* values, choosing the first argument if it is of the form *Just x*, and the second argument otherwise).

Postconditions are not always as easy to write. For example, consider a postcondition for *find*. The return value is either *Nothing*, in case the key is not found in the tree, or *Just v*, in the case where it is present with value v. So it seems that, to write a postcondition for *find*, we need to be able to determine whether a given key is present in a tree, and if so, with what associated value. *But this is exactly what find does!* So it seems we are in the awkward situation discussed in the introduction: in order to test *find*, we need to reimplement it.

We can finesse this problem using a very powerful and general idea, that of *constructing a test case whose outcome is easy to predict*. In this case, we *know* that a tree must contain a key k, *if we have just inserted it*. Likewise, we know that a tree cannot contain a key k, if we have just deleted it. Thus we can write *two* postconditions for *find*, covering the two cases:

$$prop\_FindPostPresent\ k\ v\ t = find\ k\ (insert\ k\ v\ t) == Just\ v$$
$$prop\_FindPostAbsent\ k\ t = find\ k\ (delete\ k\ t) == Nothing$$

But there is a risk, when we write properties in this form, that we are only testing very special cases. Can we be certain that *every* tree, containing key k with value v, can be expressed in the form *insert k v t*? Can we be certain that every tree *not* containing k can be expressed in the form *delete k t*? If not, then the postconditions we wrote for *find* may be less effective tests than we think.

Fortunately, for this data structure, every tree *can* be expressed in one of these two forms, because inserting a key that is already present, or deleting one that is not, is a no-op. We express this as another property to test:

$$prop\_InsertDeleteComplete\ k\ t = \textbf{case}\ find\ k\ t\ \textbf{of}$$
$$Nothing \rightarrow t == delete\ k\ t$$
$$Just\ v \rightarrow t == insert\ k\ v\ t$$

Summary: *A postcondition tests a single function, calling it with random arguments, and checking an expected relationship between its arguments and its result.*

4.3   Metamorphic Properties

"Related calls return related results."

Metamorphic testing is a successful approach to the oracle problem in many contexts [7]. The basic idea is this: even if the expected result of a function call such as *insert k v t* may be difficult to predict, we may still be able to express an expected *relationship* between this result, and the result of a related call. In this case, if we insert an additional key into t before calling *insert k v*, then we expect the additional key to appear in the result also. We formalize this as the following *metamorphic property*:

$$prop\_InsertInsert\ (k, v)\ (k', v')\ t =$$
$$insert\ k\ v\ (insert\ k'\ v'\ t) == insert\ k'\ v'\ (insert\ k\ v\ t)$$

A metamorphic property, like this one, (almost) always *relates two calls* to the function under test. Here the function under test is *insert*, and the two calls are *insert k v t* and *insert k v (insert k' v' t)*. The latter is constructed by *modifying* the argument, in this case also using *insert*, and the property expresses an expected relationship between the values of the two calls. Metamorphic testing is a fruitful source of property ideas, since if we are given $O(n)$ operations to test, each of which can also be used as a modifier, then there are potentially $O(n^2)$ properties that we can define.

However, the property above is not true: testing it yields

```
=== prop_InsertInsert from BSTSpec.hs:78 ===
*** Failed! Falsified (after 2 tests and 5 shrinks):
(0,0)
(0,1)
Leaf
Branch Leaf 0 0 Leaf /= Branch Leaf 0 1 Leaf
```

This is not surprising. The property states that the order of insertions does not matter, while the failing test case inserts the same key twice with different values—of course the order of insertion matters in this case, because "the last insertion wins". A first stab at a metamorphic property may often require correction; QuickCheck is good at showing us what it is that needs fixing. We just need to consider two equal keys as a special case:

$$prop\_InsertInsert\ (k, v)\ (k', v')\ t = \\ insert\ k\ v\ (insert\ k'\ v'\ t)$$

$$===$$

$$\textbf{if } k \equiv k' \textbf{ then } insert\ k\ v\ t \textbf{ else } insert\ k'\ v'\ (insert\ k\ v\ t)$$

Unfortunately, this property *still* fails:

```
=== prop_InsertInsert from BSTSpec.hs:78 ===
*** Failed! Falsified (after 2 tests):
(1,0)
(0,0)
Leaf
Branch Leaf 0 0 (Branch Leaf 1 0 Leaf) /=
Branch (Branch Leaf 0 0 Leaf) 1 0 Leaf
```

Inspecting the two resulting trees, we can see that changing the order of insertion results in trees with *different shapes*, but containing the *same* keys and values. Arguably this does not matter: we should not care what shape of tree each operation returns, provided it contains the right information[7]. To make our property pass, we must make this idea explicit. We therefore define an equivalence relation on trees that is true if they have the same contents,

$$t1 \simeq t2 = toList\ t1 === toList\ t2$$

and re-express the property in terms of this equivalence:

$$prop\_InsertInsert\ (k, v)\ (k', v')\ t = \\ insert\ k\ v\ (insert\ k'\ v'\ t)$$

$$\simeq$$

$$\textbf{if } k \equiv k' \textbf{ then } insert\ k\ v\ t \textbf{ else } insert\ k'\ v'\ (insert\ k\ v\ t)$$

[7] Recall that we have not imposed any *balance condition* on our trees. If we were to repeat this entire exercise for balanced trees, then we would need a stronger invariant to capture the balance condition, but we would still face the same problem in this property, since balance conditions don't require a *unique* tree shape. Both trees in this example are balanced—they are just different balanced representations of the same information.

Now, at last, the property passes. (We discuss why we need *both* this equivalence, and structural equality on trees, in Sect. 7).

There is a different way to address the first problem—that the order of insertions *does* matter, when inserting the same key twice. That is to *require* the keys to be different, via a precondition:

$$prop\_InsertInsertWeak\ (k, v)\ (k', v')\ t =$$
$$k \not\equiv k' \implies insert\ k\ v\ (insert\ k'\ v'\ t) \simeq insert\ k'\ v'\ (insert\ k\ v\ t)$$

This lets us keep the property in a simpler form, but is weaker, since it no longer captures that "the last insert wins". We will return to this point later.

We can go on to define further metamorphic properties for *insert*, with different modifiers—*delete* and *union*:

$$prop\_InsertDelete\ (k, v)\ k'\ t =$$
$$insert\ k\ v\ (delete\ k'\ t)$$
$$\simeq$$
$$\textbf{if } k \equiv k' \textbf{ then } insert\ k\ v\ t \textbf{ else } delete\ k'\ (insert\ k\ v\ t)$$
$$prop\_InsertUnion\ (k, v)\ t\ t' =$$
$$insert\ k\ v\ (union\ t\ t') \simeq union\ (insert\ k\ v\ t)\ t'$$

and, in a similar way, metamorphic properties for the other functions in the API under test. We derived sixteen different properties in this way, which are listed in Appendix A. The trickiest case is *union* which, as a binary operation, can have *either* argument modified—or both. We also found that some properties could be motivated in more than one way. For example, *prop_InsertUnion* (above) can be motivated as a metamorphic test for *insert*, in which the argument is modified by *union*, or as a metamorphic test for *union*, in which the argument is modified by *insert*. Likewise, the metamorphic tests we wrote for *find* replicated the postconditions we wrote above for *insert*, *delete* and *union*. We do not see this as a problem: that there is more than one way to motivate a property does not make it any less useful, or any harder to come up with!

Summary: *A metamorphic property tests a single function by making (usually) two related calls, and checking the expected relationship between the two results.*

Preservation of Equivalence. Now that we have an equivalence relation on trees, we may wonder whether the operations under test *preserve* it. For example, we might try to test whether *insert* preserves equivalence as follows:

$$prop\_InsertPreservesEquiv\ k\ v\ t\ t' =$$
$$t \simeq t' \implies insert\ k\ v\ t \simeq insert\ k\ v\ t'$$

This kind of property is important, since many of our metamorphic properties only allow us to conclude that two expressions are equivalent; to use these conclusions in further reasoning, we need to know that equivalence is preserved by each operation.

Unfortunately, testing the property above does not work; it is very, very unlikely that two randomly generated trees t and t' will be equivalent, and thus almost all generated tests are discarded. To test this kind of property, we need to *generate equivalent pairs of trees* together. We can do so be defining a *type* of equivalent pairs, with a custom generator and shrinker—see Fig. 4. This generator constructs two equivalent trees by inserting the *same* list of keys and values in two different orders; the shrinker is omitted for brevity. The properties using this type appear in Fig. 5, along with properties to test the new generator and shrinker.

data *Equivs k v = BST k v :≏: BST k v* **deriving** *Show*

instance *(Arbitrary k, Arbitrary v, Ord k)* ⇒ *Arbitrary (Equivs k v)* **where**
   arbitrary = **do**
     .kvs ← L.nubBy ((≡) 'on' fst) < $ > arbitrary
     kvs' ← shuffle kvs
     return (tree kvs :≏: tree kvs')
     where *tree = foldr (uncurry insert) nil*
   shrink (t1 :≏: t2) = ...

Fig. 4. Generating equivalent trees.

prop_InsertPreservesEquiv k v (t :≏: t') = insert k v t ≏ insert k v t'
prop_DeletePreservesEquiv k (t :≏: t') = delete k t ≏ delete k t'
prop_UnionPreservesEquiv (t1 :≏: t1') (t2 :≏: t2') = union t1 t2 ≏ union t1' t2'
prop_FindPreservesEquiv k (t :≏: t') = find k t == find k t'
prop_Equivs (t :≏: t') = t ≏ t'
prop_ShrinkEquivs (t :≏: t') =
   t ≏ t' ⟹ all (λ(t :≏: t') → t ≏ t') (shrink (t :≏: t'))
   where *t ≏ t' = toList t ≡ toList t'*

Fig. 5. Preservation of equivalence.

4.4 Inductive Testing

"Inductive proofs inspire inductive tests."

Metamorphic properties do not, in general, *completely* specify the behaviour of the code under test. However, in some cases, a subset of metamorphic properties *does* form a complete specification. Consider, for example, the following two properties of *union*:

$$prop\_UnionNil1\ t = union\ nil\ t \Longrightarrow t$$
$$prop\_UnionInsert\ t\ t'\ (k, v) =$$
$$union\ (insert\ k\ v\ t)\ t' \simeq insert\ k\ v\ (union\ t\ t')$$

We can argue that these two properties characterize the behaviour of *union* precisely (up to equivalence of trees), *by induction on the size of union's first argument*. This idea is due to Claessen [8].

However, there is a hidden assumption in the argument above—namely, that *any non-empty tree t can be expressed in the form insert k v t', for some smaller tree t'*, or equivalently, that any tree can be constructed using insertions only. There is no reason to believe this *a priori*—it might be that some tree shapes can only be constructed by *delete* or *union*. So, to confirm that these two properties uniquely characterize *union*, we must test this assumption.

One way to do so is to define a function that maps a tree to a list of insertions that recreate it. It is sufficient to insert the key in each node before the keys in its subtrees:

$$insertions\ Leaf = [\,]$$
$$insertions\ (Branch\ l\ k\ v\ r) = (k, v) : insertions\ l \,+\!\!+\, insertions\ r$$

Now we can write a property to check that *every* tree can be reconstructed from its list of insertions:

$$prop\_InsertComplete\ t = t \Longrightarrow foldl\ (flip\ \$\ uncurry\ insert)\ nil\ (insertions\ t)$$

However, this is not sufficient! Recall that the generator we are using, defined in Sect. 3, generates a tree by *performing a list of insertions*! It is clear that any *such* tree can be built using only *insert*, and so the property above can never fail, but what we need to know is that the same is true of trees returned by *delete* and *union*! We must thus define additional properties to test this:

$$prop\_InsertCompleteForDelete\ k\ t = prop\_InsertComplete\ (delete\ k\ t)$$
$$prop\_InsertCompleteForUnion\ t\ t' = prop\_InsertComplete\ (union\ t\ t')$$

Together, these properties also justify our choice of generator—they show that we really *can* generate any tree constructible using the tree API. If we could *not* demonstrate that trees returned by *delete* and *union* can also be constructed using *insert*, then we could define a more complex generator for trees that uses all the API operations, rather than just *insert*—a workable approach, but considerably trickier, and harder to tune for a good distribution of test data.

Finally, we note that in these completeness properties, it is vital to check *structural equality* between trees, and not just equivalence. The whole point is to show that *delete* and *union* cannot construct otherwise unreacheable *shapes* of trees, which might provoke bugs in the implementation.

Summary: *Inductive properties relate a call of the function-under-test to calls with smaller arguments. A set of inductive properties covering all possible cases together test the base case(s) and induction step(s) of an inductive proof-of-correctness. If all the properties hold, then we know the function is correct–inductive properties together make up a complete test.*

4.5   Model-Based Properties

"Abstract away from details to simplify properties."

In 1972, Hoare published an approach to proving the correctness of data representations [14], by relating them to abstract data using an *abstraction function*. Hoare defines a concrete and abstract implementation for each operation, and then proves that diagrams such as this one commute:

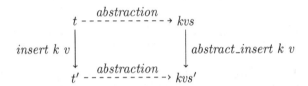

In this case we abstract trees t (the concrete implementation) as *ordered lists of key–value pairs kvs* (the abstract data), using an abstraction function which is just *toList*. The diagram says that both paths from top left to bottom right should yield the same result: applying the concrete version of insertion to a tree, and then abstracting the result to a list of key–value pairs, yields the *same* list as the abstract version of insertion, applied to the abstracted input. If a similar diagram commutes for every operation in an API, then it follows that any sequence of concrete operations behaves in the same way as the same sequence of abstract ones.

We can use the same idea for testing. Since *Data.List* already provides an insertion function for ordered lists, it is tempting to define

$$prop\_InsertModel \; k \; v \; t = toList \; (insert \; k \; v \; t) == L.insert \; (k, v) \; (toList \; t)$$

(in which *Data.List* is imported under the name L). However, this property fails:

```
*** Failed! Falsified (after 5 tests and 6 shrinks):
0
0
Branch Leaf 0 0 Leaf
[(0,0)] /= [(0,0),(0,0)]
```

The problem is that the insertion function in *Data.List* may create duplicate elements, but *insert* for trees does not. So it is not quite the correct abstract implementation; we can correct this by deleting the key if it is initially present—see the correct properties in Fig. 6.

We refer to these properties as "model-based" properties, and we refer to the abstract datatype, in this case an ordered list of keys and values, as the

$prop\_NilModel = toList\ (nil :: Tree) \mathrel{==} [\,]$

$prop\_InsertModel\ k\ v\ t =$
    $toList\ (insert\ k\ v\ t) \mathrel{==} L.insert\ (k, v)\ (deleteKey\ k\ \$\ toList\ t)$

$prop\_DeleteModel\ k\ t = toList\ (delete\ k\ t) \mathrel{==} deleteKey\ k\ (toList\ t)$

$prop\_UnionModel\ t\ t' =$
    $toList\ (union\ t\ t') \mathrel{==} L.sort\ (L.unionBy\ ((\equiv)\ `on`\ fst)\ (toList\ t)\ (toList\ t'))$

$prop\_FindModel\ k\ t = find\ k\ t \mathrel{==} L.lookup\ k\ (toList\ t)$

$deleteKey\ k = filter\ ((\not\equiv k) \circ fst)$

Fig. 6. Model-based properties.

"model". The model can be thought of as a kind of *reference implementation* of the operations under test, though with a much simpler representation. Model-based properties are very powerful: they make up a complete specification of the behaviour of the operations under test, with only a single property per operation. On the other hand, they do require us to construct a model, which in more complex situations may be quite expensive, or may resemble the actual implementation more than is healthy.

Summary: *A model-based property tests a single function by making a single call, and comparing its result to the result of a related "abstract operation" applied to related abstract arguments. An abstraction function maps the real, concrete arguments and results to abstract values, which we also call the "model".*

4.6 A Note on Generation

Throughout this paper, we have used integers as test data, for both keys and values. This is generally an acceptable choice, although not necessarily ideal. It is useful to *measure the distribution* of test data, to judge whether or not tests are likely to find bugs efficiently. In this case, many properties refer to one or more keys, and a tree, generated independently. We may therefore wonder, how often does such a key actually occur in an independently generated tree?

To find out, we can define a property just for *measurement*. QuickCheck allows properties to label test cases with one or more strings; the labelling strings are collected as tests are run, and their distribution displayed in a table afterwards. In this case, we measure how often k appears in t, and also *where* among the keys of t it appears:

prop_Measure k t =
    label (**if** $k \in keys\ t$ **then** "present" **else** "absent") $
    label (**if** $t \equiv nil$ **then** "empty" **else**
        if $keys\ t \equiv [k]$ **then** "just k" **else**
        if $(all\ (\geqslant k)\ (keys\ t))$ **then** "at start" **else**
        if $(all\ (\leqslant k)\ (keys\ t))$ **then** "at end" **else**
        "middle") $
    True

Two tables are generated by testing this property, one for each of the calls of the *label* function. After a million tests, we saw the following distributions:

```
79.1973% absent
20.8027% present

75.0878% middle
 9.6716% at end
 9.6534% at start
 5.1782% empty
 0.4090% just k
```

From the second table, we can see that k appears at the beginning or end of the keys in t about 10% of the time for each case, while it appears somewhere in the middle of the sequences of keys 75% of the time. This looks quite reasonable. On the other hand, *in almost 80% of tests, k is not found in the tree at all!*

For some of the properties we defined, this will result in quite inefficient testing. For example, consider the postcondition for *insert*:

prop_InsertPost k v t k' =
    find k' (*insert k v t*) $\Longrightarrow$ **if** $k \equiv k'$ **then** *Just v* **else** *find k' t*

In almost 80% of tests k' will not be present in t, and since k' is rarely equal to k, then in most of these cases both sides of the equation will be *Nothing*. In effect, we spend most of our effort testing that inserting key k does not insert an *unrelated key k'* into the tree! While this would be a serious bug if it occurred, it seems disproportionate to devote so much test effort to this kind of case.

More reasonable would be to divide our test effort roughly equally between cases in which the given key *does* occur in the random tree, and cases in which it does not. We can achieve this by *changing the generation of keys*. If we choose keys *from a smaller set*, then we will generate equal keys more often. For example, we might define a **newtype** of keys containing a smaller non-negative integer:

newtype *Key = Key Int* **deriving** (*Eq, Ord, Show*)

instance *Arbitrary Key* **where**
    arbitrary = **do**
        NonNegative n $\leftarrow$ *scale* ('*div*'2) *arbitrary*
        return $ *Key n*
    shrink (*Key k*) = *Key* <$> *shrink k*

Here *scale* adjusts QuickCheck's internal size parameter in the generation of n, resulting in random values whose average is half that of QuickCheck's normal random non-negative integers. Testing *prop_Measure* using this type for keys results in the following, much better, distribution:

```
55.3881% present
44.6119% absent

70.6567% middle
11.6540% at end
10.8601% at start
 5.1937% empty
 1.6355% just k
```

This example illustrates that "collisions" (that is, cases in which we randomly choose the same value in two places) can be important test cases. Indeed, consider the following (obviously false) property:

$$prop\_Unique \; x \; y = x \not\equiv y$$

If we were to choose x and y uniformly from the entire range of 64-bit integers, then QuickCheck would never be able to falsify it, in practice. If we use QuickCheck's built-in *Int* generator, then the property fails in around 3.3% of cases. Using the *Key* generator we have just defined, the property fails in 9.3% of cases. The choice of generator should be made on the basis of how important collisions are as test cases.

5   Bug Hunting

To evaluate the properties we have written, we created eight buggy implementations of binary search trees, with bugs ranging from subtle to blatant. These implementations are listed in Fig. 7.

The results of testing each property for each buggy version are shown in Fig. 8. We make the following observations.

5.1   Bug Finding Effectiveness

Validity properties miss many bugs (five of eight), as do "preservation of equivalence" and "completeness of insertion" properties. In contrast, every bug is found by at least one postcondition, metamorphic property, and model-based property.

Invalid test data provokes false positives. Bug #2, which causes invalid trees to be generated as test cases, causes many properties that *do not use insert* to fail. This is why *prop_ArbitraryValid* is so important—when it fails, we need not waste time debugging false positives in properties unrelated to the bug. Because of these false positives, we ignore bug #2 in the rest of this discussion.

Bug #	Description
1	*insert* discards the existing tree, returning a single-node tree just containing the newly inserted value.
2	*insert* fails to recognize and update an existing key, inserting a duplicate entry instead.
3	*insert* fails to update an existing key, leaving the tree unchanged instead.
4	*delete* fails to rebuild the tree above the key being deleted, returning only the remainder of the tree from that point on (an easy mistake for those used to imperative programming to make).
5	Key comparisons reversed in *delete*; only works correctly at the root of the tree.
6	*union* wrongly assumes that all the keys in the first argument precede those in the second.
7	*union* wrongly assumes that if the key at the root of t is smaller than the key at the root of t', then all the keys in t will be smaller than the key at the root of t'.
8	*union* works correctly, except that when both trees contain the same key, the left argument does not always take priority.

Fig. 7. The eight buggy implementations.

Model-based properties are effective at finding bugs; each property tests just one operation, and finds every bug in that operation. In fact, the model-based properties together form a complete specification of the code, and so should be expected to find every bug.

Postconditions are quite effective; each postcondition for a buggy operation finds all the bugs we planted in it, but some postconditions are less effective than we might expect. For example, *prop_FindPostPresent* uses both *find* and *insert*, so we might expect it to reveal the three bugs in *insert*, but it reveals only two of them.

Metamorphic properties are less effective individually, but powerful in combination. Weak properties miss bugs (compare each line ending in *Weak* with the line below), because their preconditions to exclude tricky test cases result in tricky bugs escaping detection. But even stronger-looking properties that we might expect to find bugs miss them—*prop_InsertDelete* misses bug #1 in *insert*, *prop_DeleteInsert* misses bug #3 in *insert*, and so on. Degenerate metamorphic properties involving *nil* are particularly ineffective. Metamorphic properties are essentially an axiomatization of the API under test, and there is no guarantee that this axiomitization is complete, so some bugs might be missed altogether.

Property	insert bugs #1	#2	#3	delete bugs #4	#5	union bugs #6	#7	#8
Validity properties								
prop_ArbitraryValid		X						
prop_NilValid								
prop_InsertValid		X						
prop_DeleteValid		X						
prop_UnionValid		X				X	X	
prop_ShrinkValid								
Postconditions								
prop_InsertPost	X	X	X					
prop_DeletePost		X		X	X			
prop_FindPostPresent		X	X					
prop_FindPostAbsent		X			X			
prop_InsertDeleteComplete		X		X				
prop_UnionPost						X	X	X
Metamorphic properties								
prop_InsertInsertWeak	X							
prop_InsertInsert	X	X	X					
prop_InsertDeleteWeak				X				
prop_InsertDelete		X	X	X				
prop_InsertUnion	X	X	X			X	X	X
prop_DeleteNil								
prop_DeleteInsertWeak				X				
prop_DeleteInsert	X	X		X	X			
prop_DeleteDelete				X	X			
prop_DeleteUnion		X		X	X	X	X	X
prop_UnionNil1								

Property	insert bugs #1	#2	#3	delete bugs #4	#5	union bugs #6	#7	#8
Metamorphic properties contd.								
prop_UnionNil2								
prop_UnionDeleteInsert	X	X	X	X	X	X	X	X
prop_UnionUnionIdem						X		
prop_UnionUnionAssoc						X	X	X
prop_FindNil								
prop_FindInsert	X	X	X					
prop_FindDelete		X		X	X			
prop_FindUnion						X	X	X
Preservation of equivalence								
prop_InsertPreservesEquivWeak								
prop_InsertPreservesEquiv	X			X	X			
prop_DeletePreservesEquiv	X						X	X
prop_UnionPreservesEquiv	X						X	X
prop_FindPreservesEquiv	X							
Completeness of insertion								
prop_InsertComplete								
prop_InsertCompleteForDelete								
prop_InsertCompleteForUnion	X					X	X	
Model-based properties								
prop_NilModel								
prop_InsertModel	X	X	X					
prop_DeleteModel		X		X	X			
prop_UnionModel		X				X	X	X
prop_FindModel								
Total failures	12	17	8	12	9	10	10	8

Fig. 8. Failing properties for each bug.

5.2 Bug Finding Performance

Property type	Min	Max	Mean
Postcondition	7.1	245	77
Metamorphic	2.4	714	56
Model-based	3.1	9.8	5.8

Fig. 9. Average mean number of tests required to make a property of each type fail.

Hitherto we have discussed which properties *can* find bugs, given enough testing time. But it also matters *how quickly* a property can find a bug. For seven of our eight bugs (omitting bug #2, which causes invalid test cases to be generated), and for each postcondition, metamorphic property, and model-based property that detects the bug, we found a counterexample to the property using QuickCheck 1,000 times with different random seeds, and recorded the *mean number of tests* needed to make that property fail for that bug. Note that finding a counterexample 1,000 times requires running far more than 1,000 random tests: we ran over 700,000 tests of the hardest-to-falsify property in total, in order to find a counterexample 1,000 times. We then averaged the mean-time-to-failure across all bugs, and all properties of the same type. The results are summarized in Fig. 9.

In this example model-based properties find bugs far faster than postconditions or metamorphic properties, while metamorphic properties find bugs a little faster than postconditions on average, but their mean time to failure varies more.

Digging a little deeper, for the same bug in *union*, *prop_UnionPost* fails after 50 tests on average, while *prop_UnionModel* fails after only 8.4 tests, *even though they are logically equivalent*. The reason is that after computing a *union* that is affected by the bug, the model-based property checks that the *model* of the result is correct—which requires *every* key and value to be correct. The post-condition, on the other hand, checks that a *random* key has the correct value in the result. Thus *prop_UnionPost* may exercise the bug many times without detecting it. Each model-based test may take a little longer to run, because it validates the result of *union* more thoroughly, but this is not significant compared to the enormous difference in the *number* of tests required to find the bug—the entire test case must be generated, and the *union* computed, in either case, so the difference in validation time is not really important.

5.3 Lessons

These results suggest that, if time is limited, then writing model-based properties may offer the best return on investment, in combination with validity properties to ensure we don't encounter confusing failures caused by invalid data. In situations where the model is complex (and thus expensive) to define, or where the model resembles the implementation so closely that the same bugs are likely in each, then metamorphic properties offer an effective alternative, at the cost of writing many more properties.

6 Related Work

Pre- and post-conditions were introduced by Hoare [15] for the purpose of proving programs correct, inspired by Floyd [11]. The notion of a data representation invariant, which we use here for "validity testing", comes from Hoare's 1972 paper on proving data representations correct [14]. Pre- and post-conditions and invariants also form an integral part of Meyer's "Design by Contract" approach to designing software [18], in which an invariant is specified for each class, and pre- and post-conditions for each class method, and these can optionally be checked at run-time—for example during testing.

Metamorphic testing was introduced by Chen, Cheung and Yiu as a way of deriving tests that do not require an oracle [6]. They consider, for example, an algorithm to find shortest-paths in a graph. While it is difficult to check whether a path found by the algorithm is actually shortest, it is easy to compare the path found from a node with the paths found from its neighbours, and check that it is no longer than the shortest path via a neighbour. As in this case, the key idea is to compare results from multiple invocations of the code-under-test, and check that an appropriate "metamorphic relation" holds between them.

We have used equalities and equivalences as metamorphic relations in this paper, but the idea is much more general—for example, one might test that *insert* does not *reduce the size* of a tree, which would catch bugs that accidentally discard part of the structure. Metamorphic testing is useful in many contexts, and is now the subject of an annual workshop series[8].

Metamorphic properties which are equations or equivalences are a form of *algebraic specification* [13]. Guttag and Horning divide the operations into those that return the type of interest (*nil*, *insert*, *delete*, and *union*, in our case), and *observations* that return a different type (*find*). They give conditions for "sufficient completeness", meaning that the specification precisely determines the value of any observation.

We already saw that the idea behind model-based properties comes from Hoare's seminal paper [14]. Using an abstract model as a specification is also at the heart of the Z specification language [25], and the field of model-based testing [5], an active research area with two workshop series devoted to it[9,10].

The title of the paper is of course inspired by Polya's classic book [22].

7   Discussion

We have discussed a number of different kinds of properties that a developer can try to formulate to test an implementation: invariant properties, postconditions, metamorphic properties, inductive properties, and model-based properties. Each kind of property is based on a widely applicable idea, usable in many different settings. When writing metamorphic properties, we discovered the need to define *equivalence* of data structures, and thus also to define properties that test for preservation of equivalence. We discussed the importance of *completeness*—our test data generator should be able to generate any test case—and saw how to test this. We saw the importance of testing both our generators and our shrinkers, to ensure that other properties are tested with valid data. We saw how to *measure* the distribution of test data, to ensure that test effort is well spent.

Model-based testing seemed the most effective approach overall, revealing all our bugs with a small number of properties, and generally finding bugs fast. But metamorphic testing was a fertile source of ideas, and was almost as effective at revealing bugs, so is a useful alternative, especially in situations where a model is expensive to construct.

We saw that some properties must use equivalence to compare values, while other properties must use structural equality. Thus, we need *two* notions of "equality" for the data structures under test. In fact, it is the *equivalence* which ought to be exported as the equality instance for binary search trees, because structural equality distinguishes representations that ought to be considered equal outside the abstraction barrier of the abstract data type. Yet we need to use structural equality in some properties, and of course, we want to use the

---

[8] http://metwiki.net/MET19/.

[9] http://mbt-workshop.org/.

[10] https://conf.researchr.org/series/a-most.

derived *Eq* instance for the representation datatype for this. So we appear to need *two Eq* instances for the same type! The solution to this conundrum is to define *two* types: a data type of representations with a derived structural equality, which is *not* exported to clients, and a **newtype** isomorphic to this datatype, which is exported, with an *Eq* instance which defines equality to be equivalence. This approach does mean that some properties must be *inside* the abstraction barrier of the data type, and thus must be placed in the same module as the implementation, which may not be desirable as it mixes test code and implementation code. An alternative is to define an *Internals* module which exports the representation type, and can be imported by test code, but is not used by client modules.

The choice of properties (and generators) may also depend on whether the tester takes a "white box" or "black box" view of the code. From the perspective of an *implementor*, it makes sense to use properties such as validity properties, that depend on the representation of the data. From the perspective of a *user*, properties should use only the API exported by the implementor—as do metamorphic and model-based properties. In this paper we generated random trees using the exported API, but of course we could also have generated the representation directly. This is certainly possible, but more complicated and error-prone, and often no more effective.

The ideas in this paper are applicable to testing any *pure* code, but code with side-effects demands a somewhat different approach. In this case, every operation has an implicit "state" argument, and an invisible state result, making properties harder to formulate. Test cases are *sequences* of operations, to set up the state for each operation under test, and to observe changes made to the state afterwards. Nevertheless, the same ideas can be adapted to this setting; in particular, there are a number of state-machine modelling libraries for property-based testing tools that support a "model-based" approach in a stateful setting. State machine modelling is heavily used at Quviq AB[11] for testing customer software, and an account of some of these examples can be found in [16].

We hope the reader will find the ideas in this paper helpful in developing effective property-based tests in the future.

Acknowledgements. I'm grateful to the anonymous referees for many useful suggested improvements, and to Vetenskapsrådet for funding this work under the SyTeC grant.

---

[11] A company founded in 2006 by the author and Thomas Arts, to commercialize property based testing. See http://quviq.com.

A Metamorphic Properties

$prop\_InsertInsertWeak\ (k, v)\ (k', v')\ t = k \not\equiv k' \implies$
$\quad insert\ k\ v\ (insert\ k'\ v'\ t) \simeq insert\ k'\ v'\ (insert\ k\ v\ t)$

$prop\_InsertInsert\ (k, v)\ (k', v')\ t =$
$\quad insert\ k\ v\ (insert\ k'\ v'\ t)$
$\quad \simeq \mathbf{if}\ k \equiv k'\ \mathbf{then}\ insert\ k\ v\ t\ \mathbf{else}\ insert\ k'\ v'\ (insert\ k\ v\ t)$

$prop\_InsertDeleteWeak\ (k, v)\ k'\ t = k \not\equiv k' \implies$
$\quad insert\ k\ v\ (delete\ k'\ t) \simeq delete\ k'\ (insert\ k\ v\ t)$

$prop\_InsertDelete\ (k, v)\ k'\ t =$
$\quad insert\ k\ v\ (delete\ k'\ t)$
$\quad \simeq \mathbf{if}\ k \equiv k'\ \mathbf{then}\ insert\ k\ v\ t\ \mathbf{else}\ delete\ k'\ (insert\ k\ v\ t)$

$prop\_InsertUnion\ (k, v)\ t\ t' = insert\ k\ v\ (union\ t\ t') \simeq union\ (insert\ k\ v\ t)\ t'$

$prop\_DeleteInsertWeak\ k\ (k', v')\ t = k \not\equiv k' \implies$
$\quad delete\ k\ (insert\ k'\ v'\ t) \simeq insert\ k'\ v'\ (delete\ k\ t)$

$prop\_DeleteNil\ k = delete\ k\ nil === (nil :: Tree)$

$prop\_DeleteInsert\ k\ (k', v')\ t =$
$\quad delete\ k\ (insert\ k'\ v'\ t)$
$\quad \simeq \mathbf{if}\ k \equiv k'\ \mathbf{then}\ delete\ k\ t\ \mathbf{else}\ insert\ k'\ v'\ (delete\ k\ t)$

$prop\_DeleteDelete\ k\ k'\ t = delete\ k\ (delete\ k'\ t) \simeq delete\ k'\ (delete\ k\ t)$

$prop\_DeleteUnion\ k\ t\ t' =$
$\quad delete\ k\ (union\ t\ t') \simeq union\ (delete\ k\ t)\ (delete\ k\ t')$

$prop\_UnionNil1\ t = union\ nil\ t === t$

$prop\_UnionNil2\ t = union\ t\ nil === t$

$prop\_UnionDeleteInsert\ t\ t'\ (k, v) =$
$\quad union\ (delete\ k\ t)\ (insert\ k\ v\ t') \simeq insert\ k\ v\ (union\ t\ t')$

$prop\_UnionUnionIdem\ t = union\ t\ t \simeq t$

$prop\_UnionUnionAssoc\ t1\ t2\ t3 =$
$\quad union\ (union\ t1\ t2)\ t3 === union\ t1\ (union\ t2\ t3)$

$prop\_FindNil\ k = find\ k\ (nil :: Tree) === Nothing$

$prop\_FindInsert\ k\ (k', v')\ t =$
$\quad find\ k\ (insert\ k'\ v'\ t) === \mathbf{if}\ k \equiv k'\ \mathbf{then}\ Just\ v'\ \mathbf{else}\ find\ k\ t$

$prop\_FindDelete\ k\ k'\ t =$
$\quad find\ k\ (delete\ k'\ t) === \mathbf{if}\ k \equiv k'\ \mathbf{then}\ Nothing\ \mathbf{else}\ find\ k\ t$

$prop\_FindUnion\ k\ t\ t' = find\ k\ (union\ t\ t') === (find\ k\ t <|> find\ k\ t')$

References

1. Amaral, C., Florido, M., Santos Costa, V.: PrologCheck – property-based testing in prolog. In: Codish, M., Sumii, E. (eds.) FLOPS 2014. LNCS, vol. 8475, pp. 1–17. Springer, Cham (2014). https://doi.org/10.1007/978-3-319-07151-0_1

2. Arts, T., Hughes, J., Johansson, J., Wiger, U.T.: Testing telecoms software with Quviq QuickCheck. In: Feeley, M., Trinder, P.W. (eds.) Proceedings of the 2006 ACM SIGPLAN Workshop on Erlang, Portland, Oregon, USA, 16 September 2006, pp. 2–10. ACM (2006)

3. Barr, E.T., Harman, M., McMinn, P., Shahbaz, M., Yoo, S.: The oracle problem in software testing: a survey. IEEE Trans. Soft. Eng. **41**(5), 507–525 (2015)

4. Braquehais, R.M.: Tools for discovery, refinement and generalization of functional properties by enumerative testing. Ph.D. thesis, University of York, UK (2017)

5. Broy, M., Jonsson, B., Katoen, J.-P., Leucker, M., Pretschner, A. (eds.): Model-Based Testing of Reactive Systems. LNCS, vol. 3472. Springer, Heidelberg (2005). https://doi.org/10.1007/b137241

6. Chen, T.Y., Cheung, S.C., Yiu, S.M.: Metamorphic testing: a new approach for generating next test cases. Technical report, HKUST-CS98-01, Department of Computer Science, Hong Kong (1998)

7. Chen, T.Y., et al.: Metamorphic testing: a review of challenges and opportunities. ACM Comput. Surv. **51**(1), 4:1–4:27 (2018)

8. Claessen, K.: Inductive testing. Private communication. https://docs.google.com/presentation/d/1pejW9foV4ZAw5e03kYR3urNQsIPobomY_5HshxZQpLc/edit?usp=drivesdk

9. Claessen, K., Hughes, J.: QuickCheck: a lightweight tool for random testing of Haskell programs. In: Proceedings of 5th ACM SIGPLAN International Conference on Functional Programming, ICFP 2000 (2000)

10. Lindley, S., McBride, C., Trinder, P., Sannella, D. (eds.): A List of Successes That Can Change the World. LNCS, vol. 9600. Springer, Cham (2016). https://doi.org/10.1007/978-3-319-30936-1

11. Floyd, R.W.: Assigning meanings to programs. In: Colburn, T.R., Fetzer, J.H., Rankin, T.L. (eds.) Program Verification, vol. 14, pp. 65–81. Springer, Dordrecht (1993). https://doi.org/10.1007/978-94-011-1793-7_4

12. Godefroid, P., Klarlund, N., Sen, K.: DART: directed automated random testing. ACM SIGPLAN Not. **40**, 213–223 (2005)

13. Guttag, J.V., Horning, J.J.: The algebraic specification of abstract data types. Acta Inform. **10**(1), 27–52 (1978)

14. Hoare, C.A.: Proof of correctness of data representations. Acta Inform. **1**(4), 271–281 (1972)

15. Hoare, C.A.R.: An axiomatic basis for computer programming. Commun. ACM **12**(10), 576–580 (1969)

16. Hughes, J.: Experiences with QuickCheck: testing the hard stuff and staying sane. In: Lindley et al. [10], pp. 169–186 (2016)

17. Löscher, A., Sagonas, K.: Targeted property-based testing. In: Proceedings of the 26th ACM SIGSOFT International Symposium on Software Testing and Analysis, pp. 46–56. ACM (2017)

18. Meyer, B.: Applying 'design by contract'. Computer **25**(10), 40–51 (1992)

19. Nilsson, R.: ScalaCheck: The Definitive Guide. Artima Press, Mountain View (2014)

20. Papadakis, M., Sagonas, K.: A proper integration of types and function specifications with property-based testing. In: Proceedings of the 10th ACM SIGPLAN Workshop on Erlang, pp. 39–50. ACM (2011)

21. Pike, L.: SmartCheck: automatic and efficient counterexample reduction and generalization. In: Swierstra, W. (ed.) Proceedings of the 2014 ACM SIGPLAN Symposium on Haskell, Gothenburg, Sweden, 4–5 September 2014, pp. 53–64. ACM (2014)

22. Polya, G.: How To Solve It! A System of Thinking Which Can Help You Solve Any Problem. Princeton University Press, Princeton (1945)
23. Runciman, C., Naylor, M., Lindblad, F.: SmallCheck and lazy SmallCheck: automatic exhaustive testing for small values. In: Gill, A. (ed.) Proceedings of the 1st ACM SIGPLAN Symposium on Haskell, Haskell 2008, Victoria, BC, Canada, 25 September 2008, pp. 37–48. ACM (2008)
24. Sen, K., Marinov, D., Agha, G.: CUTE: a concolic unit testing engine for C. ACM SIGSOFT Softw. Eng. Notes **30**, 263–272 (2005)
25. Spivey, J.M.: Understanding Z: A Specification Language and Its Formal Semantics, vol. 3. Cambridge University Press, Cambridge (1988)

Type Inference for Rank 2 Gradual Intersection Types

Pedro Ângelo[(✉)] and Mário Florido

Faculdade de Ciências & LIACC, Universidade do Porto, Porto, Portugal
pedro.angelo@fc.up.pt, amf@dcc.fc.up.pt

Abstract. In this paper, we extend a rank 2 intersection type system with gradual types. We then show that the problem of finding a principal typing for a lambda term, in a rank 2 gradual intersection type system is decidable. We present a type inference algorithm which builds the principal typing of a term through the generation of type constraints which are solved by a new extended unification algorithm constructing the most general unifier for rank 2 gradual intersection types.

1 Introduction

Gradual typing [5,6,11,12] has earned a great deal of attention in the types research community. Aiming to seamlessly integrate static and dynamic typing, its focus is on enabling the fine-tuning of the distribution of static and dynamic type checking in a program, and to harness the strengths of both typing disciplines. The successful application [11] of gradual typing to the parametric polymorphic Hindley-Milner (HM) type system [9,14,20] marks an important breakthrough, showing that it is possible to apply it to statically typed functional programming languages such as Haskell or ML.

Intersection types [7,8,18,25] extend the simply typed lambda-calculus [13], adding to the language of types an intersection operator $\cap$ and allowing to type terms with different types belonging to an intersection $(T_1 \cap \ldots \cap T_n)$. Intersection types provide a form of polymorphism in which it is possible to explicitly indicate every single instance of a type. Thus a term may have multiple types belonging to a finite set (intersection) of type possibilities. Although the type inference problem for intersection types is not decidable in general, it becomes decidable for finite rank fragments of the general system [17].

Recently there has been an increasing interest in intersection types for general purpose programming languages. Examples include TypeScript [26] and Flow [4]. These systems use intersection types to combine different types into one. This enables its use in contexts where the classic object-oriented model does not apply. Rank 2 intersection types [15,16] are particularly interesting for languages with type inference: they are more powerful than parametric polymorphic types [9] for functional programming languages such as ML, because they type more terms, and this extra power comes for free, since the complexity of typability is identical in both systems. In fact, in the two systems typability is DEXPTIME-complete.

© Springer Nature Switzerland AG 2020
W. J. Bowman and R. Garcia (Eds.): TFP 2019, LNCS 12053, pp. 84–120, 2020.
https://doi.org/10.1007/978-3-030-47147-7_5

In this paper, we present a type inference algorithm for a rank 2 intersection gradual type system which automatically deduces the type of an expression, allowing the programmer to write code without worrying about type annotations.

If dynamic types, which are only introduced by a programmer, are allowed as instances of intersection types, expressions may be typed with both static and dynamic types simultaneously. For example, consider the following expression:

$$\lambda x : Int \cap Dyn \, . \, x \, x$$

The occurrences of the variable x may be assigned both the Dyn and the Int type. A possible assignment of types which well-types the expression is the following:

$$\lambda x : Int \cap Dyn \, . \, x^{Dyn} \, x^{Int}$$

Here we define a type inference algorithm which first generates a set of constraints on types and then solves them using an extended type unification algorithm. The first phase of type inference is to assign initial types to expressions and then generate constraints between these types. For example, consider the expression referred previously:

$$\lambda x : Int \cap Dyn \, . \, x \, x$$

Let $\lesssim$ denote a consistent subtyping [12] constraint between two types, which means that the two types might satisfy the consistent subtyping relation. The constraint generation algorithm generates the following initial typings and corresponding constraints for the expression (several typings are generated due to different choices of where to assign types to variables):

$$\lambda x : Int \cap Dyn \, . \, x^{Dyn} \, x^{Int} : (Int \cap Dyn) \rightarrow Dyn$$
$$\{Int \lesssim Dyn\}$$

$$\lambda x : Int \cap Dyn \, . \, x^{Dyn} \, x^{Dyn} : Dyn \rightarrow Dyn$$
$$\{Dyn \lesssim Dyn\}$$

The $\lesssim$ constraint guarantees that, when applying a function, the type of the argument is a consistent subtype of the domain type of the function. The constraint solving algorithm solves the constraints and produces a substitution of types for type variables, which when applied to the initial type assigned to the expression returns a final type for the expression. For the previous example, we will end up with the following well-typed expression as result:

$$\lambda x : Int \cap Dyn \, . \, x \, x : (Int \cap Dyn \rightarrow Dyn) \cap (Dyn \rightarrow Dyn)$$

Thus, this paper makes the following main contributions:

1. A *type inference algorithm*: following [11], our approach first generates type constraints and then solves these constraints using a new unification algorithm for gradual intersection types of rank 2.

2. Theorems of *soundness* and *completeness* of the type inference algorithm, which show that the types returned by the algorithm are derivable in the type system and that, given an expression, the algorithm produces a syntactic description of all the types which type the expression using the type system.
3. The existence of *principal typings*, typings which represent all other typings for the same expression, for rank 2 gradual intersection types.

Related Work. In [2], intersections were used to type overloaded functions which can discriminate on the type of the argument and execute different code for different types. Functions typed with intersections run different pieces of code accordingly to the type of their arguments. These systems extended semantic subtyping [10] with gradual types, and types are interpreted as sets of values. Another view of intersection types originated in the Turin group of intersection type systems [7,8], and was also used in the programming language Forsythe [21,22]. Intersection types are used as finitely parametric polymorphic types where functions with intersection types have a uniform behaviour: when applied to arguments of different types, they always execute the same code for all of these types. Here we follow this second approach. In previous work, we integrated gradual types with intersection types on a gradual intersection type system [29], which considered intersection types without a finite rank restriction, thus the type inference problem was not decidable. In this paper, by restricting intersection types to rank 2, we can define a type inference algorithm.

Type inference for a system with intersection and gradual types was presented before in [3]. In this contribution, constraint solving reused existing solving algorithms such as unification and tallying and, in the type inference algorithm, intersections were coded in a type language with union types, an empty type and negation types. In [3], type inference is sound but not complete, and it is semi-decidable for set-theoretical gradual types. Here we present a sound and complete type inference algorithm, where decidability is achieved by restricting the type system to types of a finite rank.

Type inference for gradual type systems is the topic of other previous works described in [24] and [11]. These systems inferred gradual types for a given expression and were also based on extended type unification algorithms which deal with type equality in the presence of dynamic types. Both systems deal with gradual types, but not intersection types. For intersection type systems, type inference [15–18] was previously defined for finite-rank intersection types, using a generalization of the unification algorithm dealing with the complicated operation of *type expansion*. These systems deal with intersection types but not gradual types.

2   Rank 2 Gradual Intersection Types

We consider a type language where intersection types are limited to rank 2, following a definition of rank 2 inspired in [16,19]. Thus, we define rank 2 gradual intersection types here:

$$T^0 ::= X \mid B \mid Dyn \mid T^0 \rightarrow T^0$$
$$T^1 ::= T^0 \mid T^0 \cap \ldots \cap T^0$$
$$T^2 ::= T^0 \mid T^1 \rightarrow T^2$$

X represents a type variable, B is the set of base types, such as Int and $Bool$, T^0 is the set of simple types, containing type variables, base types and the dynamic type and also arrow types. T^1 is the set of rank 1 types, which contain finite and non-empty intersections of simple types. Finally, T^2 represents the set of rank 2 types, which may contain intersections, but only to the left of a single arrow. We refer to the set of possible types under our system, $T^1 \cup T^2$, simply as T. The following types are considered rank 2 gradual intersection types:

$$(T_1 \rightarrow T_1 \cap T_2 \rightarrow T_2) \rightarrow (T_1 \cap T_2) \rightarrow T$$
$$((T_1 \rightarrow T_2) \cap T_1) \rightarrow T_2$$

However, these do not belong to the set of rank 2 gradual intersection types:

$$((T_1 \rightarrow T_1) \cap (T_2 \rightarrow T_2)) \rightarrow (T_1 \cap T_2) \rightarrow (T_1 \cap T_2)$$
$$((T_1 \cap T_2) \rightarrow T_1) \rightarrow T_2$$

Therefore, intersection types are not allowed in the codomain of an arrow type, agreeing with the original definition in [7]. Intersections are commutative (e.g. $T_1 \cap T_2 = T_2 \cap T_1$), idempotent (e.g. $T_1 \cap T_1 = T_1$) and associative (e.g. $(T_1 \cap T_2) \cap T_3 = T_1 \cap (T_2 \cap T_3)$). There is no distinction between a singleton intersection of types and its sole element, so for any type T, T can be considered an intersection of types of size 1. The intersection type connective $\cap$ has higher precedence (binds tighter) than the arrow type. Also, we can abbreviate an intersection type with the following definition:

$$T_1 \cap \ldots \cap T_n = \bigcap_{i=1}^{n} T_i$$

These two representations are used interchangeably.

In presenting the syntax of our language we will follow the convention that c ranges over constants such as integers and truth values, x ranges over variables, e ranges over expressions and T ranges over types. The language of expressions in our system is given by the following grammar:

$$Expressions\ e ::= x \mid \lambda x : T^1 . e \mid \lambda x . e \mid e\,e \mid c$$

Note that there are two lambda abstraction expressions, one for typed code, allowing the insertion of type annotations, and another one for untyped code, which does not require type annotations. We impose one restriction on type annotations in lambda abstractions, besides being rank 1 types, they may not contain type variables X. As we are presenting a type inference algorithm, type annotations are not required since types will be inferred automatically by the algorithm. We also fix a set of term constants for the base types. For example, we might assume a base type *Int*, and the term constants are the natural numbers. In the type system, term constants have the appropriate base types. Note that if the language is only implicitly typed (without type annotations) the inferred types are static. Dynamic types are introduced only by type annotations. This design option goes back to previous work regarding type inference for gradual typing [11] where also *"there can be no dynamism without annotation"*.

A typing context is a finite set, represented by $\{x_1 : T_1^1, \ldots, x_n : T_n^1\}$, of (type variable, T^1 type) pairs called bindings. We use Γ to range over typing contexts. We write $\Gamma(x)$ for the type bounded by the variable x in the typing context Γ and define $\Gamma(x)$ as: $\Gamma(x) = T$, if $x : T \in \Gamma$. We write $dom(\Gamma)$ for the set $\{x \mid x : T \in \Gamma\}$, for all T, and $cod(\Gamma)$ for the set $\{T \mid x : T \in \Gamma\}$, for all x. We write Γ_x for the typing context Γ with any binding for the variable x removed. We define Γ_x as: $\Gamma_x = \Gamma/\{x : T\}$, for any type T.

An annotation context is a finite set, represented by $\{x_1 : T_1^1, \ldots, x_n : T_n^1\}$, of (type variable, T^1 type) pairs called bindings. We use A to range over annotation contexts. We write $A(x)$ for the type paired with the variable x in the annotation context A, defined as: $A(x) = T$ if $x : T \in A$. We write $dom(A)$ for the set $\{x \mid x : T \in A\}$, for all T. We write $cod(A)$ for the set $\{T \mid x : T \in A\}$, for all x. We write A_x for the annotation context A with any pair for the variable x removed. We define A_x as: $A_x = A/\{x : T\}$, for any type T.

3   Type System

In this section, we present the rank 2 gradual intersection type system (GITS), in Fig. 1. The GITS system type checks an explicitly typed lambda-calculus language with integers and booleans. This type system is composed of type rules that originate from both gradual typing [5] and intersection types, particularly from [7]. As with gradual typing, to declare terms as either dynamically typed or statically typed, we simply add an explicit domain-type declaration in lambda abstractions.

The cornerstone of gradual typing is the $\sim$ (consistency) relation on types. We say that two types are consistent if the parts where both types are defined (static) are equal. If the expected type of an expression is an arrow type, in the T-APP rule for example, but that expression is typed with the *Dyn* type, then the system assumes that the type of the expression is an arrow type. Therefore, pattern matching ($\triangleright$) is a feature of gradual typing that enables the *Dyn* type to be treated as a function type from *Dyn* to *Dyn* ($Dyn \rightarrow Dyn$), or if the type is already an arrow type, it gets its domain and codomain. Rule T-ABS: generalizes a similar rule for abstractions for the Forsythe programming language [22]. In this rule, the type of the formal parameter must be a subset of the set of types declared explicitly in the abstraction (as an intersection type).

We now define the subtyping ($\leq$) relation, which in this system is just a simplified version of the subtyping (or type inclusion) relation from [1]. Albeit having no use in the type system, we include subtyping in this paper because it

Syntax

$$Types\ T, PM ::= \ B \mid Dyn \mid T \to T \mid T \cap \ldots \cap T$$

$$Expressions\ e\ ::=\ x \mid \lambda x\,.\,e \mid \lambda x : T^1\,.\,e \mid e\,e \mid c$$

$\boxed{\Gamma \vdash_{\cap G} e : T}$ Typing

$$\frac{x : T_1 \cap \ldots \cap T_n \in \Gamma}{\Gamma \vdash_{\cap G} x : T_i} \ \text{T-VAR} \qquad \frac{\Gamma, x : T_1 \vdash_{\cap G} e : T_2 \qquad static(T_1)}{\Gamma \vdash_{\cap G} \lambda x\,.\,e : T_1 \to T_2} \ \text{T-ABS}$$

$$\frac{\Gamma, x : T_1 \cap \ldots \cap T_m \vdash_{\cap G} e : T \qquad m \le n}{\Gamma \vdash_{\cap G} \lambda x : T_1 \cap \ldots \cap T_n\,.\,e : T_1 \cap \ldots \cap T_m \to T} \ \text{T-ABS:}$$

$$\frac{\begin{array}{cc} \Gamma \vdash_{\cap G} e_1 : PM \qquad PM \rhd T_1 \cap \ldots \cap T_n \to T \\ \Gamma \vdash_{\cap G} e_2 : T_1' \cap \ldots \cap T_n' \qquad T_1' \lesssim T_1 \ldots T_n' \lesssim T_n \end{array}}{\Gamma \vdash_{\cap G} e_1\,e_2 : T} \ \text{T-APP}$$

$$\frac{\Gamma \vdash_{\cap G} e : T_1 \ \cdots \ \Gamma \vdash_{\cap G} e : T_n}{\Gamma \vdash_{\cap G} e : T_1 \cap \ldots \cap T_n} \ \text{T-GEN} \qquad \frac{\Gamma \vdash_{\cap G} e : T_1 \cap \ldots \cap T_n}{\Gamma \vdash_{\cap G} e : T_i} \ \text{T-INST}$$

$$\frac{c\ is\ a\ constant\ of\ type\ T}{\Gamma \vdash_{\cap G} c : T} \ \text{T-CONST}$$

$\boxed{T \rhd T}$ Pattern Matching

$$T_1 \to T_2 \rhd T_1 \to T_2 \qquad\qquad Dyn \rhd Dyn \to Dyn$$

Fig. 1. Gradual intersection type system ($\vdash_{\cap G}$)

is necessary for soundness and completeness properties. The subtyping relation is inductively defined using the following rules (bear in mind that subtyping is transitive):

Definition 1 (Subtyping)

1. $T \le T$
2. $T_1 \cap \ldots \cap T_n \le T_1 \cap \ldots \cap T_m$ *with* $m \le n$
3. $T_1 \to T_2 \le T_3 \to T_4 \iff T_3 \le T_1 \wedge T_2 \le T_4$
4. $T \le T_1 \cap \ldots \cap T_n \iff T \le T_1$ *and* $\ldots$ *and* $T \le T_n$
5. $(T \to T_1) \cap \ldots \cap (T \to T_n) \le T \to T_1 \cap \ldots \cap T_n$

At first glance, gradual typing and intersection types seem rather incompatible for two reasons: types in these two systems are compared using different relations, $\sim$ for gradual types and $\le$ for intersection types; and also type inference rules for gradual typing know what type to assign a variable since only one type is annotated in abstractions while type inference rules for intersection types don't know which instance will be used for a particular occurrence of a term variable, hence assigning a type variable instead. Approaching the first incompatibility, an obvious solution would be to combine these two key relations so that they can be used in the same system while maintaining their purposes. Keeping in mind that the $\leq$ relation is not commutative, the following definition captures the essence of both relations. The consistent subtyping [12] relation is inductively defined using the following rules:

Definition 2 (Consistent Subtyping)

1. $Dyn \lesssim T$
2. $T \lesssim Dyn$
3. $T \lesssim T$
4. $T_1 \cap \ldots \cap T_n \lesssim T_1 \cap \ldots \cap T_m$ with $m \leq n$
5. $T_1 \rightarrow T_2 \lesssim T_3 \rightarrow T_4 \iff T_3 \lesssim T_1 \wedge T_2 \lesssim T_4$
6. $T \lesssim T_1 \cap \ldots \cap T_n \iff T \lesssim T_1 \wedge \ldots \wedge T \lesssim T_n$
7. $(T \rightarrow T_1) \cap \ldots \cap (T \rightarrow T_n) \lesssim T \rightarrow T_1 \cap \ldots \cap T_n$

In a sense, $\lesssim$ represents the $\leq$ relation from intersection types but extended to take into account the consistency of all types with the Dyn type, hence rules 1 and 2. Also, bear in mind that consistent subtyping is not transitive. The following cases hold under $\lesssim$:

$$Int \rightarrow Int \lesssim Int \rightarrow Int \cap Dyn$$
$$Int \rightarrow Dyn \lesssim Dyn \rightarrow Dyn$$

Now that we have overcome this first obstacle, we now define substitutions, our constraints and how they relate with substitutions.

Substitutions are the standard substitution on types but extended to deal with the Dyn type and intersection types. Let $[X \mapsto T^0]$ be a type substitution of X to T^0, meaning that when applied to a type T' ($[X \mapsto T^0]T'$), every occurrence of X in T' is replaced with T^0. We restrict T^0 to be a simple type, therefore, substitution cannot introduce intersection types, but only substitute type variables with simple types. A substitution applied to an intersection type is the same as applying the same substitution to each instance of the intersection type. The composition of substitutions is written as $S_1 \circ S_2$ and it is the same as applying the substitutions S_2 and then S_1, similar to the standard function composition. We sometimes write the composition of substitutions as $[X_1 \mapsto T_1, \ldots, X_n \mapsto T_n]$, which is equivalent to writing $[X_1 \mapsto T_1] \circ \ldots \circ [X_n \mapsto T_n]$. We lift substitutions to apply to expressions, by leaving the expression unchanged and substituting type annotations.

Constraints are defined by the following grammar:

$$Constraints\ C ::= T \lesssim T \mid T \doteq T \mid C \cup C$$

We define two types of constraints: the $\lesssim$ constraint states that two types should satisfy the consistent subtyping [12] relation and the $\doteq$ constraint is the standard equality constraint. A substitution S models a constraint C ($S \models C$) between two types, T_1 and T_2, if the relation associated with that constraint holds for $S(T_1)$ and $S(T_2)$.

Definition 3 (Constraint Satisfaction)

1. $S \models \emptyset$
2. $S \models T_1 \precsim T_2 \iff S(T_1) \precsim S(T_2)$
3. $S \models T_1 \doteq T_2 \iff S(T_1) = S(T_2)$
4. $S \models C_1 \cup C_2 \iff S \models C_1 \text{ and } S \models C_2$

The type inference algorithm will be defined bottom-up regarding the assignment of types, thus different occurrences of the same term variable may be typed with different type variables. The application of expressions containing different bindings for the same variable must join the bindings in the same typing context. The following operation combines typing contexts resulting from different derivations of the type inference algorithm. For two typing contexts Γ_1 and Γ_2, we define $\Gamma_1 + \Gamma_2$ as follows:

Definition 4 ($\Gamma_1 + \Gamma_2$). *For each $x \in dom(\Gamma_1) \cup dom(\Gamma_2)$,*

$$(\Gamma_1 + \Gamma_2)(x) = \begin{cases} \Gamma_1(x), & if \ x \notin dom(\Gamma_2) \\ \Gamma_2(x), & if \ x \notin dom(\Gamma_1) \\ \Gamma_1(x) \cap \Gamma_2(x), & otherwise \end{cases}$$

Combining typing contexts is essentially gathering the types bound to a certain variable, in multiple typing contexts, in an intersection type, for each variable in each typing context. We can abbreviate the sum of various typing contexts as following, and these two representations are used interchangeably:

$$\Gamma_1 + \ldots + \Gamma_n = \sum_{i=1}^{n} \Gamma_i$$

4   Type Inference

Adapting ideas from the type inference algorithms for gradual typing [11] and intersection types [15], we adopt the common scheme for type inference, introduced by [27], which is to generate constraints for typeability and solve them through a constraint unification phase.

4.1   Constraint Generation

Given an annotation context A (whose elements are provided by user-supplied annotations in lambda-abstractions) and an expression e, the constraint generation algorithm $A \mid \Gamma \vdash_{\cap G} e : T \mid C$ (in Fig. 2, see auxiliary definitions in Figs. 3 and 4) returns a set of tuples containing a typing context Γ, a type T and a set of constraints C.

$$\boxed{A \mid \Gamma \vdash_{\cap G} e : T \mid C} \quad \text{Constraint Generation}$$

$$\frac{A(x) = T_1 \cap \ldots \cap T_n \quad i \in 1..n \quad \text{if } x \in dom(A)}{A \mid \{x : T_i\} \vdash_{\cap G} x : T_i \mid \{\}} \text{ C-Var1}$$

$$\frac{X \text{ is a fresh type variable} \quad \text{if } x \notin dom(A)}{A \mid \{x : X\} \vdash_{\cap G} x : X \mid \{\}} \text{ C-Var2}$$

$$\frac{c \text{ is a constant of type } T}{A \mid \{\} \vdash_{\cap G} c : T \mid \{\}} \text{ C-Const} \qquad \frac{A \mid \Gamma \vdash_{\cap G} e : T \mid C \quad \text{if } x \in dom(\Gamma)}{A \mid \Gamma_x \vdash_{\cap G} \lambda x \,.\, e : \Gamma(x) \to T \mid C} \text{ C-Abs1}$$

$$\frac{A \mid \Gamma \vdash_{\cap G} e : T \mid C \quad \text{if } x \notin dom(\Gamma) \quad X \text{ is a fresh type variable}}{A \mid \Gamma \vdash_{\cap G} \lambda x \,.\, e : X \to T \mid C} \text{ C-Abs2}$$

$$\frac{A_x \cup \{x : T_1 \cap \ldots \cap T_n\} \mid \Gamma \vdash_{\cap G} e : T \mid C \quad \text{if } x \in dom(\Gamma)}{A \mid \Gamma_x \vdash_{\cap G} \lambda x : T_1 \cap \ldots \cap T_n \,.\, e : \Gamma(x) \to T \mid C} \text{ C-Abs:1}$$

$$\frac{A_x \cup \{x : T_1 \cap \ldots \cap T_n\} \mid \Gamma \vdash_{\cap G} e : T \mid C \quad \text{if } x \notin dom(\Gamma)}{A \mid \Gamma \vdash_{\cap G} \lambda x : T_1 \cap \ldots \cap T_n \,.\, e : (T_1 \to T) \cap \ldots \cap (T_n \to T) \mid C} \text{ C-Abs:2}$$

$$\frac{A \mid \Gamma_1 \vdash_{\cap G} e_1 : T_1 \mid C_1 \quad A \mid \Gamma_2 \vdash_{\cap G} e_2 : T_2 \mid C_2}{cod(T_1) \doteq T_3 \mid C_3 \quad T_2 \stackrel{.}{\lesssim} dom(T_1) \mid C_4 \quad T_1 \text{ is simple type}}{A \mid \Gamma_1 + \Gamma_2 \vdash_{\cap G} e_1 \, e_2 : T_3 \mid C_1 \cup C_2 \cup C_3 \cup C_4} \text{ C-App}$$

$$\frac{A \mid \Gamma \vdash_{\cap G} e_1 : T_1 \cap \ldots \cap T_n \to T \mid C}{A \mid \Gamma_1 \vdash_{\cap G} e_2 : T_1' \mid C_1 \ldots A \mid \Gamma_n \vdash_{\cap G} e_2 : T_n' \mid C_n}{A \mid \Gamma + \Gamma_1 + \ldots + \Gamma_n \vdash_{\cap G} e_1 \, e_2 : T \mid C \cup C_1 \cup \{T_1' \stackrel{.}{\lesssim} T_1\} \cup \ldots \cup C_n \cup \{T_n' \stackrel{.}{\lesssim} T_n\}} \text{ C-App}\cap$$

Fig. 2. Constraint generation

The constraint generation algorithm follows bottom-up traversing the syntactic tree of the expression. So, when assigning types to expressions, the algorithm will first assign types to the leaves of the syntactic tree of the expression, and then work its way up. This is useful for intersection types because we can assign different type variables to different instances of the same variable. This allows generating different typings for the same variable, which can be joined in the same intersection type. An issue we overcome arises from having the assignment of types working as bottom-up while also forcing certain variables to be typed with certain types, using annotations in lambda abstractions. The algorithm cannot decide which instance of the type bound by a variable in the typing context by lambda abstractions, will be assigned to a certain occurrence of that variable, before checking the context in which that variable is located. Therefore, the types of variables must be chosen before knowing how the variable's type is constrained by its use in the program.

For example, consider the following expression:

$$\lambda f \,.\, \lambda x : Int \cap Dyn \,.\, f \, (x \, x)$$

$$\boxed{cod(T_1) \doteq T_2 \mid C}$$

$$\frac{X_1, \ X_2 \text{ are fresh}}{cod(X) \doteq X_2 \mid \{X \doteq X_1 \rightarrow X_2\}} \qquad \overline{cod(T_1 \rightarrow T_2) \doteq T_2 \mid \{\}}$$

$$\overline{cod(Dyn) \doteq Dyn \mid \{\}}$$

Fig. 3. Constraint Codomain Judgment

$$\boxed{T_2 \stackrel{.}{\lesssim} dom(T_1) \mid C}$$

$$\frac{X_1, \ X_2 \text{ are fresh}}{T_2 \stackrel{.}{\lesssim} dom(X) \mid \{X \doteq X_1 \rightarrow X_2, T_2 \stackrel{.}{\lesssim} X_1\}} \qquad \overline{T_2 \stackrel{.}{\lesssim} dom(T_{11} \rightarrow T_{12}) \mid \{T_2 \stackrel{.}{\lesssim} T_{11}\}}$$

$$\overline{T_2 \stackrel{.}{\lesssim} dom(Dyn) \mid \{T_2 \stackrel{.}{\lesssim} Dyn\}}$$

Fig. 4. Constraint Domain judgment

The algorithm cannot decide if it should assign type Int or Dyn to the first occurrence of variable x. According to the context, it is clear that the first occurrence should have an arrow type, which can be converted from the Dyn type. However, when typing x the algorithm hasn't accessed this information yet. Since in the gradual type inference defined in [11] we know what type to assign to a variable before reaching that variable, the adaptation of gradual type inference to support intersection types is not trivial. To solve this difficulty, the type inference algorithm produces various typings, each corresponding to a choice of what type to assign to that particular variable.

According to rule C-VAR1, we choose an instance of the type bound by x in the annotation context A. This leads to the generation of various typings (a more complete explanation is provided in Subsection 4.4). For the choices which originate an ill-typed expression, the algorithm fails, returning only the choices leading to a well-typed expression. This way we avoid committing to a single choice, which could cause a typeable expression to be rejected by the type inference. Regarding the variables x, in the previous example, the following typings are produced:

$$\{x : Int \cap Dyn\} \mid \{x : Int\} \vdash_{\cap G} x : Int \mid \{\}$$
$$\{x : Int \cap Dyn\} \mid \{x : Int\} \vdash_{\cap G} x : Int \mid \{\}$$

$$\{x : Int \cap Dyn\} \mid \{x : Int\} \vdash_{\cap G} x : Int \mid \{\}$$
$$\{x : Int \cap Dyn\} \mid \{x : Dyn\} \vdash_{\cap G} x : Dyn \mid \{\}$$

$$\{x : Int \cap Dyn\} \mid \{x : Dyn\} \vdash_{\cap G} x : Dyn \mid \{\}$$
$$\{x : Int \cap Dyn\} \mid \{x : Int\} \vdash_{\cap G} x : Int \mid \{\}$$

$$\{x : Int \cap Dyn\} \mid \{x : Dyn\} \vdash_{\cap G} x : Dyn \mid \{\}$$
$$\{x : Int \cap Dyn\} \mid \{x : Dyn\} \vdash_{\cap G} x : Dyn \mid \{\}$$

Then, by rule C-APP, the algorithm checks if the type of the expression in the left-hand side is an arrow type or can be converted to one. In the first two typings, this is not true. Therefore the algorithm fails for those alternatives and proceeds for the last two alternatives.

Regarding the rules for application, the expression on the left-hand side can be typed with a type whose domain is an intersection type or a simple type. Therefore, we require two rules to discriminate between these two cases. When the domain type of the expression is a simple type, the rule for application, C-APP, is the standard one from [11] with a few minor changes. Constraint Codomain Judgment (Fig. 3) and the Constraint Domain Judgment (Fig. 4) are adapted to deal with the $\lesssim$ relation instead of the $\sim$ relation, and thus rule C-APP ensures that the type of the expression on the left-hand side of an application is an arrow type and that the domain of this arrow type is a supertype (i.e. it includes it using the subtype relation) of the type of the argument (the expression on the right-hand side of the application).

When the type of the expression on the left-hand side is an intersection type, the rule C-APP$\cap$ requires the generation of different typings, one for each instance of the intersection type in the domain of the expression. Then it checks if the different types for the argument are consistent with the instances of the intersection type in the domain. This rule is inspired by an analogous rule in [15].

Both constraint generation rules will then join together the typing contexts of the two subexpressions, or in the case of rule C-APP$\cap$, the typing contexts of the different typings, by combining the types bound to the same variables as an intersection type, according to Definition 4.

The next lemmas show that the constraint generation algorithm is both sound and complete, w.r.t. the type system.

Lemma 1 (Constraint Soundness). *If* $A \mid \Gamma \vdash_{\cap G} e : T \mid C$ *and* $S \models C$ *then* $S(\Gamma) \vdash_{\cap G} S(e) : S(T)$.

Proof. By induction on the length of the derivation tree of $A \mid \Gamma \vdash_{\cap G} e : T \mid C$.

Lemma 2 (Constraint Completeness). *If* $\Gamma_1 \vdash_{\cap G} e : T_1$ *then*

1. *there exists a derivation* $A \mid \Gamma_2 \vdash_{\cap G} e : T_2 \mid C$ *such that* $\exists S . S \models C$
2. *for* $A \mid \Gamma_{21} \vdash_{\cap G} e : T_{21} \mid C_1$ *such that* $\exists S_1 . S_1 \models C_1$ *and* ... *and* $A \mid \Gamma_{2n} \vdash_{\cap G}$
   $e : T_{2n} \mid C_n$ *such that* $\exists S_n . S_n \models C_n$ *then*
   (a) *for each* $x \in dom(\Gamma_1) \cap dom(\sum_{i=1}^{n} \Gamma_{2i})$, $\Gamma_1(x) \leq S_i(\Gamma_{2i}(x))$, $\forall i \in 1..n$
   (b) $\bigcap_{i=1}^{n} S_i(T_{2i}) \leq T_1$

Proof. By induction on the length of the derivation tree of $\Gamma_1 \vdash_{\cap G} e : T_1$.

$\boxed{C \Rightarrow S}$ Constraint Solving

$$\frac{}{\emptyset \Rightarrow \emptyset} \text{ EM} \qquad \frac{C \Rightarrow S}{\{Dyn \lesssim T\} \cup C \Rightarrow S} \text{ CS-DYNL} \qquad \frac{C \Rightarrow S}{\{T \lesssim Dyn\} \cup C \Rightarrow S} \text{ CS-DYNR}$$

$$\frac{C \Rightarrow S \qquad T \in \{Int, Bool\} \cup TVar}{\{T \lesssim T\} \cup C \Rightarrow S} \text{ CS-REFL} \qquad \frac{C \Rightarrow S \qquad m \leq n}{\{T_1 \cap \ldots \cap T_n \lesssim T_1 \cap \ldots \cap T_m\} \cup C \Rightarrow S} \text{ CS-INST}$$

$$\frac{C \Rightarrow S}{\{(T \to T_1) \cap \ldots \cap (T \to T_n) \lesssim T \to T_1 \cap \ldots \cap T_n\} \cup C \Rightarrow S} \text{ CS-ASSOC}$$

$$\frac{\{T_3 \lesssim T_1, T_2 \lesssim T_4\} \cup C \Rightarrow S}{\{T_1 \to T_2 \lesssim T_3 \to T_4\} \cup C \Rightarrow S} \text{ CS-ARROW} \qquad \frac{\{T \lesssim T_1, \ldots, T \lesssim T_n\} \cup C \Rightarrow S}{\{T \lesssim T_1 \cap \ldots \cap T_n\} \cup C \Rightarrow S} \text{ CS-INSTR}$$

$$\frac{\begin{array}{c} \{X_1 \lesssim T_1, T_2 \lesssim X_2, T \doteq X_1 \to X_2\} \cup C \Rightarrow S \\ X_1, \ X_2 \text{ are fresh type variables} \end{array}}{\{T_1 \to T_2 \lesssim T\} \cup C \Rightarrow S} \text{ CS-ARROWL}$$

$$\frac{\begin{array}{c} \{T_1 \lesssim X_1, X_2 \lesssim T_2, T \doteq X_1 \to X_2\} \cup C \Rightarrow S \\ X_1, \ X_2 \text{ are fresh type variables} \end{array}}{\{T \lesssim T_1 \to T_2\} \cup C \Rightarrow S} \text{ CS-ARROWR}$$

$$\frac{\{T_1 \doteq T_2\} \cup C \Rightarrow S \qquad T_1, T_2 \in \{Int, Bool\} \cup TVar}{\{T_1 \lesssim T_2\} \cup C \Rightarrow S} \text{ CS-EQ}$$

$$\frac{C \Rightarrow S \qquad T \in \{Int, Bool\} \cup TVar}{\{T \doteq T\} \cup C \Rightarrow S} \text{ EQ-REFL} \qquad \frac{\{T_1 \doteq T_3, T_2 \doteq T_4\} \cup C \Rightarrow S}{\{T_1 \to T_2 \doteq T_3 \to T_4\} \cup C \Rightarrow S} \text{ EQ-ARROW}$$

$$\frac{\{X \doteq T\} \cup C \Rightarrow S \qquad T \notin TVar}{\{T \doteq X\} \cup C \Rightarrow S} \text{ EQ-VARR} \qquad \frac{[X \mapsto T]C \Rightarrow S \qquad X \notin Vars(T)}{\{X \doteq T\} \cup C \Rightarrow S \circ [X \mapsto T]} \text{ EQ-VARL}$$

Fig. 5. Constraint solving

4.2   Constraint Solving

Given a set of constraints C, obtained by constraint generation, we shall define, in Fig. 5, a solving relation between a set of constraints C and a substitution S ($C \Rightarrow S$) meaning: solving the set of constraints C results in S. Rules in Fig. 5 are syntax-directed and define a decision algorithm by successively applying these rules using a bottom-up proof search strategy.

Our constraint solving algorithm extends Robinson unification [23] to deal with new equality definitions which account for dynamic types and intersection types. Most of these rules are adapted from [5] and [15], with a few exceptions. Since there are two types of constraints, there are two groups of constraint solving rules, and also a base case to halt the algorithm (rule EM). The constraint solving algorithm first transforms any $\lesssim$ constraint into an equivalent standard unification problem involving only equality constraints. Thus, there is an order of application of rules in the constraint solver defined in Fig. 5. First, rules CS transform $\lesssim$ constraints into a set of equations. Then, rules EQ, solve the resulting set of equations yielding a substitution as the solution for the initial set of constraints.

Given that $\dot{\lesssim}$ constraints are a new concept, a brief walkthrough of the rules will clarify their meaning. Most rules that deal with $\dot{\lesssim}$ are a direct adaptation of [15] and relate to subtyping (Definition 1). Only rules CS-DynL and CS-DynR stand out, since they are used to simulate $\sim$ from [11]. The remaining rules, which regard $\dot{=}$ constraints, come from [11]. When we have a $\dot{\lesssim}$ constraint between different type variables or base types, we constrain those types to be equal, since they cannot be solved further. The remaining rules, for the $\dot{=}$ constraint, are based on standard unification rules for equality.

Going back to the example above, the two alternatives that haven't failed, produce the following typings and constraints:

$$\lambda f . \lambda x : Int \cap Dyn . f\ (x\ x) : X_1 \to (Int \cap Dyn) \to X_3$$
$$\{Int \dot{\lesssim} Dyn, X_1 \dot{=} X_2 \to X_3, X_1 \dot{=} X_4 \to X_5, Dyn \dot{\lesssim} X_4\}$$

$$\lambda f . \lambda x : Int \cap Dyn . f\ (x\ x) : X_1 \to Dyn \to X_3$$
$$\{Dyn \dot{\lesssim} Dyn, X_1 \dot{=} X_2 \to X_3, X_1 \dot{=} X_4 \to X_5, Dyn \dot{\lesssim} X_4\}$$

Since the step by step solving of the constraints produced for each typing are equal, only one solving will be shown. Applying the first step (rule CS-DynR) leads both constraint sets to:

$$\{X_1 \dot{=} X_2 \to X_3, X_1 \dot{=} X_4 \to X_5, Dyn \dot{\lesssim} X_4\}$$

By rule EQ-VarL, the constraint set is reduced to

$$\{X_2 \to X_3 \dot{=} X_4 \to X_5, Dyn \dot{\lesssim} X_4\}$$

and the first substitution is produced: $[X_1 \mapsto X_2 \to X_3]$. Then, by rule EQ-Arrow, the constraint set is further reduced to

$$\{X_2 \dot{=} X_4, X_3 \dot{=} X_5, Dyn \dot{\lesssim} X_4\}$$

Applying rule EQ-VarL two times reduces the constraint set to just one constraint

$$\{Dyn \dot{\lesssim} X_4\}$$

and updates the substitutions to $[X_3 \mapsto X_5, X_2 \mapsto X_4, X_1 \mapsto X_2 \to X_3]$. Finally, solving the remaining constraint gives as final the substitutions:

$$[X_3 \mapsto X_5, X_2 \mapsto X_4, X_1 \mapsto X_2 \to X_3]$$

The final typings of the expressions are then:

$$\lambda f . \lambda x : Int \cap Dyn . f\ (x\ x) : (X_4 \to X_5) \to (Int \cap Dyn \to X_5)$$
$$\lambda f . \lambda x : Int \cap Dyn . f\ (x\ x) : (X_4 \to X_5) \to (Dyn \to X_5)$$

This extended unification algorithm used for constraint solving is both sound and complete, with respect to constraint satisfaction (Definition 3). Note that completeness means that the extended unification algorithm produces most general unifiers.

Lemma 3 (Unification Soundness). *If $C \Rightarrow S$ then $S \models C$.*

Proof. By induction on the length of the derivation tree of $C \Rightarrow S$.

Lemma 4 (Unification Completeness). *If $S_1 \models C$ then $C \Rightarrow S_2$ for some S_2, and furthermore $S_1 = S \circ S_2$ for some S.*

Proof. We proceed by induction on the breakdown of constraint sets by the unification rules.

4.3 Gradual Types

Any type is a consistent subtype, or consistent supertype, of the Dyn type, thus there is no need for further checks, such as recursively checking consistent subtyping through the structure of the type. Constraints which require a type to be consistent subtype, or supertype, with the Dyn type have been discarded up until now using our definition of constraint solving since they are satisfiable with any substitution. Discarding these constraints brings a problem regarding the instantiation of type variables. A type variable that is only constrained to be consistent with the Dyn type will not be substituted since no substitution concerning that variable will be produced. However, as that type variable is only constrained by the Dyn type, it should be instantiated to the Dyn type, so a substitution from that variable to the Dyn type should be produced. Implementing this only takes a simple extension [11] to our constraint solving algorithm. Therefore, given a set of constraints C, the constraint solving algorithm $G \mid C \Rightarrow S$ will produce a set of substitutions S and a set of gradual types G. The extension is shown in Fig. 6.

$\boxed{G \mid C \Rightarrow S}$ Constraint Unification

$$\frac{}{G \mid \emptyset \Rightarrow \overline{[Vars(G) \mapsto Dyn]}} \text{ EM} \qquad \frac{G \cup \{T\} \mid C \Rightarrow S}{G \mid \{Dyn \lesssim T\} \cup C \Rightarrow S} \text{ CS-DynL}$$

$$\frac{G \cup \{T\} \mid C \Rightarrow S}{G \mid \{T \lesssim Dyn\} \cup C \Rightarrow S} \text{ CS-DynR}$$

$$\frac{[X \mapsto T]G \mid [X \mapsto T]C \Rightarrow S \qquad X \notin Vars(T)}{G \mid \{X \doteq T\} \cup C \Rightarrow S \circ [X \mapsto T]} \text{ Eq-VarL}$$

Fig. 6. Constraint solving with gradual types

To instantiate these unconstrained type variables to Dyn, we first need to collect them. When any constraint of the form $T \lesssim Dyn$ or $Dyn \lesssim T$ is encountered by the solver, we store the type T, per rules CS-DynL and CS-DynR. Note that these types might be constrained by other constraints, however, we collect them nonetheless. These will be considered gradual types since they potentially contain the *Dyn* type. When a constraint is solved and a substitution is produced, the constraint solver applies the substitution to the remaining constraints to avoid unconstrained type variables. This behaviour must also be implemented, regarding the gradual types stored. In rule EQ-VARL, when a substitution is produced, it is applied to the remaining constraints and also to the collection of gradual types. Finally, when all constraints have been solved and all the substitutions have been produced, we will get the complete collection of gradual types. These will possibly contain base types, such as *Int*, compound types such as the arrow type and type variables. Then, we take the type variables from these types and produce substitutions from those type variables to *Dyn*. This is done by rule EM. $Vars(G)$ is the set of all the type variables present in all the types in G. The overline means that a substitution will be produced for each type variable obtained by $Vars(G)$.

Since the constraint unification algorithm has been updated, we need to update the soundness and completeness lemmas to match the new algorithm's specification.

Lemma 5 (Unification Soundness). *If $G \mid C \Rightarrow S$ then $S \models C$.*

Proof. Extends proof of Lemma 3. By induction on the length of the derivation tree of $G \mid C \Rightarrow S$.

Lemma 6 (Unification Completeness). *If $S_1 \circ \overline{[Vars(G) \mapsto Dyn]} \models C$ then $G \mid C \Rightarrow S_2$ for some S_2, and furthermore $S_1 \circ \overline{[Vars(G) \mapsto Dyn]} = S \circ S_2$ for some S.*

Proof. Extends proof of Lemma 4. By induction on the breakdown of constraint sets by the unification rules.

Continuing the example above, with the extended constraint solving algorithm, a final substitution is added:

$$[X_4 \mapsto Dyn, X_3 \mapsto X_5, X_2 \mapsto X_4, X_1 \mapsto X_2 \to X_3]$$

The final typings of the expressions are then:

$$\lambda f \,.\, \lambda x : Int \cap Dyn \,.\, f\,(x\,x) : (Dyn \to X_5) \to (Int \cap Dyn \to X_5)$$
$$\lambda f \,.\, \lambda x : Int \cap Dyn \,.\, f\,(x\,x) : (Dyn \to X_5) \to (Dyn \to X_5)$$

Notice that only in the first solution all the instances of the type in the annotation of the lambda abstraction are used.

4.4   Multiple Solutions

In the language described in Sect. 2, variables may be annotated with intersection types in lambda abstractions. In these cases, the type inference algorithm assigns a particular instance of that intersection type to a particular occurrence of that variable. However, given the fact that we are dealing with idempotent intersection types, we cannot know in advance which instance to assign to a particular occurrence of a variable since some choices lead to ill-typed expressions while other choices lead to well-typed expressions. For example, consider the following expression,

$$\lambda x : Int \cap Dyn \;.\; x \; x \; x$$

We must choose, for each of the three occurrences of x, either the Int or the Dyn type. Some choices lead to the expression becoming ill-typed, such as:

$$\lambda x : Int \cap Dyn \;.\; x^{Int} \; x^{Dyn} \; x^{Int}$$

Other choices lead the expression to become well-typed, such as:

$$\lambda x : Int \cap Dyn \;.\; x^{Dyn} \; x^{Dyn} \; x^{Int}$$
$$\lambda x : Int \cap Dyn \;.\; x^{Dyn} \; x^{Int} \; x^{Int}$$

Therefore, our type inference algorithm first produces several typings for an expression. Since there are many different choices to type variables, we generate different typings according to each choice. The generation of multiple typings is clear in rule C-Var1, which generates a typing for a variable for each instance of intersection type bound to that variable in the annotation context.

Constraint generation produces several sets of constraints and each set of constraints is solved by the constraint solving algorithm leading to multiple incomparable solutions. We will show that the type inference algorithm is sound and complete and that the set of substitutions computed by the algorithm is principal in the sense that any other solution is an instance of one in the set returned by the solver when it is applied to the different constraint sets produced in the constraint generation phase.

The expression $\lambda x : Int \cap Dyn \;.\; x \; x \; x$ has a total of 8 typings, which correspond to choosing different combinations of Int and Dyn for the three occurrences of the variable x. We can see that of those choices, only 4 will produce a typeable expression. Choosing Int for the first occurrence of x leads to an ill-typed expression. Therefore, we end up with 4 different typings:

$$\lambda x : Int \cap Dyn \;.\; x^{Dyn} \; x^{Int} \; x^{Int} : Int \cap Dyn \rightarrow Dyn$$
$$\lambda x : Int \cap Dyn \;.\; x^{Dyn} \; x^{Dyn} \; x^{Int} : Int \cap Dyn \rightarrow Dyn$$
$$\lambda x : Int \cap Dyn \;.\; x^{Dyn} \; x^{Int} \; x^{Dyn} : Int \cap Dyn \rightarrow Dyn$$
$$\lambda x : Int \cap Dyn \;.\; x^{Dyn} \; x^{Dyn} \; x^{Dyn} : Dyn \rightarrow Dyn$$

However, note that the last typing does not use all the instances in typing variables. The type inference algorithm is then described as follows:

Definition 5 (Type Inference). *Let e be an expression, Γ a context, T a type, S a substitution and Sol a set of triples of the form (Γ, T, S). The type inference function I from expressions to sets of triples (Γ, T, S), is defined by the following steps:*

1. $Sol = \emptyset$
2. for every derivation of $\emptyset \mid \Gamma \vdash_{\cap G} e : T \mid C$ that holds
   (a) if $\emptyset \mid C \Rightarrow S$ holds then

$$Sol = Sol \cup \{(S(\Gamma), S(T), S)\}$$

3. return Sol

Step 2 generates constraints with derivations in the constraint generation system. Given an empty annotation context and the expression e, $\emptyset \mid \Gamma \vdash_{\cap G} e : T \mid C$ gets us the typing context Γ, the type of the expression T and the set of constraints C. In step 2.a, given an empty set of gradual types and the constraints C, if the constraint solver algorithm $\emptyset \mid C \Rightarrow S$ produces a substitution S, then that substitutions S is added to the solutions.

4.5   Decidability

Different typings in the constraint generation system in Fig. 2 arise from intersections, and intersections are always finite, thus the number of derivations for a given expression is also finite. Also, since constraint generation follows the syntactic tree of the expression, each constraint generation derivation terminates.

Lemma 7 (Termination of Constraint Generation). *Given a context A and an expression e, the number of derivations by the constraint generation system for $A \mid \Gamma \vdash_{\cap G} e : T \mid C$ is finite.*

Proof. The proof follows by structural induction on e.

Now, to prove that the successive application of constraint solving rules in Fig. 5 always halt, note that, every rule, when applied to a consistent subtyping constraint, reduces the number of type constructors in consistent subtyping constraints or reduces the number of consistent subtyping constraints. If the rule applies to an equality constraint then every rule reduces the number of type constructors in equality constraints or reduces the number of equality constraints. The only rule that has a different behaviour is EQ-VARR, but it will be followed by rule EQ-VARL which reduces the number of equality constraints. Thus to prove termination we use a metric well-ordered by a lexicographical order on the tuples $(\text{NICS}, \text{NCCS}, \text{NCS})$ and $(\text{NVEQ}, \text{NCEQ}, \text{NTXEQ}, \text{NEQ})$, where NICS is the number of unique intersection types in the left of an $\lesssim$ constraint + the number of unique intersection types in the right of an $\lesssim$ constraint; NCCS is the number of type constructors in $\lesssim$ constraints; NCS is the number of $\lesssim$ constraints; NVEQ is the number of different type variables in $\doteq$ constraints; NCEQ is the number of type constructors in $\doteq$ constraints; NTXEQ is the number of $\doteq$ constraints of the form $T \doteq X$; and NEQ is the number of $\doteq$ constraints. The result is stated in the following lemma.

Lemma 8 (Termination of Constraint Solving). *$C \Rightarrow S$ terminates for every set of constraints C.*

Proof. By a metric well-ordered by a lexicographical order. The full proof can be consulted in Appendix A.

Finally, decidability of the type inference algorithm follows from the two last lemmas.

Theorem 1 (Decidability). *Type inference is decidable.*

Proof. By Lemmas 7 and 8

4.6   Soundness and Completeness

Soundness and completeness are two important properties which show the correctness and usefulness of the type inference algorithm. Soundness guarantees that if the type inference algorithm returns a type, then that type is derivable in the type system. Completeness states that the output of the type inference algorithm represents the *most general type judgment able to type the expression,* a property known as *principal typing*. The full proofs of the following theorems can be consulted in Appendix A.

Theorem 2 (Soundness). *If $(\Gamma, T, S) \in I(e)$ then $S(\Gamma) \vdash_{\cap G} S(e) : S(T)$.*

Proof. By Lemmas 1 and 5.

Principal Typing. A type judgment, or typing, for a term, is *principal if and only if all other typings for the same expression can be derived from it by some set of operations.* Thus principal typings can be seen as the most general typings. The notion of principal typing and its relation with the slightly different notion of principal type was studied in detail in [16,28].

Definition 6 (Principal Typing). *If $\Gamma_p \vdash_{\cap G} e : T_p$, then we say that (Γ_p, T_p) is a principal typing of e if whenever $\Gamma_1 \vdash_{\cap G} e : T_1$ holds, then for some substitutions S, for each $x \in dom(\Gamma_1) \cap dom(\Gamma_p)$, we have $\Gamma_1(x) \leq S(\Gamma_p(x))$ and $S(T_p) \leq T_1$.*

As the following theorem shows, our language has principal typings for every well-typed expression.

Theorem 3 (Principal Typings). *If $\Gamma_1 \vdash_{\cap G} e : T_1$ then there are $\Gamma_{21}, \ldots,$ $\Gamma_{2n}, T_{21}, \ldots, T_{2n}, S_{21}, \ldots, S_{2n}$ and $S_1, \ldots, S_n$ such that $((\Gamma_{21}, T_{21}, S_{21}), \ldots,$ $(\Gamma_{2n}, T_{2n}, S_{2n})) = I(e)$ and, for each $x \in dom(\Gamma_1) \cap dom(\Gamma_{21} + \ldots + \Gamma_{2n})$, we have $\Gamma_1(x) \leq S_1 \circ S_{21}(\Gamma_{21}(x))$ and $\ldots$ and $\Gamma_1(x) \leq S_n \circ S_{2n}(\Gamma_{2n}(x))$ and $S_1 \circ S_{21}(T_{21}) \cap \ldots \cap S_n \circ S_{2n}(T_{2n}) \leq T_1$.*

Proof. By Lemmas 2 and 6.

Principal typings are clearly a quite relevant feature of our type system. They allow compositional type inference, where type inference for a given expression uses only the typings inferred for its subexpressions, which can be inferred independently in any order.

5   Conclusion

Here we study the type inference problem for the rank 2 fragment of our general system and prove that it is decidable, by defining a type inference algorithm, sound w.r.t. the type system and complete in the sense that returns principal typings. This strongly indicates that rank 2 intersection gradual types may be safely and successfully applied to the design and implementation of gradually typed programming languages able to type values which are all of many different types.

Acknowledgments. This work is partially funded by FCT within project Elven POCI-01-0145-FEDER-016844, Project 9471 - Reforçar a Investigação, o Desenvolvimento Tecnológico e a Inovação (Project 9471-RIDTI) and by Fundo Comunitário Europeu FEDER.

A   Proofs

Lemma 9 (Weakening). *If $\Gamma \vdash_{\cap G} e : T$ then $\Gamma + \Gamma' \vdash_{\cap G} e : T$ for any typing context Γ'.*

Proof. We proceed by induction on the derivation tree of $\Gamma \vdash_{\cap G} e : T$.

Base cases:

- Rule T-VAR. If $\Gamma \vdash_{\cap G} x : T_i$ then $x : T_1 \cap \ldots \cap T_n \in \Gamma$. If $x : T'_1 \cap \ldots \cap T'_m \in \Gamma'$, then $x : T_1 \cap \ldots \cap T_n \cap T'_1 \cap \ldots \cap T'_m \in \Gamma + \Gamma'$. Therefore, $\Gamma + \Gamma' \vdash_{\cap G} x : T_i$.
- Rule T-CONST. If $\Gamma \vdash_{\cap G} c : T$ and c is a constant of type T, then $\Gamma + \Gamma' \vdash_{\cap G} c : T$.

Induction step:

- Rule T-ABS. To avoid capture we assume that $\alpha-reduction$ is made whenever needed to rename formal parameters. If $\Gamma \vdash_{\cap G} \lambda x \,.\, e : T_1 \to T_2$ then $\Gamma, x : T_1 \vdash_{\cap G} e : T_2$. By induction hypothesis, $\Gamma, x : T_1 + \Gamma' \vdash_{\cap G} e : T_2$. By rule T-ABS, $\Gamma + \Gamma' \vdash_{\cap G} \lambda x \,.\, e : T_1 \to T_2$.
- Rule T-ABS. To avoid capture we assume that $\alpha-reduction$ is made whenever needed to rename formal parameters. If $\Gamma \vdash_{\cap G} \lambda x : T_1 \cap \ldots \cap T_n \,.\, e : T_1 \cap \ldots \cap T_m \to T$ then $\Gamma, x : T_1 \cap \ldots \cap T_m \vdash_{\cap G} e : T$. By induction hypothesis, $\Gamma, x : T_1 \cap \ldots \cap T_m + \Gamma' \vdash_{\cap G} e : T$. By rule T-ABS:, $\Gamma + \Gamma' \vdash_{\cap G} \lambda x : T_1 \cap \ldots \cap T_n \,.\, e : T_1 \cap \ldots \cap T_m \to T$.
- Rule T-APP. If $\Gamma \vdash_{\cap G} e_1 \, e_2 : T$ then $\Gamma \vdash_{\cap G} e_1 : PM$, $PM \rhd T_1 \cap \ldots \cap T_n \to T$, $\Gamma \vdash_{\cap G} e_2 : T'_1 \cap \ldots \cap T'_n$ and $T'_1 \lesssim T_1 \ldots T'_n \lesssim T_n$. By induction hypothesis, $\Gamma + \Gamma' \vdash_{\cap G} e_1 : PM$ and $\Gamma + \Gamma' \vdash_{\cap G} e_2 : T'_1 \cap \ldots \cap T'_n$. By rule T-APP, $\Gamma + \Gamma' \vdash_{\cap G} e_1 \, e_2 : T$.
- Rule T-GEN. If $\Gamma \vdash_{\cap G} e : T_1 \cap \ldots \cap T_n$ then $\Gamma \vdash_{\cap G} e : T_1$ and $\ldots$ and $\Gamma \vdash_{\cap G} e : T_n$. By induction hypothesis, $\Gamma + \Gamma' \vdash_{\cap G} e : T_1$ and $\ldots$ and $\Gamma + \Gamma' \vdash_{\cap G} e : T_n$. By rule T-GEN, $\Gamma + \Gamma' \vdash_{\cap G} e : T_1 \cap \ldots \cap T_n$.

- Rule T-INST. If $\Gamma \vdash_{\cap G} e : T_i$ then $\Gamma \vdash_{\cap G} e : T_1 \cap \ldots \cap T_n$. By induction hypothesis, $\Gamma + \Gamma' \vdash_{\cap G} e : T_1 \cap \ldots \cap T_n$. By rule T-INST, $\Gamma + \Gamma' \vdash_{\cap G} e : T_i$

Lemma 1 (Constraint Soundness). *If* $A \mid \Gamma \vdash_{\cap G} e : T \mid C$ *and* $S \models C$ *then* $S(\Gamma) \vdash_{\cap G} S(e) : S(T)$.

Proof. We proceed by induction on the length of the derivation tree of $A \mid \Gamma \vdash_{\cap G} e : T \mid C$.

Base cases:

- Rule C-VAR1. If $A \mid \{x : T_i\} \vdash_{\cap G} x : T_i \mid \{\}$ and $S \models \{\}$ then $\{x : S(T_i)\} \vdash_{\cap G} x : S(T_i)$. Since $S(\{x : T_i\}) = \{x : S(T_i)\}$ and $S(x) = x$, then $S(\{x : T_i\}) \vdash_{\cap G} S(x) : S(T_i)$.
- Rule C-VAR2. If $A \mid \{x : X\} \vdash_{\cap G} x : X \mid \{\}$ and $S \models \{\}$ then $\{x : S(X)\} \vdash_{\cap G} x : S(X)$. Since $S(\{x : X\}) = \{x : S(X)\}$ and $S(x) = x$, then $S(\{x : X\}) \vdash_{\cap G} S(x) : S(X)$.
- Rule C-CONST. If $A \mid \{\} \vdash_{\cap G} c : T \mid \{\}$ and $S \models \emptyset$ then c is a constant of type T. Therefore, $S(\{\}) \vdash_{\cap G} S(c) : S(T)$.

Induction step:

- Rule C-ABS1. If $A \mid \Gamma_x \vdash_{\cap G} \lambda x . e : \Gamma(x) \to T \mid C$ and $S \models C$ then $A \mid \Gamma \vdash_{\cap G} e : T \mid C$. By the induction hypothesis, $S(\Gamma) \vdash_{\cap G} S(e) : S(T)$. Then, by rule T-ABS, $S(\Gamma)_x \vdash_{\cap G} \lambda x . S(e) : S(\Gamma(x)) \to S(T)$. As $S(\Gamma_x) = S(\Gamma)_x$, $S(\lambda x . e) = \lambda x . S(e)$ and $S(\Gamma(x) \to T) = S(\Gamma(x)) \to S(T)$ then $S(\Gamma_x) \vdash_{\cap G} S(\lambda x . e) : S(\Gamma(x) \to T)$.
- Rule C-ABS2. If $A \mid \Gamma \vdash_{\cap G} \lambda x . e : X \to T \mid C$ and $S \models C$ then $A \mid \Gamma \vdash_{\cap G} e : T \mid C$. By the induction hypothesis, $S(\Gamma) \vdash_{\cap G} S(e) : S(T)$. As $x : S(X)$ is not used to type e and thus $x \notin \Gamma$ then we also have $S(\Gamma) \cup \{x : S(X)\} \vdash_{\cap G} S(e) : S(T)$. Then by the T-ABS, $S(\Gamma) \vdash_{\cap G} S(\lambda x . e) : S(X \to T)$.
- Rule C-ABS:1. If $A \mid \Gamma_x \vdash_{\cap G} \lambda x : T_1 \cap \ldots \cap T_n . e : \Gamma(x) \to T \mid C$ and $S \models C$ then $A_x \cup \{x : T_1 \cap \ldots \cap T_n\} \mid \Gamma \vdash_{\cap G} e : T \mid C$. By the induction hypothesis, $S(\Gamma) \vdash_{\cap G} S(e) : S(T)$. Therefore, $S(\Gamma)_x \vdash_{\cap G} \lambda x : T_1 \cap \ldots \cap T_n . S(e) : S(\Gamma(x)) \to S(T)$. As $S(\Gamma_x) = S(\Gamma)_x$, $S(\Gamma(x) \to T) = S(\Gamma(x)) \to S(T)$ and $\{x : T_1 \cap \ldots \cap T_m\} \in \Gamma$ then $S(\Gamma_x) \vdash_{\cap G} \lambda x : S(T_1 \cap \ldots \cap T_m) \cap T_{m+1} \cap \ldots \cap T_n . S(e) : S(\Gamma(x) \to T)$. As $T_{m+1} \cap \ldots \cap T_n$ does not occur in e, then those those types are not affected by substitutions. Therefore, $S(\Gamma_x) \vdash_{\cap G} S(\lambda x : T_1 \cap \ldots \cap T_n . e) : S(\Gamma(x) \to T)$.
- Rule C-ABS:2. If $A \mid \Gamma \vdash_{\cap G} \lambda x : T_1 \cap \ldots \cap T_n . e : T_1 \to T \cap \ldots \cap T_n \to T \mid C$ and $S \models C$ then $A_x \cup \{x : T_1 \cap \ldots \cap T_n\} \mid \Gamma \vdash_{\cap G} e : T \mid C$. By the induction hypothesis, $S(\Gamma) \vdash_{\cap G} S(e) : S(T)$. As $x \notin dom(\Gamma)$ then x doesn't occur in e. Therefore, we also have $S(\Gamma) \cup \{x : S(T_1)\} \vdash_{\cap G} S(e) : S(T)$ and ... and $S(\Gamma) \cup \{x : S(T_n)\} \vdash_{\cap G} S(e) : S(T)$. Then, by rule T-ABS:, $S(\Gamma) \vdash_{\cap G} S(\lambda x : T_1 \cap \ldots \cap T_n . e) : S(T_1 \to T)$ and ... and $S(\Gamma) \vdash_{\cap G} S(\lambda x : T_1 \cap \ldots \cap T_n . e) : S(T_n \to T)$. By rule T-GEN, we have $S(\Gamma) \vdash_{\cap G} S(\lambda x : T_1 \cap \ldots \cap T_n . e) : S(T_1 \to T \cap \ldots \cap T_n \to T)$.

– Rule C-App. If $A \mid \Gamma_1 + \Gamma_2 \vdash_{\cap G} e_1\ e_2 : T_3 \mid C_1 \cup C_2 \cup C_3 \cup C_4$ and $S \models C_1 \cup C_2 \cup C_3 \cup C_4$ then $A \mid \Gamma_1 \vdash_{\cap G} e_1 : T_1 \mid C_1$ and $A \mid \Gamma_2 \vdash_{\cap G} e_2 : T_2 \mid C_2$ and $cod(T_1) \doteq T_3 \mid C_3$ and $T_2 \lesssim dom(T_1) \mid C_4$. There are three possibilities:

- $T_1 = X$. Then, $T_3 = X_2$. By the induction hypothesis, $S(\Gamma_1) \vdash_{\cap G} S(e_1) : S(X)$ and $S(\Gamma_2) \vdash_{\cap G} S(e_2) : S(T_2)$. As $S \models \{X \doteq X_1 \to X_2, X \doteq X_3 \to X_4, T_2 \lesssim X_1\}$, then $S(\Gamma_1) \vdash_{\cap G} S(e_1) : S(X_1 \to X_2)$ and $S(T_2) \lesssim S(X_1)$. Therefore, $S(\Gamma_1) \vdash_{\cap G} S(e_1) : S(X_1) \to S(X_2)$. Therefore, by Lemma 9, $S(\Gamma_1 + \Gamma_2) \vdash_{\cap G} S(e_1\ e_2) : S(X_2)$.

- $T_1 = T_{11} \to T_{12}$. Then, $T_3 = T_{12}$. By the induction hypothesis, $S(\Gamma_1) \vdash_{\cap G} S(e_1) : S(T_{11} \to T_{12})$ and $S(\Gamma_2) \vdash_{\cap G} S(e_2) : S(T_2)$. Therefore, $S(\Gamma_1) \vdash_{\cap G} S(e_1) : S(T_{11}) \to S(T_{12})$. As $S \models T_2 \lesssim T_{11}$, then $S(T_2) \lesssim S(T_{11})$. Therefore, by Lemma 9, $S(\Gamma_1 + \Gamma_2) \vdash_{\cap G} S(e_1\ e_2) : S(T_{12})$.

- $T_1 = Dyn$. Then $T_3 = Dyn$. By the induction hypothesis, $S(\Gamma_1) \vdash_{\cap G} S(e_1) : S(Dyn)$ and $S(\Gamma_2) \vdash_{\cap G} S(e_2) : S(T_2)$. Therefore, $S(\Gamma_1) \vdash_{\cap G} S(e_1) : Dyn$ and $Dyn \triangleright Dyn \to Dyn$. As $S(T_2) \lesssim Dyn$ then, by Lemma 9, $S(\Gamma_1 + \Gamma_2) \vdash_{\cap G} S(e_1\ e_2) : S(Dyn)$.

– Rule C-App∩. If $A \mid \Gamma + \Gamma_1 + \ldots + \Gamma_n \vdash_{\cap G} e_1\ e_2 : T \mid C \cup C_1 \cup \{T_1' \lesssim T_1\} \cup \ldots \cup C_n \cup \{T_n' \lesssim T_n\}$ and $S \models C \cup C_1 \cup \{T_1' \lesssim T_1\} \cup \ldots \cup C_n \cup \{T_n' \lesssim T_n\}$ then $A \mid \Gamma \vdash_{\cap G} e_1 : T_1 \cap \ldots \cap T_n \to T \mid C$ and $A \mid \Gamma_1 \vdash_{\cap G} e_2 : T_1' \mid C_1$ and $\ldots$ and $A \mid \Gamma_n \vdash_{\cap G} e_2 : T_n' \mid C_n$ and $S(T_1') \lesssim S(T_1)$ and $\ldots$ and $S(T_n') \lesssim S(T_n)$. By the induction hypothesis, $S(\Gamma) \vdash_{\cap G} S(e_1) : S(T_1 \cap \ldots \cap T_n \to T)$ and $S(\Gamma_1) \vdash_{\cap G} S(e_2) : S(T_1')$ and $\ldots$ and $S(\Gamma_n) \vdash_{\cap G} S(e_2) : S(T_n')$. Since, by Lemma 9, $S(\Gamma + \Gamma_1 + \ldots + \Gamma_n) \vdash_{\cap G} S(e_1) : S(T_1 \cap \ldots \cap T_n) \to S(T)$, $S(\Gamma + \Gamma_1 + \ldots + \Gamma_n) \vdash_{\cap G} S(e_2) : S(T_1')$ and $\ldots$ and $S(\Gamma + \Gamma_1 + \ldots + \Gamma_n) \vdash_{\cap G} S(e_2) : S(T_n')$, then by rule T-App, $S(\Gamma + \Gamma_1 + \ldots + \Gamma_n) \vdash_{\cap G} S(e_1\ e_2) : S(T)$.

Lemma 10 (Consistent Subtyping to Subtyping). *If $T_1 \lesssim T_2$ and both T_1 and T_2 are static, then $T_1 \leq T_2$.*

Proof. We proceed by induction on Definition 2.

Base cases:

- $T \lesssim T$. If $T \lesssim T$ then $T \leq T$.
- $T_1 \cap \ldots \cap T_n \lesssim T_1$ and $\ldots$ and $T_1 \cap \ldots \cap T_n \lesssim T_n$. If $T_1 \cap \ldots \cap T_n \lesssim T_1$ and $\ldots$ and $T_1 \cap \ldots \cap T_n \lesssim T_n$, then $T_1 \cap \ldots \cap T_n \leq T_1$ and $\ldots$ and $T_1 \cap \ldots \cap T_n \leq T_n$.
- $(T \to T_1) \cap \ldots \cap (T \to T_n) \lesssim T \to T_1 \cap \ldots \cap T_n$. If $(T \to T_1) \cap \ldots \cap (T \to T_n) \lesssim T \to T_1 \cap \ldots \cap T_n$ then $(T \to T_1) \cap \ldots \cap (T \to T_n) \leq T \to T_1 \cap \ldots \cap T_n$.

Induction step:

- $T_1 \to T_2 \lesssim T_3 \to T_4 \iff T_3 \lesssim T_1 \wedge T_2 \lesssim T_4$. There are two possibilities:
  - We proceed first for the right direction of the implication. If $T_1 \to T_2 \lesssim T_3 \to T_4$ then $T_3 \lesssim T_1$ and $T_2 \lesssim T_4$. By the induction hypothesis, $T_3 \leq T_1$ and $T_2 \leq T_4$. Then by the Definition 1, $T_1 \to T_2 \leq T_3 \to T_4$.
  - We now proceed for the left direction of the implication. If $T_3 \lesssim T_1$ and $T_2 \lesssim T_4$ then $T_1 \to T_2 \lesssim T_3 \to T_4$. By the induction hypothesis, $T_1 \to T_2 \leq T_3 \to T_4$. By Definition 1, $T_3 \leq T_1$ and $T_2 \leq T_4$.

– $T \lesssim T_1 \cap \ldots \cap T_n \iff T \lesssim T_1 \wedge \ldots \wedge T \lesssim T_n$. There are two possibilities:
  • We proceed first for the right direction of the implication. If $T \lesssim T_1 \cap \ldots \cap T_n$ then $T \lesssim T_1$ and ... and $T \lesssim T_n$. By the induction hypothesis, $T \leq T_1$ and ... and $T \leq T_n$. Therefore, by Definition 1, $T \leq T_1 \cap \ldots \cap T_n$.
  • We now proceed for the left direction of intersection types. If $T \lesssim T_1$ and ... and $T \lesssim T_n$ then $T \lesssim T_1 \cap \ldots \cap T_n$. By the induction hypothesis, $T \leq T_1 \cap \ldots \cap T_n$. By Definition 1, $T \leq T_1$ and ... and $T \leq T_n$.

Lemma 2 (Constraint Completeness). *If $\Gamma_1 \vdash_{\cap G} e : T_1$ then*

1. *there exists a derivation $A \mid \Gamma_2 \vdash_{\cap G} e : T_2 \mid C$ such that $\exists S . S \models C$*
2. *for $A \mid \Gamma_{21} \vdash_{\cap G} e : T_{21} \mid C_1$ such that $\exists S_1 . S_1 \models C_1$ and ... and $A \mid \Gamma_{2n} \vdash_{\cap G} e : T_{2n} \mid C_n$ such that $\exists S_n . S_n \models C_n$ then*
   (a) *for each $x \in dom(\Gamma_1) \cap dom(\sum_{i=1}^{n} \Gamma_{2i})$, $\Gamma_1(x) \leq S_i(\Gamma_{2i}(x)), \forall i \in 1..n$*
   (b) $\bigcap_{i=1}^{n} S_i(T_{2i}) \leq T_1$

Proof. We proceed by induction on the length of the derivation tree of $\Gamma_1 \vdash_{\cap G} e : T_1$.

Base cases:

– Rule T-VAR. If $\Gamma_1 \vdash_{\cap G} x : T_i$ then $x : T_1 \cap \ldots \cap T_n \in \Gamma_1$. There are two possibilities:
  • $x \in dom(A)$. If $x \in dom(A)$, then $x : T_1 \cap \ldots \cap T_n \in A$, since the type $T_1 \cap \ldots \cap T_n$ came from the annotation of the lambda abstraction that binds x. To prove 1., we have that $A \mid \{x : T_1\} \vdash_{\cap G} x : T_1 \mid \emptyset$ and for a $S_1 = []$, $S_1 \models \emptyset$ and ... and $A \mid \{x : T_n\} \vdash_{\cap G} x : T_n \mid \emptyset$ and for a $S_n = []$, $S_n \models \emptyset$. To prove 2.a), we have that since $S_1(\Gamma_{21}(x)) = T_1$ and ... and $S_n(\Gamma_{2n}(x)) = T_n$ and $\Gamma_1(x) = T_1 \cap \ldots \cap T_n$ then by Definition 1, $\Gamma_1(x) \leq S_1(\Gamma_{21}(x))$ and ... and $\Gamma_1(x) \leq S_n(\Gamma_{2n}(x))$ and to prove 2.b), we have that $S_1(T_1) \cap \ldots \cap S_n(T_n) \leq T_i$.
  • $x \notin dom(A)$. To prove 1., we have that $A \mid \{x : X_1\} \vdash_{\cap G} x : X_1 \mid \emptyset$ and for a $S_1 = [X_1 \mapsto T_1]$, $S_1 \models \emptyset$ and ... and $A \mid \{x : X_n\} \vdash_{\cap G} x : X_n \mid \emptyset$ and for a $S_n = [X_n \mapsto T_n]$, $S_n \models \emptyset$. To prove 2.a), since $S_1(\Gamma_{21}(x)) = T_1$ and ... and $S_n(\Gamma_{2n}(x)) = T_n$ and $\Gamma_1(x) = T_1 \cap \ldots \cap T_n$ then by Definition 1, $\Gamma_1(x) \leq S_1(\Gamma_{21}(x))$ and ... and $\Gamma_1(x) \leq S_n(\Gamma_{2n}(x))$ and to prove 2.b), we have that $S_1(X_1) \cap \ldots \cap S_n(X_n) \leq T_i$.
– Rule T-CONST. If $\Gamma \vdash_{\cap G} c : T$, then c is an constant of type T. Therefore, to prove 1., we have that $A \mid \{\} \vdash_{\cap G} c : T \mid \{\}$ and $S \models \emptyset$. Since there is no $x \in dom(\Gamma_1) \cap dom(\{\})$, 2.a) is proved. To prove 2.b), we have that $S(T) \leq T$, by Definition 1.

Induction step:

– Rule T-ABS. If $\Gamma_1 \vdash_{\cap G} \lambda x . e : T_1 \to T_2$ then $\Gamma_1, x : T_1 \vdash_{\cap G} e : T_2$. There are two possibilities:

- $x \in dom(\Gamma_2)$. By the induction hypothesis on 1., exists $A \mid \Gamma_2 \vdash_{\cap G} e :$ $T_2' \mid C$ such that $\exists S \, . \, S \models C$.

  By the induction hypothesis on 2., we have that for $A \mid \Gamma_{21} \vdash_{\cap G} e :$ $T_{21} \mid C_1$ such that $\exists S_1 \, . \, S_1 \models C_1$ and $\ldots$ and for $A \mid \Gamma_{2n} \vdash_{\cap G} e :$ $T_{2n} \mid C_n$ such that $\exists S_n \, . \, S_n \models C_n$, then for each $y \in dom(\Gamma_1, x :$ $T_1) \cap dom(\sum_{i=1}^n \Gamma_{2i})$, we have $(\Gamma_1, x : T_1)(y) \leq S_i(\Gamma_{2i}(y))$, $\forall i \in 1..n$, and $\bigcap_{i=1}^n S_i(T_{2i}) \leq T_2$.

  To prove 1., we have that as $A \mid \Gamma_2 \vdash_{\cap G} e : T_2' \mid C$ such that $\exists S \, . \, S \models C$, then by rule C-ABS1, exists $A \mid \Gamma_{2x} \vdash_{\cap G} \lambda x \, . \, e : \Gamma_2(x) \to T_2' \mid C$ and $S \models C$.

  To prove 2., we have that for $A \mid \Gamma_{21} \vdash_{\cap G} e : T_{21} \mid C_1$ then $A \mid \Gamma_{21x} \vdash_{\cap G}$ $\lambda x \, . \, e : \Gamma_{21}(x) \to T_{21} \mid C_1$ and $S_1 \models C_1$ and $\ldots$ and for $A \mid \Gamma_{2n} \vdash_{\cap G} e :$ $T_{2n} \mid C_n$ then $A \mid \Gamma_{2nx} \vdash_{\cap G} \lambda x \, . \, e : \Gamma_{2n}(x) \to T_{2n} \mid C_n$ and $S_n \models C_n$.

  To prove 2.a), as $(\Gamma_1, x : T_1)(y) \leq S_1(\Gamma_{21}(y))$ and $\ldots$ and $(\Gamma_1, x : T_1)(y) \leq S_n(\Gamma_{2n}(y))$ for each $y \in dom(\Gamma_1, x : T_1) \cap dom(\Gamma_2)$ then $(\Gamma_1)(y) \leq S_1(\Gamma_{21x}(y))$ and $\ldots$ and $(\Gamma_1)(y) \leq S_n(\Gamma_{2nx}(y))$.

  To prove 2.b), as $S_1(T_{21}) \cap \ldots \cap S_n(T_{2n}) \leq T_2$ and $T_1 \leq S_1(\Gamma_{21}(x))$ and $\ldots$ and $T_1 \leq S_n(\Gamma_{2n}(x))$ then by Definition 1, rule 4, $T_1 \leq S_1(\Gamma_{21}(x)) \cap \ldots \cap S_n(\Gamma_{2n}(x))$. Therefore, by Definition 1, rule 3, $S_1(\Gamma_{21}(x)) \cap \ldots \cap S_n(\Gamma_{2n}(x)) \to S_1(T_{21}) \cap \ldots \cap S_n(T_{2n}) \leq T_1 \to T_2$. Therefore, by Definition 1, rule 5, $(S_1(\Gamma_{21}(x)) \cap \ldots \cap S_n(\Gamma_{2n}(x)) \to S_1(T_{21})) \cap \ldots \cap (S_1(\Gamma_{21}(x)) \cap \ldots \cap S_n(\Gamma_{2n}(x)) \to S_n(T_{2n})) \leq T_1 \to T_2$. By Definition 1, rule 2, $S_1(\Gamma_{21}(x) \to T_{21}) \cap \ldots \cap S_n(\Gamma_{2n}(x) \to T_{2n}) \leq T_1 \to T_2$.

- $x \notin dom(\Gamma_2)$. By the induction hypothesis on 1., exists $A \mid \Gamma_2 \vdash_{\cap G} e :$ $T_2' \mid C$ such that $\exists S \, . \, S \models C$.

  By the induction hypothesis on 2., we have that for $A \mid \Gamma_{21} \vdash_{\cap G} e :$ $T_{21} \mid C_1$ such that $\exists S_1 \, . \, S_1 \models C_1$ and $\ldots$ and for $A \mid \Gamma_{2n} \vdash_{\cap G} e :$ $T_{2n} \mid C_n$ such that $\exists S_n \, . \, S_n \models C_n$ then for each $y \in dom(\Gamma_1, x :$ $T_1) \cap dom(\sum_{i=1}^n \Gamma_{2i})$, we have $(\Gamma_1, x : T_1)(y) \leq S_i(\Gamma_{2i}(y))$, $\forall i \in 1..n$ and $\bigcap i = 1^n S_i(T_{2i}) \leq T_2$.

  To prove 1., we have that as $A \mid \Gamma_2 \vdash_{\cap G} e : T_2' \mid C$ such that $\exists S \, . \, S \models C$ then by rule C-ABS2, exists $A \mid \Gamma_2 \vdash_{\cap G} \lambda x \, . \, e : X \to T_2' \mid C$ and $S \models C$.

  To prove 2., we have that for $A \mid \Gamma_{21} \vdash_{\cap G} e : T_{21} \mid C_1$ then $A \mid \Gamma_{21} \vdash_{\cap G}$ $\lambda x \, . \, e : X_1 \to T_{21} \mid C_1$ and $S_1 \models C_1$ and $\ldots$ and for $A \mid \Gamma_{2n} \vdash_{\cap G} e :$ $T_{2n} \mid C_n$ then $A \mid \Gamma_{2n} \vdash_{\cap G} \lambda x \, . \, e : X_n \to T_{2n} \mid C_n$ and $S_n \models C_n$.

  Since X_1 is a fresh type variable, it is not contained in C_1 and $\ldots$ and since X_n is a fresh type variable, it is not contained in C_n. Then, we can consider $S_1 = S_1' \circ [X_1 \mapsto T_1]$ and $\ldots$ and we can consider $S_n = S_n' \circ [X_n \mapsto T_1]$.

  To prove 2.a), as for each $y \in dom(\Gamma_1, x : T_1) \cap dom(\sum_{i=1}^n \Gamma_{2i})$, we have $(\Gamma_1, x : T_1)(y) \leq S_i(\Gamma_{2i}(y))$, $\forall i \in 1..n$, then $\Gamma_1(y) \leq S_i(\Gamma_{2ix}(y))$, $\forall i \in 1..n$.

  To prove 2.b), as $T_1 \leq S_1(X_1)$ and $\ldots$ and $T_1 \leq S_n(X_n)$ then by Definition 1, rule 4, $T_1 \leq S_1(X_1) \cap \ldots \cap S_n(X_n)$. As $S_1(T_{21}) \cap \ldots \cap S_n(T_{2n}) \leq T_2$, then by Definition 1, rule 3, $S_1(X_1) \cap \ldots \cap S_n(X_n) \to S_1(T_{21}) \cap \ldots \cap S_n(T_{2n}) \leq T_1 \to T_2$. Therefore, by Definition 1, rule 5, $(S_1(X_1) \cap \ldots \cap S_n(X_n) \to S_1(T_{21})) \cap \ldots \cap (S_1(X_1) \cap \ldots \cap S_n(X_n) \to$

$S_n(T_{2n})) \leq T_1 \to T_2$. By Definition 1, rule 2, $S_1(X_1 \to T_{21}) \cap \ldots \cap S_n(X_n \to T_{2n}) \leq T_1 \to T_2$.

- Rule T-ABS. If $\Gamma_1 \vdash_{\cap G} \lambda x : T_1 \cap \ldots \cap T_n$. $e : T_1 \cap \ldots \cap T_m \to T$ then $\Gamma_1, x : T_1 \cap \ldots \cap T_m \vdash_{\cap G} e : T$. There are two possibilities:

  • $x \in dom(\Gamma_2)$. By the induction hypothesis on 1., exists $A_x \cup \{x : T_1 \cap \ldots \cap T_n\} \mid \Gamma_2 \vdash_{\cap G} e : T' \mid C$ such that $\exists S$. $S \models C$.

  By the induction hypothesis on 2., we have that for $A_x \cup \{x : T_1 \cap \ldots \cap T_n\} \mid \Gamma_{21} \vdash_{\cap G} e : T_1' \mid C_1$ such that $\exists S_1$. $S_1 \models C_1$ and ... and for $A_x \cup \{x : T_1 \cap \ldots \cap T_n\} \mid \Gamma_{2l} \vdash_{\cap G} e : T_l' \mid C_l$ such that $\exists S_l$. $S_l \models C_l$ then for each $y \in dom(\Gamma_1, x : T_1 \cap \ldots \cap T_m) \cap dom(\sum_{i=1}^{l} \Gamma_{2i})$, we have that $(\Gamma_1, x : T_1 \cap \ldots \cap T_m)(y) \leq S_i(\Gamma_{2i}(y))$, $\forall i \in 1..l$, and $\bigcap_{i=1}^{l} S_i(T_i') \leq T$.

  To prove 1., we have that as $A_x \cup \{x : T_1 \cap \ldots \cap T_n\} \mid \Gamma_2 \vdash_{\cap G} e : T' \mid C$ such that $\exists S$. $S \models C$, then $A \mid \Gamma_{2x} \vdash_{\cap G} \lambda x : T_1 \cap \ldots \cap T_n$. $e : \Gamma_2(x) \to T' \mid C$ and $S \models C$.

  To prove 2., we have that for $A_x \cup \{x : T_1 \cap \ldots \cap T_n\} \mid \Gamma_{21} \vdash_{\cap G} e : T_1' \mid C_1$ then $A \mid \Gamma_{21x} \vdash_{\cap G} \lambda x : T_1 \cap \ldots \cap T_n$. $e : \Gamma_{21}(x) \to T_1' \mid C_1$ and $S_1 \models C_1$ and ... and for $A_x \cup \{x : T_1 \cap \ldots \cap T_n\} \mid \Gamma_{2l} \vdash_{\cap G} e : T_l' \mid C_l$ then $A \mid \Gamma_{2lx} \vdash_{\cap G} \lambda x : T_1 \cap \ldots \cap T_n$. $e : \Gamma_{2l}(x) \to T_l' \mid C_l$ and $S_l \models C_l$.

  To prove 2.a), as for each $y \in dom(\Gamma_1) \cap dom(\sum_{i=1}^{l} \Gamma_{2i})$, we have $(\Gamma_1, x : T_1 \cap \ldots \cap T_m)(y) \leq S_i(\Gamma_{2i}(y))$, $\forall i \in 1..l$, then $\Gamma_1(y) \leq S_i(\Gamma_{2ix}(y))$.

  To prove 2.b), we have that $T_1 \cap \ldots \cap T_m \leq S_1(\Gamma_{21}(x))$ and ... and $T_1 \cap \ldots \cap T_m \leq S_l(\Gamma_{2l}(x))$. As $T_1 \cap \ldots \cap T_m \leq S_1(\Gamma_{21}(x))$ and ... and $T_1 \cap \ldots \cap T_m \leq S_l(\Gamma_{2l}(x))$ then by Definition 1, rule 4, $T_1 \cap \ldots \cap T_m \leq S_1(\Gamma_{21}(x)) \cap \ldots \cap S_l(\Gamma_{2l}(x))$. As $S_1(T_1') \cap \ldots \cap S_l(T_l') \leq T$, then by Definition 1, rule 3, $S_1(\Gamma_{21}(x)) \cap \ldots \cap S_l(\Gamma_{2l}(x)) \to S_1(T_1') \cap \ldots \cap S_l(T_l') \leq T_1 \cap \ldots \cap T_m \to T$. Therefore, by Definition 1, rule 5, $(S_1(\Gamma_{21}(x)) \cap \ldots \cap S_l(\Gamma_{2l}(x)) \to S_1(T_1')) \cap \ldots \cap (S_1(\Gamma_{21}(x)) \cap \ldots \cap S_l(\Gamma_{2l}(x)) \to S_l(T_l')) \leq T_1 \cap \ldots \cap T_m \to T$. By Definition 1, rule 2, $S_1(\Gamma_{21}(x) \to T_1') \cap \ldots \cap S_l(\Gamma_{2l}(x) \to T_l') \leq T_1 \cap \ldots \cap T_m \to T$.

  • $x \notin dom(\Gamma_2)$. By the induction hypothesis on 1., exists $A_x \cup \{x : T_1 \cap \ldots \cap T_n\} \mid \Gamma_2 \vdash_{\cap G} e : T' \mid C$ such that $\exists S$. $S \models C$.

  By the induction hypothesis on 2., we have that for $A_x \cup \{x : T_1 \cap \ldots \cap T_n\} \mid \Gamma_{21} \vdash_{\cap G} e : T_1' \mid C_1$ such that $\exists S_1$. $S_1 \models C_1$ and ... and for $A_x \cup \{x : T_1 \cap \ldots \cap T_n\} \mid \Gamma_{2l} \vdash_{\cap G} e : T_l' \mid C_l$ then for each $y \in dom(\Gamma_1, x : T_1 \cap \ldots \cap T_m) \cap dom(\sum_{i=1}^{l} \Gamma_{2i})$, we have that $(\Gamma_1, x : T_1 \cap \ldots \cap T_m)(y) \leq S_i(\Gamma_{2i}(y))$, $\forall i \in 1..l$, and $\bigcap_{i=1}^{l} S_i(T_i') \leq T$.

  To prove 1., we have that as $A_x \cup \{x : T_1 \cap \ldots \cap T_n\} \mid \Gamma_2 \vdash_{\cap G} e : T' \mid C$ such that $\exists S$. $S \models C$ then by rule C-ABS:2, exists $A \mid \Gamma_2 \vdash_{\cap G} \lambda x : T_1 \cap \ldots \cap T_n$. $e : T_1 \to T' \cap \ldots \cap T_n \to T' \mid C$ and $S \models C$.

  To prove 2., we have that for $A_x \cup \{x : T_1 \cap \ldots \cap T_n\} \mid \Gamma_{21} \vdash_{\cap G} e : T_1' \mid C_1$ then $A \mid \Gamma_{21} \vdash_{\cap G} \lambda x : T_1 \cap \ldots \cap T_n$. $e : T_1 \to T_1' \cap \ldots \cap T_n \to T_1' \mid C_1$ and $S_1 \models C_1$ and ... and for $A_x \cup \{x : T_1 \cap \ldots \cap T_n\} \mid \Gamma_{2l} \vdash_{\cap G} e : T_l' \mid C_l$ then $A \mid \Gamma_{2l} \vdash_{\cap G} \lambda x : T_1 \cap \ldots \cap T_n$. $e : T_1 \to T_l' \cap \ldots \cap T_n \to T_l' \mid C_l$ and $S_n \models C_n$.

  To prove 2.a), as for each $y \in dom(\Gamma_1, x : T_1 \cap \ldots \cap T_m) \cap dom(\sum_{i=1}^{l} \Gamma_{2i})$, we have that $(\Gamma_1, x : T_1 \cap \ldots \cap T_m)(y) \leq S_i(\Gamma_{2i}(y))$, $\forall i \in 1..l$, then $\Gamma_1(y) \leq S_i(\Gamma_{2i}(y))$.

To prove 2.b), as x does not occur in e, then T_1 and $\ldots$ and T_n are not affected by $S_1, \ldots, S_n$. Therefore $S_1(T_1 \cap \ldots \cap T_n) = T_1 \cap \ldots \cap T_n$ and $\ldots$ and $S_l(T_1 \cap \ldots \cap T_n) = T_1 \cap \ldots \cap T_n$. Therefore, $S_1((T_1 \to T_1') \cap \ldots \cap (T_n \to T_1')) \cap \ldots \cap S_l((T_1 \to T_l') \cap \ldots \cap (T_n \to T_l')) = (T_1 \to S_1(T_1')) \cap \ldots \cap (T_n \to S_1(T_1')) \cap \ldots \cap (T_1 \to S_l(T_l')) \cap \ldots \cap (T_n \to S_l(T_l'))$. Then, by Definition 1, rule 2, $(T_1 \to S_1(T_1')) \cap \ldots \cap (T_n \to S_1(T_1')) \cap \ldots \cap (T_1 \to S_l(T_l')) \cap \ldots \cap (T_n \to S_l(T_l')) \leq (T_1 \cap \ldots \cap T_m \to S_1(T_1')) \cap \ldots \cap (T_1 \cap \ldots \cap T_m \to S_l(T_l'))$. Then, by Definition 1, rule 5, $(T_1 \cap \ldots \cap T_m \to S_1(T_1')) \cap \ldots \cap (T_1 \cap \ldots \cap T_m \to S_l(T_l')) \leq T_1 \cap \ldots \cap T_m \to S_1(T_1') \cap \ldots \cap S_l(T_l')$. Then, by Definition 1, rule 3, $T_1 \cap \ldots \cap T_m \to S_1(T_1') \cap \ldots \cap S_l(T_l') \leq T_1 \cap \ldots \cap T_m \to T$.

- Rule T-APP. If $\Gamma \vdash_{\cap G} e_1 e_2 : T$ then $\Gamma \vdash_{\cap G} e_1 : PM$, $PM \rhd T_1 \cap \ldots \cap T_n \to T$, $\Gamma \vdash_{\cap G} e_2 : T_1' \cap \ldots \cap T_n'$ and $T_1' \lesssim T_1$ and $\ldots$ and $T_n' \lesssim T_n$. There are two possibilities:

  • Using rule C-APP. By the induction hypothesis on 1., exists $A \mid \Gamma_1 \vdash_{\cap G} e_1 : PM' \mid C_1$ such that $\exists S_1 . S_1 \models C_1$ and exists $A \mid \Gamma_2 \vdash_{\cap G} e_2 : T'' \mid C_2$ such that $\exists S_2 . S_2 \models C_2$.

  By the induction hypothesis on 2., we have that for $A \mid \Gamma_{11} \vdash_{\cap G} e_1 : PM_1 \mid C_{11}$ such that $\exists S_{11} . S_{11} \models C_{11}$ and $\ldots$ and $A \mid \Gamma_{1n'} \vdash_{\cap G} e_1 : PM_{1n'} \mid C_{1n'}$ such that $\exists S_{1n'} . S_{1n'} \models C_{1n'}$ then for each $x \in dom(\Gamma) \cap dom(\sum_{i=1}^{n'} \Gamma_{1i})$, we have that $\Gamma(x) \leq S_{1i}(\Gamma_{1i}(x))$ and $\bigcap_{i=1}^{n'} S_{1i}(PM_i) \leq PM$.

  Also, by the induction hypothesis on 2., we have that for $A \mid \Gamma_{21} \vdash_{\cap G} e_2 : T_1'' \mid C_{21}$ such that $\exists S_{21} . S_{21} \models C_{21}$ and $\ldots$ and $A \mid \Gamma_{2m'} \vdash_{\cap G} e_2 : T_{m'}'' \mid C_{2m'}$ such that $\exists S_{2m'} . S_{2m'} \models C_{2m'}$ then for each $x \in dom(\Gamma) \cap dom(\sum_{j=1}^{m'} \Gamma_{2j})$, we have that $\Gamma(x) \leq S_{2j}(\Gamma_{2j}(x))$ and $\bigcap_{j=1}^{m'} S_{2j}(T_j'') \leq T_1' \cap \ldots \cap T_n'$.

  To prove 1., we want to prove that since $A \mid \Gamma_1 \vdash_{\cap G} e_1 : PM' \mid C_1$ such that $\exists S_1 . S_1 \models C_1$ and since $A \mid \Gamma_2 \vdash_{\cap G} e_2 : T'' \mid C_2$ such that $\exists S_2 . S_2 \models C_2$, and for $cod(PM') \doteq T_3 \mid C_3$ and $T'' \lesssim dom(PM') \mid C_4$, then exists $A \mid \Gamma_1 + \Gamma_2 \vdash_{\cap G} e_1 e_2 : T_3 \mid C_1 \cup C_2 \cup C_3 \cup C_4$ such that $\exists S_k . S_k \models C_1 \cup C_2 \cup C_3 \cup C_4$.

  To prove 2., we want to prove that, for $\forall i \in 1..n'$ and $\forall j \in 1..m'$ such that $A \mid \Gamma_{1i} \vdash_{\cap G} e_1 : PM_i \mid C_{1i}$ such that $\exists S_{1i} . S_{1i} \models C_{1i}$, $A \mid \Gamma_{2j} \vdash_{\cap G} e_2 : T_j'' \mid C_{2j}$ such that $\exists S_{2j} . S_{j2} \models C_{2j}$, $cod(PM_i) \doteq T_{3i} \mid C_{3i}$ and $T_j'' \lesssim dom(PM_i) \mid C_{4k}$, with $k \in 1..i * j$ then for $A \mid \Gamma_{1i} + \Gamma_{2j} \vdash_{\cap G} e_1 e_2 : T_{3i} \mid C_{1i} \cup C_{2j} \cup C_{3i} \cup C_{4k}$, such that $\exists S_k . S_k \models C_{1i} \cup C_{2j} \cup C_{3i} \cup C_{4k}$ then 2.a) for each $x \in dom(\Gamma) \cap dom(\Gamma_{1i} + \Gamma_{2j})$ we have that $\Gamma(x) \leq S_k(\Gamma_{1i} + \Gamma_{2j})(x)$, and 2.b) $S_1(T_{13}) \cap \ldots \cap S_{n' * m'}(T_{n'3}) \leq T$. We define $dom_\rhd$ as $dom_\rhd(Dyn) = Dyn$ and $dom_\rhd(T_1 \to T_2) = T_1$ and $cod_\rhd$ as $cod_\rhd(Dyn) = Dyn$ and $cod_\rhd(T_1 \to T_2) = T_2$. Since $cod_\rhd(PM) = T$, we want to prove that $S_k(T_{i3}) \leq cod_\rhd(S_{i1}(PM_i))$.

  By Definition 1, rule 4, we have that $\Gamma(x) \leq (S_{1i}(\Gamma_{1i}) + S_{2j}(\Gamma_{2j}))(x)$. Since substitutions in S_{1i} don't affect Γ_{2j} and substitutions in S_{2j} don't affect Γ_{1i}, then $\Gamma(x) \leq (S_{1i} \circ S_{2j}(\Gamma_{1i} + \Gamma_{2j}))(x)$. For an $S_{3i} \models C_{3i}$ and $S_{4k} \models C_{4k}$, S_{3i} doesn't affect S_{2j}.

There are 3 possibilities:

* $PM_i = X$. Proof for 1. We have that exists $A \mid \Gamma_1 \vdash_{\cap G} e_1 : PM' \mid C_1$ such that $\exists S_1 \,.\, S_1 \models C_1$ and exists $A \mid \Gamma_2 \vdash_{\cap G} e_2 : T'' \mid C_2$ such that $\exists S_2 \,.\, S_2 \models C_2$, and for $cod(X) \doteq X_2 \mid \{X \doteq X_1 \to X_2\}$ and $T'' \stackrel{.}{\lesssim} dom(PM') \mid \{X \doteq X_3 \to X_4, T'' \stackrel{.}{\lesssim} X_3\}$ then, by rule C-App, $A \mid \Gamma_1 + \Gamma_2 \vdash_{\cap G} e_1 \, e_2 : T_3 \mid C_1 \cup C_2 \cup \{X \doteq X_1 \to X_2\} \cup \{X \doteq X_3 \to X_4, T'' \stackrel{.}{\lesssim} X_3\}$. We now have to prove that $\exists S \,.\, S \models C_1 \cup C_2 \cup \{X \doteq X_1 \to X_2\} \cup \{X \doteq X_3 \to X_4, T'' \stackrel{.}{\lesssim} X_3\}$. Since $S_2(T'') \leq T_1' \cap \ldots \cap T_n'$, and $T_1' \stackrel{.}{\lesssim} T_1$ and $\ldots$ and $T_n' \stackrel{.}{\lesssim} T_n$ and $T_1 \cap \ldots \cap T_n \leq dom_{\rhd} S_1(PM')$, then $S_2(T'') \stackrel{.}{\lesssim} dom_{\rhd}(S_1(PM'))$. Therefore, it is proved.

  Proof for 2. For all $i \in 1..n'$, $j \in 1..m'$, such that $A \mid \Gamma_{1i} \vdash_{\cap G} e_1 : PM_i \mid C_{1i}$ and $\exists S_{1i} \,.\, S_{1i} \models C_{1i}$, $A \mid \Gamma_{2j} \vdash_{\cap G} e_2 : T_j'' \mid C_{2j}$ and $\exists S_{2j} \,.\, S_{2j} \models C_{2j}$, $cod(PM_i) \doteq T_{3i} \mid C_{3i}$ and $T_j'' \stackrel{.}{\lesssim} dom(PM_i) \mid C_{4k}$, then $A \mid \Gamma_{1i} + \Gamma_{2j} \vdash_{\cap G} e_1 \, e_2 : T_{3i} \mid C_{1i} \cup C_{2j} \cup C_{3i} \cup C_{4k}$, with $k \in 1..i * j$.

  Since PM_i is a type variable, then there exists a term variable x such that $PM_i = \Gamma_{1i}(x)$ and so we have that $C_{3i} = \{X \doteq X_1 \to X_2\}$ and $C_{k4} = \{X \doteq X_3 \to X_4, T_j'' \stackrel{.}{\lesssim} X_3\}$. As $\Gamma(x) \leq S_{1i}(X)$ and, since we are dealing with an expression application, $\Gamma(x) = T_1 \to T$ for some simple types T_1 and T, then $T_1 \to T \leq S_{1i}(X)$. Since substitutions don't introduce intersection types, then $T_1 \to T = S_{1i}(X)$.

  Proof for 2.a). If $S_k \models T_j'' \stackrel{.}{\lesssim} X_3$, then by Definition 3, $S_k(T_j'') \stackrel{.}{\lesssim} S_k(X_3)$. If $T_j'' \in cod(S_{2j}(\Gamma_{2j}))$ and T_j'' is static, then $S_{2j}(\Gamma_{2j})(x) \leq S_k(\Gamma_{2j})(x)$. Also, since $X \in cod(S_{i1}(\Gamma_{i1}))$, then $S_{i1}(\Gamma_{i1}) \leq S_k(\Gamma_{i1})$. For a S_k such that $S_k \models C_{i1} \cup C_{j2} \cup C_{i3} \cup C_{k4}$, $\Gamma(x) \leq S_k(\Gamma_{i1} + \Gamma_{j2})(x)$.

  Proof for 2.b). We have that $T = cod_{\rhd}(S_{i1}(PM_i))$ and $S_k(T_{i3}) = T$.

* $PM_i = T_3 \to T_4$. We have that exists $A \mid \Gamma_1 \vdash_{\cap G} e_1 : PM' \mid C_1$ such that $\exists S_1 \,.\, S_1 \models C_1$ and exists $A \mid \Gamma_2 \vdash_{\cap G} e_2 : T'' \mid C_2$ such that $\exists S_2 \,.\, S_2 \models C_2$, and for $cod(T_3 \to T_4) \doteq T_4 \mid \{\}$ and $T'' \stackrel{.}{\lesssim} dom(T_3 \to T_4) \mid \{T'' \stackrel{.}{\lesssim} T_3\}$ then, by rule C-App, $A \mid \Gamma_1 + \Gamma_2 \vdash_{\cap G} e_1 \, e_2 : T_4 \mid C_1 \cup C_2 \cup \{T'' \stackrel{.}{\lesssim} T_3\}$. We now have to prove that $\exists S \,.\, S \models C_1 \cup C_2 \cup \{T'' \stackrel{.}{\lesssim} T_3\}$. Since $S_2(T'') \leq T_1' \cap \ldots \cap T_n'$, and $T_1' \stackrel{.}{\lesssim} T_1$ and $\ldots$ and $T_n' \stackrel{.}{\lesssim} T_n$ and $T_1 \cap \ldots \cap T_n \leq S_1(T_3)$, then $S_2(T'') \stackrel{.}{\lesssim} S_1(T_3)$. Therefore, it is proved.

  For all $i \in 1..n'$, $j \in 1..m'$, such that $A \mid \Gamma_{1i} \vdash_{\cap G} e_1 : PM_i \mid C_{1i}$ and $\exists S_{1i} \,.\, S_{1i} \models C_{1i}$, $A \mid \Gamma_{2j} \vdash_{\cap G} e_2 : T_j'' \mid C_{2j}$ and $\exists S_{2j} \,.\, S_{2j} \models C_{2j}$, $cod(PM_i) \doteq T_{3i} \mid C_{3i}$ and $T_j'' \stackrel{.}{\lesssim} dom(PM_i) \mid C_{4k}$, then $A \mid \Gamma_{1i} + \Gamma_{2j} \vdash_{\cap G} e_1 \, e_2 : T_{3i} \mid C_{1i} \cup C_{2j} \cup C_{3i} \cup C_{4k}$, with $k \in 1..i * j$.

  Proof for 2.a). S_{i3} doesn't affect Γ_{i1} and Γ_{j2}. We don't allow variables in annotations in lambda abstractions. If $T_3 = Dyn$ or $T_j'' = Dyn$ then $[] \models T_j'' \stackrel{.}{\lesssim} T_3$ and so, $\Gamma(x) \leq S_k(\Gamma_{i1} + \Gamma_{j2})(x)$. One way that

$PM_i = T_3 \to T_4$ is if e_1 is a term variable and T_3 is a type variable, and so $T_3 \notin \Gamma_{i1}$ then $\Gamma(x) \leq S_k(\Gamma_{i1} + \Gamma_{j2})(x)$. Another way that $PM_i = T_3 \to T_4$ is if e_1 is a lambda abstraction and $T_3 \to T_4 \in \Gamma_{i1}$, and so T_3 is not a type variable, then $\Gamma(x) \leq S_k(\Gamma_{i1} + \Gamma_{j2})(x)$. Therefore, if $T_j'' \in \Gamma_{j2}$, and as $S_k \models T_j'' \stackrel{.}{\lesssim} T_3$ then $\Gamma(x) \leq S_k(\Gamma_{i1} + \Gamma_{j2})(x)$.

Proof for 2.b). We have that $T_{i3} = T_4$, then $cod_\triangleright(S_{i1}(PM_i)) = S_{i1}(T_{i3})$. We want to prove that $S_i(T_{i3}) \leq S_{i1}(T_{i3})$. If T_{i3} is not a variable, then $S_i(T_{i3}) = S_{i1}(T_{i3})$. If T_{i3} is a variable, then either $T_{i3} \neq T_3$, in which case S_k doesn't affect $S_{i1}(T_4)$ and so $S_{i1}(T_4) = S_k(T_4)$. Otherwise, $T_3 = T_4 = T_{i3}$. Therefore, as $S_k \models T_j'' \stackrel{.}{\lesssim} T_4$. So, $S_k(T_4) \stackrel{.}{\lesssim} S_{i1}(T_4)$. Since S_k doesn't have a subtitution that turns T_4 into Dyn, then by Lemma 10, $S_k(T_4) \leq S_{i1}(T_4)$.

* $PM_i = Dyn$. Proof for 1. We have that exists $A \mid \Gamma_1 \vdash_{\cap G} e_1 : Dyn \mid C_1$ such that $\exists S_1 \;.\; S_1 \models C_1$ and exists $A \mid \Gamma_2 \vdash_{\cap G} e_2 : T'' \mid C_2$ such that $\exists S_2 \;.\; S_2 \models C_2$, and for $cod(Dyn) \stackrel{.}{=} Dyn \mid \{\}$ and $T'' \stackrel{.}{\lesssim} dom(Dyn) \mid \{T'' \stackrel{.}{\lesssim} Dyn\}$ then, by rule C-App, $A \mid \Gamma_1 + \Gamma_2 \vdash_{\cap G} e_1\, e_2 : Dyn \mid C_1 \cup C_2 \cup \{T'' \stackrel{.}{\lesssim} Dyn\}$. Since $\exists S \;.\; S \models C_1 \cup C_2 \cup \{T'' \stackrel{.}{\lesssim} Dyn\}$, it is proved.

Proof for 2. For all $i \in 1..n'$, $j \in 1..m'$, such that $A \mid \Gamma_{1i} \vdash_{\cap G} e_1 : PM_i \mid C_{1i}$ and $\exists S_{1i} \;.\; S_{1i} \models C_{1i}$, $A \mid \Gamma_{2j} \vdash_{\cap G} e_2 : T_j'' \mid C_{2j}$ and $\exists S_{2j} \;.\; S_{2j} \models C_{2j}$, $cod(PM_i) \stackrel{.}{=} T_{3i} \mid C_{3i}$ and $T_j'' \stackrel{.}{\lesssim} dom(PM_i) \mid C_{4k}$, then $A \mid \Gamma_{1i} + \Gamma_{2j} \vdash_{\cap G} e_1\, e_2 : T_{3i} \mid C_{1i} \cup C_{2j} \cup C_{3i} \cup C_{4k}$, with $k \in 1..i * j$.

Proof for 2.a). For $A \mid \Gamma_{1i} + \Gamma_{2j} \vdash_{\cap G} e_1\, e_2 : T_{3i} \mid C_{1i} \cup C_{2j} \cup C_{3i} \cup C_{4k}$, with $k \in 1..i * j$ such that $S_k \models C_{1i} \cup C_{2j} \cup C_{3i} \cup C_{4k}$, we have that $C_{i3} = \{\}$ and $C_{k4} = \{T_j'' \stackrel{.}{\lesssim} Dyn\}$. Therefore, $S_k = S_1 \circ S_2$ and then $\Gamma(x) \leq S_k(\Gamma_{i1} + \Gamma_{j2})(x)$.

Proof for 2.b). We have that $cod_\triangleright(S_{i1}(PM_i)) = Dyn$ and $S_i(T_i3) = Dyn$.

- Using rule C-App$\cap$. By the induction hypothesis on 1., exists $A \mid \Gamma' \vdash_{\cap G} e_1 : T_1 \cap \ldots \cap T_m \to T_0 \mid C$ such that $\exists S \;.\; S \models C$ and exists $A \mid \Gamma'' \vdash_{\cap G} e_2 : T'' \mid C''$ such that $\exists S'' \;.\; S'' \models C''$ and $\ldots$ and exists $A \mid \Gamma'' \vdash_{\cap G} e_2 : T'' \mid C''$ such that $\exists S'' \;.\; S'' \models C''$.

  By the induction hypothesis on 2., we have that for $A \mid \Gamma_1 \vdash_{\cap G} e_1 : T_{11} \cap \ldots \cap T_{1m^1} \to T_{10} \mid C_1$ such that $\exists S_1 \;.\; S_1 \models C_1$ and $\ldots$ and for $A \mid \Gamma_{n'} \vdash_{\cap G} e_1 : T_{n'1} \cap \ldots \cap T_{n'm^{n'}} \to T_{n'0} \mid C_{n'}$ such that $\exists S_{n'} \;.\; S_{n'} \models C_{n'}$ then for each $x \in dom(\Gamma) \cap dom(\sum_{i=1}^{n'} \Gamma_i)$, we have that $\Gamma(x) \leq S_i(\Gamma_i(x))$ and $\bigcap_{i=1}^{n'} S_i(T_{i1} \cap \ldots \cap T_{im^i} \to T_{i0}) \leq PM$.

  Also, by the induction hypothesis on 2., we have that for $A \mid \Gamma_1' \vdash_{\cap G} e_2 : T_1'' \mid C_1'$ such that $\exists S_1' \;.\; S_1' \models C_1'$ and $\ldots$ and for $A \mid \Gamma_k' \vdash_{\cap G} e_2 : T_k'' \mid C_k'$ such that $\exists S_k' \;.\; S_k' \models C_k'$ then for each $x \in dom(\Gamma) \cap dom(\sum_{l=1}^{k} \Gamma_i')$, we have that $\Gamma(x) \leq S_l'(\Gamma_l'(x))$ and $\bigcap_{l=1}^{k} S_l'(T_l'') \leq T_1' \cap \ldots \cap T_n'$.

  Proof for 1. If $S(T_1 \cap \ldots \cap T_m \to T_0) \leq PM$, then by Definition 1 and $\triangleright$, $PM = T_1 \cap \ldots \cap T_n \to T$. Therefore, $T_1 \cap \ldots \cap T_n \leq S(T_1 \cap \ldots \cap T_m)$

and $S(T_0) \leq T$. We have that $S''(T'') \leq T_1' \cap \ldots \cap T_n'$ and $T_1' \lesssim T_1$ and $\ldots$ and $T_n' \lesssim T_n$ and $T_1 \cap \ldots \cap T_n \leq S(T_1 \cap \ldots \cap T_m)$. Therefore, we have that $S''(T'') \lesssim S(T_1)$ and $\ldots$ and $S''(T'') \lesssim S(T_m)$. Therefore, we have that $A \mid \Gamma' + \Gamma'' + \ldots + \Gamma'' \vdash_{\cap G} e_1 \ e_2 : T_0 \mid C \cup C'' \cup \{T'' \lesssim T_1\} \cup \ldots \cup C'' \cup \{T'' \lesssim T_m\}$ such that $S \circ S'' \circ \ldots \circ S'' \models C \cup C'' \cup \{T'' \lesssim T_1\} \cup \ldots \cup C'' \cup \{T'' \lesssim T_m\}$.

Proof for 2. For all $i \in 1..n'$, $j \in 1..m^i$, $l, l' \in 1..k$, such that $A \mid \Gamma_i \vdash_{\cap G} e_1 : T_{i1} \cap \ldots \cap T_{im^i} \to T_{i0} \mid C_i$ such that $\exists S_i . S_i \models C_i$, $A \mid \Gamma_l' \vdash_{\cap G} e_2 : T_l'' \mid C_l'$ such that $\exists S_l' . S_l' \models C_l'$ and $\ldots$ and $A \mid \Gamma_{l'}' \vdash_{\cap G} e_2 : T_{l'}'' \mid C_{l'}'$ such that $\exists S_{l'}' . S_{l'}' \models C_{l'}'$ then $A \mid \Gamma_i + \Gamma_l' + \ldots + \Gamma_{l'}' \vdash_{\cap G} e_1 \ e_2 : T_{i0} \mid C_i \cup C_l' \cup \{T_l'' \lesssim T_{i1}\} \cup \ldots \cup C_{l'}' \cup \{T_{l'}'' \lesssim T_{im^i}\}$.

Proof for 2.a). By Definition 1, rule 4, we have that $\Gamma(x) \leq (S_i(\Gamma_i) + S_l'(\Gamma_l') + \ldots + S_{l'}'(\Gamma_{l'}'))(x)$. Since substitutions in S_i and S_l' and $\ldots$ and $S_{l'}'$, don't affect each other, then $\Gamma(x) \leq S_i \circ S_l' \circ \ldots \circ S_{l'}'(\Gamma_i + \Gamma_l' + \ldots + \Gamma_{l'}')(x)$. For all $i \in 1..n'$, $j \in 1..m^i$, $l, l' \in 1..k$, for $A \mid \Gamma_i + \Gamma_l' + \ldots + \Gamma_{l'}' \vdash_{\cap G} e_1 \ e_2 : T_{i0} \mid C_i \cup C_l' \cup \{T_l'' \lesssim T_{i1}\} \cup \ldots \cup C_{l'}' \cup \{T_{l'}'' \lesssim T_{im^i}\}$ such that $\exists S_i \circ S_l' \circ S_l'' \circ \ldots \circ S_{l'}' \circ S_{l'}'' . S_i \circ S_l' \circ S_l'' \circ \ldots \circ S_{l'}' \circ S_{l'}'' \models C_i \cup C_l' \cup \{T_l'' \lesssim T_{i1}\} \cup \ldots \cup C_{l'}' \cup \{T_{l'}'' \lesssim T_{im^i}\}$, with $S_l'' \models T_l'' \lesssim T_{i1}$ and $\ldots$ and $S_{l'}'' \models T_{l'}'' \lesssim T_{im^i}$, then we have several possibilities. If either $T_l'' = Dyn$ or $T_{ij} = Dyn$, then $[] \models T_l'' \lesssim T_{ij}$, and therefore $\Gamma(x) \leq S_i \circ S_l' \circ S_l'' \circ \ldots \circ S_{l'}' \circ S_{l'}''(\Gamma_i + \Gamma_l' + \ldots + \Gamma_{l'}')(x)$. If $T_l'' \in cod(\Gamma_l')$, since $S_l'' \models T_l'' \lesssim T_{ij}$, then $\Gamma(x) \leq S_i \circ S_l' \circ S_l'' \circ \ldots \circ S_{l'}' \circ S_{l'}''(\Gamma_i + \Gamma_l' + \ldots + \Gamma_{l'}')(x)$. If e_1 is a lambda abstraction, then $T_{im^i} \notin cod(\Gamma_i)$. If e_1 is a term variable, then $T_{ij} \to T''' \in \Gamma_i$, for some T'''. Since $S_l'' \models T_l'' \lesssim T_{ij}$, then $\Gamma(x) \leq S_i \circ S_l' \circ S_l'' \circ \ldots \circ S_{l'}' \circ S_{l'}''(\Gamma_i + \Gamma_l' + \ldots + \Gamma_{l'}')(x)$.

Proof for 2.b). If $S_1(T_{11} \cap \ldots \cap T_{1m^1} \to T_{10}) \cap \ldots \cap S_{n'}(T_{n'1}' \cap \ldots \cap T_{n'm^{n'}} \to T_{n'0}) \leq PM$, then by Definition 1 and $\triangleright$, $PM = T_1 \cap \ldots \cap T_n \to T$. Therefore, $S_1(T_{10}) \cap \ldots \cap S_{n'}(T_{n'0}) \leq T$. Since T_{i0} is not affected by substitutions besides S_i, then $\bigcap_{i=1}^{n'}(\bigcap_{l=1}^{k} \ldots \bigcap_{l'=1}^{k} S_i \circ S_l' \circ S_l'' \circ \ldots \circ S_{l'}' \circ S_{l'}''(T_{i0})) \leq T$.

– Rule T-GEN. If $\Gamma \vdash_{\cap G} e : T_1 \cap \ldots \cap T_n$ then $\Gamma \vdash_{\cap G} e : T_1$ and $\ldots$ and $\Gamma \vdash_{\cap G} e : T_n$. By the induction hypothesis on 1., exists $A \mid \Gamma_1 \vdash_{\cap G} e : T_1' \mid C_1$ such that $\exists S_1 . S_1 \models C_1$ and $\ldots$ and exists $A \mid \Gamma_n \vdash_{\cap G} e : T_n' \mid C_n$ such that $\exists S_n . S_n \models C_n$.

By the induction hypothesis on 2., we have that for $A \mid \Gamma_{11} \vdash_{\cap G} e : T_{11}' \mid C_{11}$ such that $\exists S_{11} . S_{11} \models C_{11}$ and $\ldots$ and for $A \mid \Gamma_{1m^1} \vdash_{\cap G} e : T_{1m^1}' \mid C_{1m^1}$ such that $\exists S_{1m^1} . S_{1m^1} \models C_{1m^1}$ then for each $x \in dom(\Gamma) \cap dom(\sum_{j=1}^{m^1} \Gamma_{1j})$, we have that $\Gamma(x) \leq S_{1j}(\Gamma_{1j}(x))$, $\forall j \in 1..m^1$, and $S_{11}(T_{11}') \cap \ldots \cap S_{1m^1}(T_{1m^1}') \leq T_1$ and $\ldots$ and we have that for $A \mid \Gamma_{n1} \vdash_{\cap G} e : T_{n1}' \mid C_{n1}$ such that $\exists S_{n1} . S_{n1} \models C_{n1}$ and $\ldots$ and for $A \mid \Gamma_{nm^n} \vdash_{\cap G} e : T_{nm^n}' \mid C_{nm^n}$ such that $\exists S_{nm^n} . S_{nm^n} \models C_{nm^n}$ then for each $x \in dom(\Gamma) \cap dom(\sum_{j=1}^{m^n} \Gamma_{nj})$, we have that $\Gamma(x) \leq S_{nj}(\Gamma_{nj}(x))$, $\forall j \in 1..m^n$, and $S_{n1}(T_{n1}') \cap \ldots \cap S_{nm^n}(T_{nm^n}') \leq T_n$. Proof for 2.b). By Definition 1, we have that $S_{11}(T_{11}') \cap \ldots \cap S_{1m^1}(T_{1m^1}') \cap \ldots \cap S_{n1}(T_{n1}') \cap \ldots \cap S_{nm^n}(T_{nm^n}') \leq T_1 \cap \ldots \cap T_n$.

- Rule T-INST. If $\Gamma_1 \vdash_{\cap G} e : T_i$ then $\Gamma_1 \vdash_{\cap G} e : T_1 \cap \ldots \cap T_n$. By the induction hypothesis on 1., exists $A \mid \Gamma_2 \vdash_{\cap G} e : T' \mid C$ such that $\exists S . S \models C$.
  By the induction hypothesis on 2., we have that for $A \mid \Gamma_{21} \vdash_{\cap G} e : T'_1 \mid C_1$ such that $\exists S_1 . S_1 \models C_1$ and ... and for $A \mid \Gamma_{2n} \vdash_{\cap G} e : T'_n \mid C_n$ such that $\exists S_n . S_n \models C_n$ then for each $x \in dom(\Gamma_1) \cap dom(\sum_{i=1}^n \Gamma_{2i})$, we have $\Gamma_1(x) \leq S_i(\Gamma_{2i}(x)), \forall i \in 1..n$, and $S_1(T'_1) \cap \ldots \cap S_n(T'_n) \leq T_1 \cap \ldots \cap T_n$.
  Proof for 2.b). As, by Definition 1, $T_1 \cap \ldots \cap T_n \leq T_i$, by transitivity, $S_1(T'_1) \cap \ldots \cap S_n(T'_n) \leq T_i$.

Lemma 3 (Unification Soundness). *If $C \Rightarrow S$ then $S \models C$.*

Proof. We proceed by induction on the length of the derivation tree of $C \Rightarrow S$.

Base cases:

- Rule EM. If $\emptyset \Rightarrow \emptyset$, then by Definition 3, $\emptyset \models \emptyset$.

Induction step:

- Rule CS-DYNL. If $\{Dyn \overset{.}{\lesssim} T\} \cup C \Rightarrow S$ then $C \Rightarrow S$. By the induction hypothesis, $S \models C$. Since $S(Dyn) \lesssim S(T)$ then $S \models Dyn \overset{.}{\lesssim} T$. Therefore, by Definition 3, $S \models \{Dyn \overset{.}{\lesssim} T\} \cup C$.
- Rule CS-DYNR. If $\{T \overset{.}{\lesssim} Dyn\} \cup C \Rightarrow S$ then $C \Rightarrow S$. By the induction hypothesis, $S \models C$. Since $S(T) \lesssim S(Dyn)$ then $S \models T \overset{.}{\lesssim} Dyn$. Therefore, by Definition 3, $S \models \{T \overset{.}{\lesssim} Dyn\} \cup C$.
- Rule CS-REFL. If $\{T \overset{.}{\lesssim} T\} \cup C \Rightarrow S$ then $C \Rightarrow S$. By the induction hypothesis, $S \models C$. Since $S(T) \lesssim S(T)$, then $S \models T \overset{.}{\lesssim} T$. Therefore, by Definition 3, $S \models \{T \overset{.}{\lesssim} T\} \cup C$.
- Rule CS-INST. If $\{T_1 \cap \ldots \cap T_n \overset{.}{\lesssim} T_1 \cap \ldots \cap T_m\} \cup C \Rightarrow S$ then $C \Rightarrow S$. By the induction hypothesis, $S \models C$. Since $S(T_1 \cap \ldots \cap T_n) \lesssim S(T_1 \cap \ldots \cap T_m)$, then $S \models T_1 \cap \ldots \cap T_n \overset{.}{\lesssim} T_1 \cap \ldots \cap T_m$. Therefore, by Definition 3, $S \models \{T_1 \cap \ldots \cap T_n \overset{.}{\lesssim} T_1 \cap \ldots \cap T_m\} \cup C$.
- Rule CS-ASSOC. If $\{(T \to T_1) \cap \ldots \cap (T \to T_n) \overset{.}{\lesssim} T \to T_1 \cap \ldots \cap T_n\} \cup C \Rightarrow S$ then $C \Rightarrow S$. By the induction hypothesis, $S \models C$. Since $S((T \to T_1) \cap \ldots \cap (T \to T_n)) \lesssim S(T \to T_1 \cap \ldots \cap T_n)$, then $S \models (T \to T_1) \cap \ldots \cap (T \to T_n) \overset{.}{\lesssim} T \to T_1 \cap \ldots \cap T_n$. Therefore, by Definition 3, $S \models \{(T \to T_1) \cap \ldots \cap (T \to T_n) \overset{.}{\lesssim} T \to T_1 \cap \ldots \cap T_n\} \cup C$.
- Rule CS-ARROW. If $\{T_1 \to T_2 \overset{.}{\lesssim} T_3 \to T_4\} \cup C \Rightarrow S$ then $\{T_3 \overset{.}{\lesssim} T_1, T_2 \overset{.}{\lesssim} T_4\} \cup C \Rightarrow S$. By the induction hypothesis, $S \models \{T_3 \overset{.}{\lesssim} T_1, T_2 \overset{.}{\lesssim} T_4\} \cup C$. Since $S \models \{T_3 \overset{.}{\lesssim} T_1, T_2 \overset{.}{\lesssim} T_4\}$, then $S(T_3) \lesssim S(T_1)$ and $S(T_2) \lesssim S(T_4)$. Therefore, by Definition 2, $S(T_1) \to S(T_2) \lesssim S(T_3) \to S(T_4)$. Therefore, $S(T_1 \to T_2) \lesssim S(T_3 \to T_4)$. By Definition 3, $S \models \{T_1 \to T_2 \overset{.}{\lesssim} T_3 \to T_4\}$. Therefore, by Definition 3, $S \models \{T_1 \to T_2 \overset{.}{\lesssim} T_3 \to T_4\} \cup C$.
- Rule CS-INSTR. If $\{T \overset{.}{\lesssim} T_1 \cap \ldots \cap T_n\} \cup C \Rightarrow S$ then $\{T \overset{.}{\lesssim} T_1 \wedge \ldots \wedge T \overset{.}{\lesssim} T_n\} \cup C \Rightarrow S$. By the induction hypothesis, $S \models \{T \overset{.}{\lesssim} T_1, \ldots, T \overset{.}{\lesssim} T_n\} \cup C$. Since

$S \models \{T \lesssim T_1, \ldots, T \lesssim T_n\}$, then by Definition 3, $S(T) \lesssim S(T_1) \wedge \ldots \wedge S(T) \lesssim S(T_n)$. Therefore, by Definition 2, $S(T) \lesssim S(T_1) \cap \ldots \cap S(T_n)$. Therefore, $S(T) \lesssim S(T_1 \cap \ldots \cap T_n)$. By Definition 3, $S \models T \lesssim T_1 \cap \ldots \cap T_n$. Therefore, $S \models \{T \lesssim T_1 \cap \ldots \cap T_n\} \cup C$.

- Rule CS-ARROWL. If $\{T_1 \rightarrow T_2 \lesssim T\} \cup C \Rightarrow S$ then $\{T_3 \lesssim T_1, T_2 \lesssim T_4, T = T_3 \rightarrow T_4\} \cup C \Rightarrow S$. By the induction hypothesis, $S \models \{T_3 \lesssim T_1, T_2 \lesssim T_4, T \doteq T_3 \rightarrow T_4\} \cup C$. Since $S \models \{T_3 \lesssim T_1, T_2 \lesssim T_4, T \doteq T_3 \rightarrow T_4\}$, then by Definition 3, $S(T_3) \lesssim S(T_1)$ and $S(T_2) \lesssim S(T_4)$ and $S(T) = S(T_3 \rightarrow T_4)$. By Definition of $\lesssim$, $S(T_1) \rightarrow S(T_2) \lesssim S(T_3) \rightarrow S(T_4)$. Therefore, $S(T_1 \rightarrow T_2) \lesssim S(T_3 \rightarrow T_4)$. Since $S(T) = S(T_3 \rightarrow T_4)$, then $S(T_1 \rightarrow T_2) \lesssim S(T)$. Therefore, by Definition 3, $S \models T_1 \rightarrow T_2 \lesssim T$. Therefore, $S \models \{T_1 \rightarrow T_2 \lesssim T\} \cup C$.

- Rule CS-ARROWR. If $\{T \lesssim T_1 \rightarrow T_2\} \cup C \Rightarrow S$ then $\{T_1 \lesssim T_3, T_4 \lesssim T_2, T = T_3 \rightarrow T_4\} \cup C \Rightarrow S$. By the induction hypothesis, $S \models \{T_1 \lesssim T_3, T_4 \lesssim T_2, T \doteq T_3 \rightarrow T_4\} \cup C$. Since $S \models \{T_1 \lesssim T_3, T_4 \lesssim T_2, T \doteq T_3 \rightarrow T_4\}$, then by Definition 3, $S(T_1) \lesssim S(T_3)$ and $S(T_4) \lesssim S(T_2)$ and $S(T) = S(T_3 \rightarrow T_4)$. By Definition of $\lesssim$, $S(T_3) \rightarrow S(T_4) \lesssim S(T_1) \rightarrow S(T_2)$. Therefore, $S(T_3 \rightarrow T_4) \lesssim S(T_1 \rightarrow T_2)$. Since $S(T) = S(T_3 \rightarrow T_4)$, then $S(T) \lesssim S(T_1 \rightarrow T_2)$. Therefore, by Definition 3, $S \models T \lesssim T_1 \rightarrow T_2$. Therefore, $S \models \{T \lesssim T_1 \rightarrow T_2\} \cup C$.

- Rule CS-EQ. If $\{T_1 \lesssim T_2\} \cup C \Rightarrow S$ then $\{T_1 \doteq T_2\} \cup C \Rightarrow S$. By the induction hypothesis, $S \models \{T_1 \doteq T_2\} \cup C$. By Definition 3, $S(T_1) = S(T_2)$. By Definition 2, $S(T_1) \lesssim S(T_2)$. By Definition 3, $S \models T_1 \lesssim T_2$. Therefore, $S \models \{T_1 \lesssim T_2\} \cup C$.

- Rule EQ-REFL. If $\{T \doteq T\} \cup C \Rightarrow S$ then $C \Rightarrow S$. By the induction hypothesis, $S \models C$. Since $S(T) = S(T)$, then by Definition 3, $S \models T \doteq T$. Therefore, $S \models \{T \doteq T\} \cup C$.

- Rule EQ-ARROW. If $\{T_1 \rightarrow T_2 \doteq T_3 \rightarrow T_4\} \cup C \Rightarrow S$ then $\{T_1 \doteq T_3, T_2 \doteq T_4\} \cup C \Rightarrow S$. By the induction hypothesis, $S \models \{T_1 \doteq T_3, T_2 \doteq T_4\} \cup C$. By Definition 3, $S(T_1) = S(T_3)$ and $S(T_2) = S(T_4)$. Then $S(T_1) \rightarrow S(T_2) = S(T_3) \rightarrow S(T_4)$. Therefore, $S(T_1 \rightarrow T_2) = S(T_3 \rightarrow T_4)$. By Definition 3, $S \models T_1 \rightarrow T_2 \doteq T_3 \rightarrow T_4$. Therefore, $S \models \{T_1 \rightarrow T_2 \doteq T_3 \rightarrow T_4\} \cup C$.

- Rule EQ-VARR. If $\{T \doteq X\} \cup C \Rightarrow S$ then $\{X \doteq T\} \wedge C \Rightarrow S$. By the induction hypothesis, $S \models \{X \doteq T\} \cup C$. By Definition 3, $S(X) = S(T)$. Then, $S(T) = S(X)$. By Definition 3, $S \models T \doteq X$. Therefore, $S \models \{T \doteq X\} \cup C$.

- Rule EQ-VARL. If $\{X \doteq T\} \cup C \Rightarrow S \circ [X \mapsto T]$ then $[X \mapsto T]C \Rightarrow S$. By the induction hypothesis, $S \models [X \mapsto T]C$. Then, for each constraint of the form $T_1' \doteq T_2'$ or $T_1' \lesssim T_2'$ in C, $S([X \mapsto T]T_1') = S([X \mapsto T]T_2')$ or $S([X \mapsto T]T_1') \lesssim S([X \mapsto T]T_2')$. Therefore, $S \circ [X \mapsto T](T_1') = S \circ [X \mapsto T](T_2')$ or $S \circ [X \mapsto T](T_1') \lesssim S \circ [X \mapsto T](T_2')$. Therefore, $S \circ [X \mapsto T] \models C$. It follows that $S \circ [X \mapsto T] \models \{X \doteq T\} \cup C$, because $S \circ [X \mapsto T](X) = S \circ [X \mapsto T](T)$. Therefore, $S \circ [X \mapsto T] \models \{X \doteq T\} \cup C$.

Lemma 4 (Unification Completeness). *If $S_1 \models C$ then $C \Rightarrow S_2$ for some S_2, and furthermore $S_1 = S \circ S_2$ for some S.*

Proof. We proceed by induction on the breakdown of constraint sets by the unification rules.

Base cases:

- Rule EM. If $S_1 \models \emptyset$ then $\emptyset \Rightarrow \emptyset$. As $S_1 = S \circ \emptyset$ for some S_1, it is proved.

Induction step:

- Rule CS-DYNL. If $S_1 \models \{Dyn \overset{.}{\lesssim} T\} \cup C$ then by Definition 3, $S_1 \models C$. By the induction hypothesis, $C \Rightarrow S_2$ and $S_1 = S \circ S_2$. As $C \Rightarrow S_2$, then $\{Dyn \overset{.}{\lesssim} T\} \cup C \Rightarrow S_2$.
- Rule CS-DYNR. If $S_1 \models \{T \overset{.}{\lesssim} Dyn\} \cup C$ then by Definition 3, $S_1 \models C$. By the induction hypothesis, $C \Rightarrow S_2$ and $S_1 = S \circ S_2$. As $C \Rightarrow S_2$, then $\{T \overset{.}{\lesssim} Dyn\} \cup C \Rightarrow S_2$.
- Rule CS-REFL. If $S_1 \models \{T \overset{.}{\lesssim} T\} \cup C$ then by Definition 3, $S_1 \models C$. By the induction hypothesis, $C \Rightarrow S_2$ and $S_1 = S \circ S_2$. As $C \Rightarrow S_2$, then $\{T \overset{.}{\lesssim} T\} \cup C \Rightarrow S_2$.
- Rule CS-INST. If $S_1 \models \{T_1 \cap \ldots \cap T_n \overset{.}{\lesssim} T_1 \cap \ldots \cap T_m\} \cup C$ then by Definition 3, $S_1 \models C$. By the induction hypothesis, $C \Rightarrow S_2$ and $S_1 = S \circ S_2$. As $C \Rightarrow S_2$, then $\{T_1 \cap \ldots \cap T_n \overset{.}{\lesssim} T_1 \cap \ldots \cap T_m\} \cup C \Rightarrow S_2$.
- Rule CS-ASSOC. If $S_1 \models \{(T \rightarrow T_1) \cap \ldots \cap (T \rightarrow T_n) \overset{.}{\lesssim} T \rightarrow T_1 \cap \ldots \cap T_n\} \cup C$ then by Definition 3, $S_1 \models C$. By the induction hypothesis, $C \Rightarrow S_2$ and $S_1 = S \circ S_2$. As $C \Rightarrow S_2$, then $\{(T \rightarrow T_1) \cap \ldots \cap (T \rightarrow T_n) \overset{.}{\lesssim} T \rightarrow T_1 \cap \ldots \cap T_n\} \cup C \Rightarrow S_2$.
- Rule CS-ARROW. If $S_1 \models \{T_1 \rightarrow T_2 \overset{.}{\lesssim} T_3 \rightarrow T_4\} \cup C$ then by Definition 3, $S_1(T_1 \rightarrow T_2) \lesssim S_1(T_3 \rightarrow T_4)$ and $S_1 \models C$. Then, $S_1(T_1) \rightarrow S_1(T_2) \lesssim S_1(T_3) \rightarrow S_1(T_4)$ and by Definition 2, $S_1(T_3) \lesssim S_1(T_1)$ and $S_1(T_2) \lesssim S_1(T_4)$. Then, by Definition 3, $S_1 \models \{T_3 \overset{.}{\lesssim} T_1, T_2 \overset{.}{\lesssim} T_4\} \cup C$. By the induction hypothesis, $\{T_3 \overset{.}{\lesssim} T_1, T_2 \overset{.}{\lesssim} T_4\} \cup C \Rightarrow S_2$ and $S_1 = S \circ S_2$. Therefore, $\{T_1 \rightarrow T_2 \overset{.}{\lesssim} T_3 \rightarrow T_4\} \cup C \Rightarrow S_2$.
- Rule CS-INSTR. If $S_1 \models \{T \overset{.}{\lesssim} T_1 \cap \ldots \cap T_n\} \cup C$ then by Definition 3, $S_1(T) \lesssim S_1(T_1 \cap \ldots \cap T_n)$ and $S_1 \models C$. Therefore, by Definition 2, $S_1(T) \lesssim S_1(T_1) \cap \ldots \cap S_1(T_n)$, and therefore, $S_1(T) \lesssim S_1(T_1)$ and $\ldots$ and $S_1(T) \lesssim S_1(T_n)$. By Definition 3, $S_1 \models \{T \overset{.}{\lesssim} T_1, \ldots, T \overset{.}{\lesssim} T_n\} \cup C$. By the induction hypothesis, $\{T \overset{.}{\lesssim} T_1, \ldots, T \overset{.}{\lesssim} T_n\} \cup C \Rightarrow S_2$ and $S_1 = S \circ S_2$. Therefore, $\{T \overset{.}{\lesssim} T_1 \cap \ldots \cap T_n\} \cup C \Rightarrow S_2$.
- Rule CS-ARROWL. If $S_1 \models \{T_1 \rightarrow T_2 \overset{.}{\lesssim} T\} \cup C$ then, by Definition 3, $S_1(T_1 \rightarrow T_2) \lesssim S_1(T)$ and $S_1 \models C$. Then, it exists a T_3 and T_4, such that $S_1(T) = S_1(T_3 \rightarrow T_4)$, so that $S_1(T_1 \rightarrow T_2) \lesssim S_1(T_3 \rightarrow T_4)$. By Definition 2, $S_1(T_3) \lesssim S_1(T_1)$ and $S_1(T_2) \lesssim S_1(T_4)$. By Definition 3, $S_1 \models T_3 \overset{.}{\lesssim} T_1, T_2 \overset{.}{\lesssim} T_4, T \overset{.}{=} T_3 \rightarrow T_4 \cup C$. By the induction hypothesis, $\{T_3 \overset{.}{\lesssim} T_1, T_2 \overset{.}{\lesssim} T_4, T \overset{.}{=} T_3 \rightarrow T_4\} \cup C \Rightarrow S_2$ and $S_1 = S \circ S_2$. Therefore, $\{T_1 \rightarrow T_2 \overset{.}{\lesssim} T\} \cup C \Rightarrow S_2$.

- Rule CS-ARROWR. If $S_1 \models \{T \stackrel{.}{\lesssim} T_1 \to T_2\} \cup C$ then, by Definition 3, $S_1(T) \lesssim S_1(T_1 \to T_2)$ and $S_1 \models C$. Then, it exists a T_3 and T_4, such that $S_1(T) = S_1(T_3 \to T_4)$, so that $S_1(T_1 \to T_2) \lesssim S_1(T_3 \to T_4)$. By Definition 2, $S_1(T_3) \lesssim S_1(T_1)$ and $S_1(T_2) \lesssim S_1(T_4)$. By Definition 3, $S_1 \models T_3 \stackrel{.}{\lesssim} T_1, T_2 \stackrel{.}{\lesssim} T_4, T \stackrel{.}{=} T_3 \to T_4 \cup C$. By the induction hypothesis, $\{T_3 \stackrel{.}{\lesssim} T_1, T_2 \stackrel{.}{\lesssim} T_4, T \stackrel{.}{=} T_3 \to T_4\} \cup C \Rightarrow S_2$ and $S_1 = S \circ S_2$. Therefore, $\{T_1 \to T_2 \stackrel{.}{\lesssim} T\} \cup C \Rightarrow S_2$.

- Rule CS-EQ. If $S_1 \models \{T_1 \stackrel{.}{\lesssim} T_2\} \cup C$ and $T_1, T_2 \in \{Int, Bool\} \cup TVar$ then, by Definition 3, $S_1(T_1) \lesssim S_1(T_2)$ and $S_1 \models C$. Therefore, by Definition 2, $S_1(T_1) = S_1(T_2)$. Then, $S_1 \models \{T_1 \stackrel{.}{=} T_2\}$. By the induction hypothesis, $\{T_1 \stackrel{.}{=} T_2\} \Rightarrow S_2$ and $S_1 = S \circ S_2$. Therefore, $\{T_1 \stackrel{.}{\lesssim} T_2\} \Rightarrow S_2$.

- Rule EQ-REFL. If $S_1 \models \{T \stackrel{.}{=} T\} \cup C_1$ then, by Definition 3, $S_1 \models C$. By the induction hypothesis, $C \Rightarrow S_2$ and $S_1 = S \circ S_2$. Therefore, $\{T \stackrel{.}{=} T\} \cup C \Rightarrow S_2$.

- Rule EQ-ARROW. If $S_1 \models \{T_1 \to T_2 \stackrel{.}{=} T_3 \to T_4\} \cup C$ then, by Definition 3, $S_1(T_1 \to T_2) = S_1(T_3 \to T_4)$ and $S_1 \models C$. Then, $S_1(T_1) \to S_1(T_2) = S_1(T_3) \to S_1(T_4)$ and $S_1(T_1) = S_1(T_3)$ and $S_1(T_2) = S_1(T_4)$. Then, by Definition 3, $S_1 \models \{T_1 \stackrel{.}{=} T_3, T_2 \stackrel{.}{=} T_4\} \cup C$. By the induction hypothesis, $\{T_1 \stackrel{.}{=} T_3, T_2 \stackrel{.}{=} T_4\} \cup C \Rightarrow S_2$ and $S_1 = S \circ S_2$. Therefore, $\{T_1 \to T_2 \stackrel{.}{=} T_3 \to T_4\} \cup C \Rightarrow S_2$.

- Rule EQ-VARR. If $S_1 \models \{T \stackrel{.}{=} X\} \cup C$ then, by Definition 3, $S_1(T) = S_1(X)$ and $S_1 \models C$. Then, $S_1(X) = S_1(T)$ and therefore, $S_1 \models \{X \stackrel{.}{=} T\} \cup C$. By the induction hypothesis, $\{X \stackrel{.}{=} T\} \cup C \Rightarrow S_2$ and $S_1 = S \circ S_2$. Therefore, $\{T \stackrel{.}{=} X\} \cup C \Rightarrow S_2$.

- Rule EQ-VARL. If $S_1 \models \{X \stackrel{.}{=} T\} \cup C$ then, by Definition 3, $S_1(X) = S_1(T)$ and $S_1 \models C$. Then, $S_1 \models [X \mapsto T]C$. By the induction hypothesis, $[X \mapsto T]C \Rightarrow S_2$ and $S_1 = S \circ S_2$. Therefore, $\{X \stackrel{.}{=} T\} \cup C \Rightarrow S_2 \circ [X \mapsto T]$ and $S_1 = S \circ S_2 \circ [X \mapsto T]$.

Lemma 5 (Unification Soundness). *If $G \mid C \Rightarrow S$ then $S \models C$.*

Proof. Only proofs for cases EM, CS-DYNL, CS-DYNR and EQ-VARL are included since proofs for other cases are straightforward adaptations from the proofs of Lemma 3. We proceed by induction on the length of the derivation tree of $G \mid C \Rightarrow S$.

Base cases:

- Rule EM. If $G \mid \emptyset \Rightarrow \overline{[Vars(G) \mapsto Dyn]}$, then by Definition 3, $\overline{[Vars(G) \mapsto Dyn]} \models \emptyset$.

Induction step:

- Rule CS-DYNL. If $G \mid \{Dyn \stackrel{.}{\lesssim} T\} \cup C \Rightarrow S$ then $G \cup \{T\} \mid C \Rightarrow S$. By the induction hypothesis, $S \models C$. Since $S(Dyn) \lesssim S(T)$ then $S \models Dyn \stackrel{.}{\lesssim} T$. Therefore, by Definition 3, $S \models \{Dyn \stackrel{.}{\lesssim} T\} \cup C$.

- Rule CS-DynR. If $G \mid \{T \stackrel{.}{\lesssim} Dyn\} \cup C \Rightarrow S$ then $G \cup \{T\} \mid C \Rightarrow S$. By the induction hypothesis, $S \models C$. Since $S(T) \lesssim S(Dyn)$ then $S \models T \stackrel{.}{\lesssim} Dyn$. Therefore, by Definition 3, $S \models \{T \stackrel{.}{\lesssim} Dyn\} \cup C$.
- Rule EQ-VarL. If $G \mid \{X \stackrel{.}{=} T\} \cup C \Rightarrow S \circ [X \mapsto T]$ then $[X \mapsto T]G \mid [X \mapsto T]C \Rightarrow S$. By the induction hypothesis, $S \models [X \mapsto T]C$. Then, for each constraint of the form $T_1' \stackrel{.}{=} T_2'$ or $T_1' \stackrel{.}{\lesssim} T_2'$ in C, $S([X \mapsto T]T_1') = S([X \mapsto T]T_2')$ or $S([X \mapsto T]T_1') \leq S([X \mapsto T]T_2')$. Therefore, $S \circ [X \mapsto T](T_1') = S \circ [X \mapsto T](T_2')$ or $S \circ [X \mapsto T](T_1') \leq S \circ [X \mapsto T](T_2')$. Therefore, $S \circ [X \mapsto T] \models C$. It follows that $S \circ [X \mapsto T] \models \{X \stackrel{.}{=} T\} \cup C$, because $S \circ [X \mapsto T](X) = S \circ [X \mapsto T](T)$. Therefore, $S \circ [X \mapsto T] \models \{X \stackrel{.}{=} T\} \cup C$.

Lemma 6 (Unification Completeness). If $S_1 \circ \overline{[Vars(G) \mapsto Dyn]} \models C$ then $G \mid C \Rightarrow S_2$ for some S_2, and furthermore $S_1 \circ \overline{[Vars(G) \mapsto Dyn]} = S \circ S_2$ for some S.

Proof. Only proofs for cases EM, CS-DynL, CS-DynR and EQ-VarL are included since proofs for other cases are straightforward adaptations from the proofs of Lemma 4. We proceed by induction on the breakdown of constraint sets by the unification rules.

Base cases:

- Rule EM. If $S_1 \circ \overline{[Vars(G) \mapsto Dyn]} \models \emptyset$ then $G \mid \emptyset \Rightarrow \overline{[Vars(G) \mapsto Dyn]}$. As $S_1 \circ \overline{[Vars(G) \mapsto Dyn]} = S \circ \overline{[Vars(G) \mapsto Dyn]}$ for some S, it is proved.

Induction step:

- Rule CS-DynL. If $S_1 \circ \overline{[Vars(G) \mapsto Dyn]} \models \{Dyn \stackrel{.}{\lesssim} T\} \cup C$ then by Definition 3, $S_1 \circ \overline{[Vars(G) \mapsto Dyn]} \models C$. By the induction hypothesis, $G \cup \{T\} \mid C \Rightarrow S_2$ and $S_1 \circ \overline{[Vars(G) \mapsto Dyn]} = S \circ S_2$. As $G \cup \{T\} \mid C \Rightarrow S_2$, then $G \mid \{Dyn \stackrel{.}{\lesssim} T\} \cup C \Rightarrow S_2$.
- Rule CS-DynR. If $S_1 \circ \overline{[Vars(G) \mapsto Dyn]} \models \{T \stackrel{.}{\lesssim} Dyn\} \cup C$ then by Definition 3, $S_1 \circ \overline{[Vars(G) \mapsto Dyn]} \models C$. By the induction hypothesis, $G \cup \{T\} \mid C \Rightarrow S_2$ and $S_1 \circ \overline{[Vars(G) \mapsto Dyn]} = S \circ S_2$. As $G \cup \{T\} \mid C \Rightarrow S_2$, then $G \mid \{T \stackrel{.}{\lesssim} Dyn\} \cup C \Rightarrow S_2$.
- Rule EQ-VarL. If $S_1 \circ \overline{[Vars(G) \mapsto Dyn]} \models \{X \stackrel{.}{=} T\} \cup C$ then, by Definition 3, $S_1 \circ \overline{[Vars(G) \mapsto Dyn]}(X) = S_1 \circ \overline{[Vars(G) \mapsto Dyn]}(T)$ and $S_1 \circ \overline{[Vars(G) \mapsto Dyn]} \models C$. Then, $S_1 \models [X \mapsto T]C$. By the induction hypothesis, $[X \mapsto T]G \mid [X \mapsto T]C \Rightarrow S_2$ and $S_1 \circ \overline{[Vars(G) \mapsto Dyn]} = S \circ S_2$. Therefore, $G \mid \{X \stackrel{.}{=} T\} \cup C \Rightarrow S_2 \circ [X \mapsto T]$.

Theorem 2 (Soundness). *If* $(\Gamma, T, S) \in I(e)$ *then* $S(\Gamma) \vdash_{\cap G} S(e) : S(T)$.

Proof. If $(\Gamma, T, S) \in I(e)$ then by Definition 5, $\emptyset \mid \Gamma \vdash_{\cap G} e : T \mid C, \emptyset \mid C \Rightarrow S$. By Lemma 5, $S \models C$. Therefore, by Lemma 1, $S(\Gamma) \vdash_{\cap G} S(e) : S(T)$.

Theorem 3 (Principal Typings). *If* $\Gamma_1 \vdash_{\cap G} e : T_1$ *then there are* $\Gamma_{21}, \ldots,$ $\Gamma_{2n}, T_{21}, \ldots, T_{2n}, S_{21}, \ldots, S_{2n}$ *and* $S_1, \ldots, S_n$ *such that* $((\Gamma_{21}, T_{21}, S_{21}), \ldots, (\Gamma_{2n},$ $T_{2n}, S_{2n})) = I(e)$ *and, for each* $x \in dom(\Gamma_1) \cap dom(\Gamma_{21} + \ldots + \Gamma_{2n})$, *we have* $\Gamma_1(x) \leq S_1 \circ S_{21}(\Gamma_{21}(x))$ *and* $\ldots$ *and* $\Gamma_1(x) \leq S_n \circ S_{2n}(\Gamma_{2n}(x))$ *and* $S_1 \circ S_{21}(T_{21}) \cap$ $\ldots \cap S_n \circ S_{2n}(T_{2n}) \leq T_1$.

Proof. If $\Gamma_1 \vdash_{\cap G} e : T_1$ then by Lemma 2, for $A \mid \Gamma_{21} \vdash_{\cap G} e : T_{21} \mid C_1$ such that $\exists S_{11} . S_{11} \models C_1$ and $\ldots$ and for $A \mid \Gamma_{2n} \vdash_{\cap G} e : T_{2n} \mid C_n$ such that $\exists S_{1n} . S_{1n} \models C_n$ then for each $x \in dom(\Gamma_1) \cap dom(\Gamma_{21} + \ldots + \Gamma_{2n})$, we have $\Gamma_1(x) \leq S_{11}(\Gamma_{21}(y))$ and $\ldots$ and $\Gamma_1(x) \leq S_{1n}(\Gamma_{2n}(y))$ and $S_{11}(T_{21}) \cap \ldots \cap$ $S_{1n}(T_{2n}) \leq T_1$. By Lemma 6, $G_1 \mid C_1 \Rightarrow S_{21}$ for some S_{21} and furthermore $S_{11} = S_1 \circ S_{21}$, for some S_1 and $\ldots$ and $G_n \mid C_n \Rightarrow S_{2n}$ for some S_{2n} and furthermore $S_{1n} = S_n \circ S_{2n}$, for some S_n. As $A \mid \Gamma_{21} \vdash_{\cap G} e : T_{21} \mid C_1$ and $G_1 \mid C_1 \Rightarrow S_{21}$ and $\ldots$ and $A \mid \Gamma_{2n} \vdash_{\cap G} e : T_{2n} \mid C_n$ and $G_n \mid C_n \Rightarrow S_{2n}$, then by Definition 5, $((\Gamma_{21}, T_{21}, S_{21}), \ldots, (\Gamma_{2n}, T_{2n}, S_{2n})) = I(e)$ and for each $x \in dom(\Gamma_1) \cap dom(\Gamma_{21} + \ldots + \Gamma_{2n})$, $\Gamma_1(x) \leq S_1 \circ S_{21}(\Gamma_{21}(x))$ and $\ldots$ and $\Gamma_1(x) \leq S_n \circ S_{2n}(\Gamma_{2n}(x))$ and $S_1 \circ S_{21}(T_{21}) \cap \ldots \cap S_n \circ S_{2n}(T_{2n}) \leq T_1$.

Lemma 8 (Termination of Constraint Solving). $C \Rightarrow S$ *terminates for every set of constraints* C.

Proof. A unification problem $C \Rightarrow S$ is solved if $C = \emptyset$. We define the following metrics with respect to the unification problem $C \Rightarrow S$:

- NICS is the number of unique intersection types in the left of an $\lesssim$ constraint + the number of unique intersection types in the right of an $\lesssim$ constraint
- NCCS is the number of type constructors in $\lesssim$ constraints
- NCS is the number of $\lesssim$ constraints
- NVEQ is the number of different type variables in $\doteq$ constraints
- NCEQ is the number of type constructors in $\doteq$ constraints
- NTXEQ is the number of $\doteq$ constraints of the form $T \doteq X$
- NEQ is the number of $\doteq$ constraints

We will prove termination by showing that both NCS and NEq reduce to 0.

The first part of the proof consists of reducing only $\lesssim$ constraints. Termination of $C \Rightarrow S$, is proved by a measure function that maps the constraint set C to a tuple (NICS, NCCS, NCS). The following table shows that each step decreases the tuple w.r.t. the lexicographic order:

	NICS	NCCS	NCS
CS-DynL	$\geq$	$\geq$	$>$
CS-DynR	$\geq$	$\geq$	$>$
CS-Refl	$=$	$=$	$>$
CS-Inst	$>$		
CS-Assoc	$>$		
CS-Arrow	$=$	$>$	
CS-InstR	$>$		
CS-ArrowL	$\geq$	$>$	
CS-ArrowR	$\geq$	$>$	
CS-Eq	$=$	$=$	$>$

Note that the number of $\lesssim$ constraints decreases to 0, leaving only $\doteq$ constraints in C.

The second part of the proof consists of reducing the remaining $\doteq$ constraints. Termination of $C \Rightarrow S$, where now only $\doteq$ are in C, is proved by a measure function that maps the constraint set C to a tuple (NVEQ, NCEQ, NTXEQ, NEQ). The following table shows that each step decreases the tuple w.r.t. the lexicographic order:

	NVEq	NCEq	NTXEq	NEq
Eq-Refl	$\geq$	$\geq$	$\geq$	$>$
Eq-Arrow	$=$	$>$		
Eq-VarR	$=$	$=$	$>$	
Eq-VarL	$>$			

Note that the number of $\doteq$ constraints decreases to 0, leaving C empty.

References

1. Barendregt, H., Coppo, M., Dezani-Ciancaglini, M.: A filter lambda model and the completeness of type assignment. J. Symbolic Logic **48**(4), 931–940 (1983)
2. Castagna, G., Lanvin, V.: Gradual typing with union and intersection types. Proc. ACM Program. Lang. **1**(ICFP), 41:1–41:28 (2017)
3. Castagna, G., Lanvin, V., Petrucciani, T., Siek, J.G.: Gradual typing: a new perspective. Proc. ACM Program. Lang. **3**(POPL), 16:1–16:32 (2019)
4. Chaudhuri, A.: Flow: abstract interpretation of Javascript for type checking and beyond. In: Proceedings of the 2016 ACM Workshop on Programming Languages and Analysis for Security, PLAS 2016. ACM (2016)
5. Cimini, M., Siek, J.G.: The gradualizer: a methodology and algorithm for generating gradual type systems. In: Proceedings of the 43rd Annual ACM SIGPLAN-SIGACT Symposium on Principles of Programming Languages, POPL 2016, pp. 443–455 (2016)
6. Cimini, M., Siek, J.G.: Automatically generating the dynamic semantics of gradually typed languages. In: Proceedings of the 44th ACM SIGPLAN Symposium on Principles of Programming Languages, POPL 2017, pp. 789–803 (2017)

7. Coppo, M., Dezani-Ciancaglini, M.: An extension of the basic functionality theory for the λ-calculus. Notre Dame J. Form. Log. **21**(4), 685–693 (1980)
8. Coppo, M., Dezani-Ciancaglini, M., Venneri, B.: Functional characters of solvable terms. Math. Logic Quart. **27**(2–6), 45–58 (1981)
9. Damas, L., Milner, R.: Principal type-schemes for functional programs. In: Proceedings of the 9th ACM SIGPLAN-SIGACT Symposium on Principles of Programming Languages, POPL 1982, pp. 207–212 (1982)
10. Frisch, A., Castagna, G., Benzaken, V.: Semantic subtyping: dealing set-theoretically with function, union, intersection, and negation types. J. ACM **55**(4), 19:1–19:64 (2008)
11. Garcia, R., Cimini, M.: Principal type schemes for gradual programs. In: Proceedings of the 42nd Annual ACM SIGPLAN-SIGACT Symposium on Principles of Programming Languages, POPL 2015, pp. 303–315 (2015)
12. Garcia, R., Clark, A.M., Tanter, É.: Abstracting gradual typing. In: Proceedings of the 43rd Annual ACM SIGPLAN-SIGACT Symposium on Principles of Programming Languages, POPL 2016, pp. 429–442 (2016)
13. Roger Hindley, J.: Basic Simple Type Theory. Cambridge Tracts in Theoretical Computer Science. Cambridge University Press, Cambridge (1997)
14. Hindley, R.: The principal type-scheme of an object in combinatory logic. Trans. Am. Math. Soc. **146**, 29–60 (1969)
15. Jim, T.: Rank 2 type systems and recursive definitions. Technical report (1995)
16. Jim, T.: What are principal typings and what are they good for? In: Proceedings of the 23rd ACM SIGPLAN-SIGACT Symposium on Principles of Programming Languages, POPL 1996, pp. 42–53 (1996)
17. Kfoury, A.J., Wells, J.B.: Principality and decidable type inference for finite-rank intersection types. In: Proceedings of the 26th ACM SIGPLAN-SIGACT Symposium on Principles of Programming Languages, POPL 1999, pp. 161–174 (1999)
18. Kfoury, A.J., Wells, J.B.: Principality and type inference for intersection types using expansion variables. Theoret. Comput. Sci. **311**(1), 1–70 (2004)
19. Leivant, D.: Polymorphic type inference. In: Proceedings of the 10th ACM SIGACT-SIGPLAN Symposium on Principles of Programming Languages, POPL 1983, pp. 88–98 (1983)
20. Milner, R.: A theory of type polymorphism in programming. J. Comput. Syst. Sci. **17**(3), 348–375 (1978)
21. Reynolds, J.C.: The coherence of languages with intersection types. In: Ito, T., Meyer, A.R. (eds.) TACS 1991. LNCS, vol. 526, pp. 675–700. Springer, Heidelberg (1991). https://doi.org/10.1007/3-540-54415-1_70
22. Reynolds, J.C.: Design of the Programming Language Forsythe, pp. 173–233. Birkhäuser Boston, Boston (1997)
23. Robinson, J.A.: A machine-oriented logic based on the resolution principle. J. ACM **12**(1), 23–41 (1965)
24. Siek, J.G., Vachharajani, M.: Gradual typing with unification-based inference. In: Proceedings of the 2008 Symposium on Dynamic Languages, DLS 2008, pp. 7:1–7:12 (2008)
25. van Bakel, S.: Intersection type assignment systems. Theoret. Comput. Sci. **151**(2), 385–435 (1995)
26. Vekris, P., Cosman, B., Jhala, R.: Refinement types for typescript. SIGPLAN Not. **51**(6), 310–325 (2016)
27. Wand, M.: A simple algorithm and proof for type inference. Fundamenta Informaticae **10**(2), 115–121 (1987)

28. Wells, J.B.: The essence of principal typings. In: Widmayer, P., Eidenbenz, S., Triguero, F., Morales, R., Conejo, R., Hennessy, M. (eds.) ICALP 2002. LNCS, vol. 2380, pp. 913–925. Springer, Heidelberg (2002). https://doi.org/10.1007/3-540-45465-9_78

29. Ângelo, P., Florido, M.: Gradual intersection types. In: Ninth Workshop on Intersection Types and Related Systems, ITRS 2018, Oxford, UK, 8 July 2018 (2018)

Set Constraints, Pattern Match Analysis, and SMT

Joseph Eremondi[✉]

University of British Columbia, Vancouver, Canada
`jeremond@cs.ubc.ca`

Abstract. Set constraints provide a highly general way to formulate program analyses. However, solving arbitrary boolean combinations of set constraints is NEXPTIME-hard. Moreover, while theoretical algorithms to solve arbitrary set constraints exist, they are either too complex to realistically implement or too slow to ever run.

We present a translation that converts a set constraint formula into an SMT problem. Our technique allows for arbitrary boolean combinations of set constraints, and leverages the performance of modern SMT solvers. To show the usefulness of unrestricted set constraints, we use them to devise a pattern match analysis for functional languages, which ensures that missing cases of pattern matches are always unreachable. We implement our analysis in the Elm compiler and show that our translation is fast enough to be used in practical verification.

Keywords: Program analysis · SMT · Pattern-matching · Set constraints

1 Introduction

Set constraints are a powerful tool for expressing a large number of program analyses in a generic way. Featuring recursive equations and inequations over variables denoting sets of values, set constraints allow us to model the sets of values an expression could possibly take. While they were an active area of research in decades prior, they have not seen widespread adoption. In their most general form, finding solutions for a conjunction of set constraints is NEXPTIME-complete. While efficient solvers have been developed for restricted versions of the set constraint problem [4,26], solvers for unrestricted set constraints are not used in practice.

However, since the development of set constraints, there have been significant advances in solvers for SAT modulo theories (SMT). Although SMT requires exponential time in theory, solvers such as Z3 [31] and CVC4 [8] are able to solve a wide range of satisfiability problems in practice. Given the success of SMT solvers in skirting the theoretical intractability of SAT, one wonders, can these solvers be used to solve set constraints? We show that this is possible with reasonable performance. Our full contributions are as follows:

This material is based on work supported by the NSERC CGS-D scholarship.

W. J. Bowman and R. Garcia (Eds.): TFP 2019, LNCS 12053, pp. 121–141, 2020.
https://doi.org/10.1007/978-3-030-47147-7_6

- We devise a pattern match analysis for a strict functional language, expressed in terms of unrestricted set constraints (Sect. 2).
- We provide a method for translating unrestricted set constraint problems into SAT modulo UF, a logical theory with booleans, uninterpreted functions, and first order quantification (Sect. 3). Additionally, we show that projections, a construct traditionally difficult to formulate with set constraints, are easily formulated using disjunctions in SMT (Sect. 3.1).
- We implement our translation and analysis, showing that they are usable for verification despite NEXPTIME-completeness (Sect. 4).

Motivation: Pattern Match Analysis

Our primary interest in set constraints is using them to devise a functional *pattern match analysis*. Many functional programming languages feature *algebraic datatypes*, where values of a datatype D are formed by applying a *constructor* function to some arguments. Values of an algebraic type can be decomposed using pattern matching, where the programmer specifies a number of branches with free variables, and the program takes the first branch that matches the given value, binding the corresponding values to the free variables. If none of the patterns match the value, a runtime error is raised.

Many modern languages, such as Elm [12] and Rust [25] require that pattern matches be *exhaustive*, so that each pattern match has a branch for every possible value of the given type. This ensures that runtime errors are never raised due to unmatched patterns, and avoids the null-pointer exceptions that plague many procedural languages. However, the type systems of these languages cannot express all invariants. Consider the following pseudo-Haskell, with an algebraic type for shapes, and a function that calculates their area.

```
                            area :: Shape -> Double
                            area shape = case shape of
        data Shape =          NGon sides -> ...
          Square Double       _ -> simpleArea shape
          | Circle Double     where simpleArea sshape = case sshape of
          | NGon [Double]        Square len -> len * len
                                 Circle r -> pi * r * r
                                 _ -> error "This␣cannot␣happen"
```

The above code is perfectly safe, since `simpleArea` can only be called from `area`, and will never be given an `NGon`. However, it is not robust to changes. If we add the constructor `Triangle Double Double Double` to our `Shape` definition, then both matches are still exhaustive, since the _ pattern covers every possible case. However, we now may face a runtime error if `area` is given a `Triangle`. In general, requiring exhaustiveness forces the programmer to either manually raise an error or return a dummy value in an unreachable branch.

$x \in \text{PROGVARIABE}, X \in \text{TYPEVARIABLE}, D \in \text{DATATYPE}, K \in \text{DATACONSTRUCTOR}$

Terms

$$t ::= x \mid \lambda x.t \mid \texttt{match } t \texttt{ with } \{\overrightarrow{P \Rightarrow t;}\}$$

$$\mid t_1 \; t_2 \mid K_D(\overrightarrow{t}) \mid \texttt{let } x = t_1 \texttt{ in } t_2$$

Patterns

$$P ::= x \mid K_D(\overrightarrow{P})$$

Underlying Types

$$\tau ::= X \mid D \mid \tau_1 \to \tau_2$$

Datatype environments

$$\Delta ::= \cdot \mid D = \overrightarrow{K(\overrightarrow{T})}, \Delta$$

Underlying Type Schemes

$$\sigma ::= \forall \overrightarrow{X}.\tau$$

Type Environments

$$\Gamma ::= \cdot \mid X, \Gamma \mid x : T, \Gamma$$

Fig. 1. λ_{MATCH}: syntax

We propose an alternate approach: remove the catch-all case of `simpleArea`, and use a static analysis to determine that only values matching `Circle` or `Square` will be passed in. Such analysis would mark the above code safe, but would signal unsafety if `Triangle` were added to the definition of `Shape`.

The analysis for this particular case is intuitive, but can be complex in general:

- Because functions may be recursive, we need to be able to handle recursive equations (or inequations) of possible pattern sets. For example, a program dealing with lists may generate a constraint of the form $X \subseteq Nil \cup Cons(\top, Cons(\top, X))$.
- We wish to encode *first-match semantics*: if a program takes a certain branch in the pattern match, then the matched value cannot possibly match any of the previous cases.
- We wish to avoid false negatives by tracking what conditions must be true for a branch to be taken, and to only enforce constraints from that branch when it is reachable. If we use logical implication, we can express constraints of the form "if x matches pattern P_1, then y must match pattern P_2".

Section 2 gives such an analysis, while Sect. 3 describes solving these constraints. Both are implemented and evaluated in Sect. 4.

2   A Set Constraint-Based Pattern Match Analysis

Here, we describe an annotated type system for *pattern match analysis*. It tracks the possible values that expressions may take. Instead of requiring that each match be exhaustive, we restrict functions to reject inputs that may not be covered by a pattern match in the function's body. Types are refined by constraints, which are solved using an external solver (Sect. 3).

2.1 λ_{Match} Syntax

We present λ_{MATCH}, a small, typed functional language, whose syntax we give in Fig. 1. Throughout, for a given metavariable $\mathcal{M}$ we write $\overrightarrow{\mathcal{M}}^i$ for a sequence of objects matching $\mathcal{M}$. We omit the positional index i when it is unneeded.

$$\boxed{\Gamma \vdash t : \tau} \text{ (Expression typing)}$$

$$\text{CTOR}\frac{\begin{array}{c}K(\overrightarrow{\tau}) \in \Delta(D)\\ \overrightarrow{\Gamma \vdash t : \tau}\end{array}}{\Gamma \vdash K_D(\overrightarrow{t}) : D} \qquad \text{LAM}\frac{x : \tau_1, \Gamma \vdash t : \tau_2}{\Gamma \vdash \lambda x.t : \tau_1 \to \tau_2} \qquad \text{APP}\frac{\begin{array}{c}\Gamma \vdash t_1 : \tau_1 \to \tau_2\\ \Gamma \vdash t_2 : \tau_1\end{array}}{\Gamma \vdash t_1\, t_2 : \tau_2}$$

$$\text{VAR}\frac{\Gamma(x) = \forall \overrightarrow{X}.\tau}{\Gamma \vdash x : [\overrightarrow{\tau'/X}]\tau} \qquad \text{MAT}\frac{\Gamma \vdash t : \tau \quad \overrightarrow{\Gamma \vdash P : \tau | \Gamma'} \quad \overrightarrow{\Gamma' \vdash t' : \tau'}}{\Gamma \vdash \texttt{match } t \texttt{ with } \{\overrightarrow{P \Rightarrow t';}\} : \tau'}$$

$$\text{LET}\frac{x : \tau_1, \overrightarrow{X}, \Gamma \vdash t_1 : \tau_1 \quad x : \forall \overrightarrow{X}.\tau_1, \Gamma \vdash t_2 : \tau_2}{\Gamma \vdash \texttt{let } x = t_1 \texttt{ in } t_2 : \tau_2}$$

$$\boxed{\Gamma \vdash P : \tau | \Gamma'} \text{ (Pattern typing and binding generation)}$$

$$\text{VAR}\frac{}{\Gamma \vdash x : \tau | (x : \tau), \Gamma} \qquad \text{CTOR}\frac{K(\overrightarrow{\tau}) \in \Delta(D) \quad \overrightarrow{\Gamma \vdash P : \tau | \Gamma'}}{\Gamma \vdash K_D(\overrightarrow{P}) : D | \bigcup \overrightarrow{\Gamma'}}$$

Fig. 2. Underlying typing for expressions and patterns

In addition to functions and applications, we have a form $K_D(\overrightarrow{t})$ which applies the data constructor K to the argument sequence $\overrightarrow{t}$ to make a term of type D. Conversely, the form $\texttt{match } t' \texttt{ with } \{\overrightarrow{P \Rightarrow t;}\}$ chooses the first branch $P_i \Rightarrow t_i$; for which t' matches pattern P_i, and then evaluates t_i after binding the matching parts of t' to the variables of P_i. We use Haskell-style shadowing for non-linear patterns: e.g. (x, x) matches any pair, and binds the second element to x. We omit advanced matching features, such as guarded matches, since these can be desugared into nested simple matches. We use type environments Γ store free type variables and types for program variables. We assume a fixed datatype environment Δ that stores the names of each datatype D, along with the name and argument-types of each constructor of D.

2.2 The Underlying Type System

The underlying type system is in the style of Damas and Milner [13], where monomorphic types are separated from polymorphic type schemes. The declarative typing rules for the underlying system are standard (Fig. 2). We do not check the exhaustiveness of matches, as this overly-conservative check is precisely what we aim to replace. The analysis we present below operates on these underlying typing derivations, so each expression has a known underlying type.

$$
\begin{array}{lll}
V & \in & \text{SET VARIABLE} \\
& & \textbf{Set constraints} \\
C & ::= & E_1 \subseteq E_2 \mid C_1 \wedge C_2 \mid C_1 \vee C_2 \mid \neg C \\
& & \textbf{Annotated Types} \\
T & ::= & X^E \mid D^E \mid (T_1 \to T_2)^E
\end{array}
$$

$$
\begin{array}{lll}
& & \textbf{Set expressions} \\
E & ::= & V \mid E_1 \cup E_2 \mid E_1 \cap E_2 \mid \neg E \\
& & \mid K_D(\overrightarrow{E}) \mid K_D^{-i}(E) \mid \top \mid \bot \\
& & \textbf{Annotated Schemes} \\
S & ::= & \forall \overrightarrow{X}, \overrightarrow{V}. C \Rightarrow T
\end{array}
$$

Fig. 3. λ_{MATCH}: annotations

2.3 Annotated Types

For our analysis, we annotate types with *set expressions* (Fig. 3). We define their semantics formally in Sect. 3, but intuitively, they represent possible shapes that the value of an expression might have in some context. We have variables, along with intersection, union and negation, and $\top$ and $\bot$ representing the sets of all and no values respectively. The form $K_D(E_1 \ldots E_a)$ denotes applying the arity-a constructor K of datatype D to each combination of values from the sets denoted by $\overrightarrow{E}$. Conversely, $K_D^{-i}(E)$ denotes the ith *projection* of K: it takes the ith argument of each value constructed using K from the set denoted by E.

Set constraints then specify the inclusion relationships between those sets. These are boolean combinations of atomic constraints of the form $E_1 \subseteq E_2$. Our analysis uses these in *annotated type schemes*, to constrain which annotations a polymorphic type accepts as instantiations. The idea is similar to Haskell's type-class constraints, and we adopt a similar notation. Since each syntactic variant has a top-level annotation E, we use T^E to denote an annotated type T along with its top-level annotation E. Annotated types T^E replace underlying types τ in our rules, and our analysis emits constraints on E that dictate its value. We note that boolean operations such as $\implies$ and $\iff$, can be decomposed into $\wedge$, $\vee$, and $\neg$. Similarly, we use $E_1 = E_2$ as a shorthand for $E_1 \subseteq E_2 \wedge E_2 \subseteq E_1$, and **T** and **F** as shorthands for $\bot \subseteq \top$ and $\top \subseteq \bot$ respectively.

2.4 The Analysis

We present our pattern match analysis in Fig. 4. The analysis is phrased as an annotated type system in the style of Nielson and Nielson [32]. The judgment $\Gamma | C_p \vdash t : T^E \mid C$ says that, under context Γ, if C_p holds, then t has the underlying type of T and can take only forms from E, where the constraint C holds. C_p is an input to the judgment called the *path constraint*, which must hold for this part of the program to have been reached. The set expression E

$\boxed{\Gamma | C_p \vdash t : T_E \mid C}$ (Pattern Match Analysis)

$$\text{AVAR} \frac{\begin{array}{c} \Gamma(x) = \forall \vec{X}, \vec{V}. C \Rightarrow T^E \\ \overrightarrow{V'} \text{ fresh} \end{array}}{\begin{array}{c} \Gamma | C_p \vdash x : [V'/V][\tau'/X](T^E) \\ | (C_p \implies \overrightarrow{[V'/V]}C) \end{array}}$$

$$\text{AAPP} \frac{\begin{array}{c} \Gamma | C_p \vdash t_1 : (T_1^{E_1} \to T_2^{E_2})^{E_3} \mid C_1 \\ \Gamma | C_p \vdash t_2 : T_1^{E_1'} \mid C_2 \end{array}}{\begin{array}{c} \Gamma | C_p \vdash t_1 \ t_2 : T_2^{E_2} \\ | C_1 \wedge C_2 \wedge (C_p \implies T_1^{E_1} \equiv T_1^{E_1'}) \end{array}}$$

$$\text{ACTOR} \frac{\begin{array}{c} \overrightarrow{K(\vec{T}) \in \Delta(D)} \\ \Gamma | C_p \vdash t : T^E \mid C \end{array}}{\Gamma | C_p \vdash K_D(\vec{t}) : D^{K(\vec{E})} \mid \bigwedge \vec{C}}$$

$$\text{ALAM} \frac{\begin{array}{c} V \text{ fresh} \\ x : T_1^V, \Gamma | C_p \vdash t : T_2^E \mid C \end{array}}{\Gamma | C_p \vdash \lambda x.t : (T_1^V \to T_2^E)^\top \mid C}$$

$$\text{AMAT} \frac{\begin{array}{c} V \text{ fresh} \qquad \Gamma | C_p \vdash t : T^E \mid C_{dsc} \qquad \overrightarrow{\Gamma | C_p \vdash P_i : T^{E \cap \overline{\mathcal{P}_i}(\vec{P})} | \Gamma_i}^i \\ \overrightarrow{C_i := (E \cap \mathcal{P}[\![P_i]\!] \cap \overline{\mathcal{P}_i}(\vec{P}) \not\subseteq \bot)}^i \qquad \overrightarrow{\Gamma_i | C_i \wedge C_p \vdash t_i' : T'^{E_i'}}^i \\ C_{res} := \overrightarrow{\bigwedge C_i \implies E_i' \subseteq V}^i \qquad C_{saf} := \overrightarrow{(C_p \implies (E \subseteq \bigcup \mathcal{P}[\![P_i]\!]))}^i \end{array}}{\Gamma | C_p \vdash \mathbf{match}\ t\ \mathbf{with}\ \overrightarrow{\{P_i \Rightarrow t_i'\}} : T'^V \mid C_{dsc} \wedge C_{res} \wedge C_{saf}}$$

$$\text{ALET} \frac{\begin{array}{c} T'^{V'}_1 := \mathbf{freshen}(T_1) \qquad x : T'_1, \vec{X}, \Gamma | C_p \vdash t_1 : T_1^E \mid C_1 \\ \vec{V} = (FV(E) \cup FV(C_1)) \setminus (FV(\Gamma) \cup FV(C_p)) \qquad T'^{V'}_1 \equiv T_1^E \wedge C_1 \text{ satisfiable} \\ x : (\forall \vec{X}, \vec{V}. (T'^{V'}_1 \equiv T_1^E \wedge C_1) \Rightarrow T_1^E), \Gamma | C_p \vdash t_2 : T_2^{E_2} \mid C_2 \end{array}}{\Gamma | C_p \vdash \mathbf{let}\ x = t_1\ \mathbf{in}\ t_2 : T_2^{E_2} \mid C_2}$$

$\boxed{\Gamma \vdash P : T^E | \Gamma'}$ (Analysis pattern environments. P, T^E are input, Γ' is output)

$$\text{VAR} \frac{}{\Gamma \vdash x : T^E | (x : T^E), \Gamma}$$

$$\text{CTOR} \frac{\begin{array}{c} K(T_1, \ldots, T_n) \in \Delta(D) \\ \overrightarrow{\Gamma \vdash P : T^{K^{-i}(E)} : \Gamma'_1}^i \end{array}}{\Gamma \vdash K_D(\vec{P}) : D^E | \bigcup \overrightarrow{\Gamma'}^i}$$

Fig. 4. Pattern match analysis

and constraint C are outputs of the judgment, synthesized by traversing the expression. We need an external solver for set constraints to find a value for each variable V that satisfies C. This is precisely what we define in Sect. 3. We write the conversion between patterns and set-expressions as $\mathcal{P}[\![P]\!]$.

The analysis supports higher-order functions, and it is *polyvariant*: refined types use polymorphism, so that precise analysis can be performed at each instantiation site. A variant of Damas-Milner style inference with let-generalization is used to generate these refined types. Moreover, the analysis is push-button: no additional input need be provided by the programmer. It is sound but conservative: it accounts for all possible values an expression may take, but may declare some matches unsafe when they will not actually crash.

$$\boxed{T_1 \equiv T_2 := C} \qquad \text{(Type equating)}$$

$$(T_1 \rightarrow T_1')^{E_1} \equiv (T_2 \rightarrow T_2')^{E_2} := (T_1 \equiv T_2) \wedge (T_1' \equiv T_2') \wedge E_1 = E_2$$

$$X^{E_1} \equiv X^{E_2} := E_1 = E_2 \qquad D^{E_1} \equiv D^{E_2} := E_1 = E_2 \qquad T_1 \equiv T_2 := \mathbf{F} \; otherwise$$

$$\boxed{\mathbf{freshen}(T) := T} \qquad \text{(Annotation freshening where } V \text{ fresh)}$$

$$\mathbf{freshen}(X^E) := X^V \qquad \mathbf{freshen}(D^E) := D^V$$

$$\mathbf{freshen}((T_1 \rightarrow T_2)^E) := (\mathbf{freshen}(T_1) \rightarrow \mathbf{freshen}(T_2))^V$$

$$\boxed{\mathcal{P}[\![P]\!] := E} \; \text{(Set expression matched by pattern)}$$

$$\mathcal{P}[\![x]\!] := \top \qquad \mathcal{P}[\![K(\vec{P})]\!] := K(\overrightarrow{\mathcal{P}[\![P]\!]})$$

$$\boxed{\overline{\mathcal{P}}_i(\vec{P}) := C} \qquad \text{(Not-yet covered pattern at branch } i)$$

$$\overline{\mathcal{P}}_0(P_0 \ldots P_n) = \top \qquad \overline{\mathcal{P}}_i(P_0 \ldots P_n) = \neg \mathcal{P}[\![P_0]\!] \cap \ldots \neg \mathcal{P}[\![P_{i-1}]\!] \text{ when } 0 < i \leq n$$

Fig. 5. Auxiliary metafunctions

The lack of polymorphic recursion is a source of imprecision, but a necessary one for preserving termination without requiring annotations from the programmer.

We generate two sorts of constraints. First, we constrain what values expressions could possibly take. For example, if we apply a constructor $K_D(\vec{t})$, and we know the possible forms $\vec{E}$ for $\vec{t}$, then in any context, this expressions can only ever evaluate to values in the set $K(\vec{E})$. Second, we generate safety constraints, which must hold to ensure that the program encounters no runtime errors. Specifically, we generate a constraint that when we match on a term t, all of its possible values are covered by the left-hand side of one of the branches.

Variables: Our analysis rule AVAR for variables looks up a scheme from Γ. However, typing schemes now quantify over type and set variables, and carry a constraint along with the type. We then take instantiation of type variables as given, since we know the underlying type of each expression. Each set variable is instantiated with a fresh variable. We then give x the type from the scheme, with the constraint that the instantiated version of the scheme's constraint must hold if this piece of code is reachable (i.e. if the path condition is satisfiable).

Functions and Applications: The analysis rule ALAM for functions is straightforward. We generate a fresh set variable with which to annotate the argument type in the environment, and check the body in this extended environment. Since functions are not algebraic datatypes and cannot be matched upon, we emit $\top$ as a trivial set of possible forms for the function itself.

We know nothing about the forms that the parameter-type annotation V may take, since it depends entirely on what concrete argument is given when the function is applied. However, when checking the body, we may encounter a pattern match that constraints what values V may take without risking runtime failure. So our analysis may emit safety constraints involving V, but it will not constrain it otherwise. Generally, $(T_1^{E_1} \to T_2^{E_2})$ means that the function can safely accept any expression matching E_1, and may return values matching E_2.

Applications are analyzed using AAPP. Annotations and constraints for the function and argument are both generated, and we emit a constraint equating the argument's annotated type with its domain, under the assumption that the path condition holds and this function call is actually reachable. The metafunction $T_1^{E_1} \equiv T_1^{E_1'}$ (defined in Fig. 5) traverses the structure of the argument and function domain type, constraining that parallel annotations are equal. This traversal is possible because the underlying type system guarantees that the function domain and argument have identical underlying types.

Constructors: As we mentioned above, applying a constructor to arguments can only produce a value that is that constructor wrapped around its argument's values. The rule ACTOR for a constructor K infers annotations and constraints for each argument, then emits those constraints and applies K to those annotations.

Pattern Matching: It is not surprising that in a pattern match analysis, the interesting details are found in the case for pattern matching. The rule AMAT begins by inferring the constraint C_{dsc} and annotation E for the discriminee t.

For each branch, we perform two tasks. First, for each branch's pattern P_i, we use an auxiliary judgment to generate the environment Γ_i binding the pattern variables to the correct types and annotations, using projection to access the relevant parts. For P_1, the annotation of the whole pattern is E i.e. the annotation for t. However, the first-match semantics mean that if we reach P_i, then the discriminee does not match any of $P_1 \ldots P_{i-1}$. So for each P_i, we extend the environment with annotations obtained by intersecting E with the negation of all previous patterns, denoted $\overline{\mathcal{P}}_i(\vec{P})$ (Fig. 5).

Having obtained the extended environment for each branch, we perform our second task: we check each right-hand-side in the new environment, obtaining an annotation E_i'. When checking the results, we augment the path constraint with C_i, asserting that some possible input matches this branch's pattern, obtained via $\mathcal{P}[\![]\!]$ (Fig. 5), but none of the previous. This ensures that safety constraints for the branch are only enforced when the branch can actually be taken.

To determine the annotation for the entire expression, we could naively take the union of the annotations for each branch. However, we can be more precise than this. We generate a fresh variable V for the return annotation, and constrain that it contains the result E_i' of each branch, provided that it C_i holds, and it is possible we actually took that branch. This uses implication, justifying the need for a solver that supports negation and disjunction.

Finally, we emit a safety constraint C_{saf}, saying that if it is possible to reach this part of the program (that is, if C_p holds), then the inputs to the match must be contained within the values actually matched.

Let-Expressions: Our ALET rule deals with the generalization of types into type schemes. This rule essentially performs Damas-Milner style inference, but for the annotations, rather than the types. When defining $x = t_1$, we check t_1 in a context extended with its type variables, and a monomorphic version of its own type. The metafunction **freshen** takes the underlying type for t_1 and adds fresh annotation variables across the entire type. This allows for monomorphic recursion. The metafunction $\equiv$ constrains the freshly generated variables on T' to be equal to the corresponding annotations on T_1 obtained when checking t_1. Again this traversal is possible because the underlying types must be identical. Once we have a constraint for the definition, we check that its constraint is in fact satisfiable, ensuring that none of the safety constraints are violated. In our implementation, this is where the call to the external solver is made.

To generate a type scheme for our definition, we generalize over all variables free in the inferred annotation or constraint but not free in Γ or C_p. Finally, we check the body of the let-expression in a context extended with the new variable and type scheme. Because let-expressions are where constraints are actually checked, we assume that all top-level definitions of a program are wrapped in let-declarations, and are typed with environment $\cdot$ and path constraint **T**.

Example - Safety Constraints: To illustrate our analysis, we return to the Ngon code from Sect. 1. We assume that all Double terms are given annotation $\top$. Then, the simpleArea function would be given the annotated type scheme $\forall V_1, V_2.\, C_1 \wedge C_2 \wedge C_3 \Rightarrow \text{Ngon}^{V_1} \rightarrow \text{Double}^{V_2}$, where

$$C_1 := V_1 \subseteq \text{Square}(\top) \cup \text{Circle}(\top) \quad C_2 := (V_1 \cap \text{Square}(\top) \not\subseteq \bot) \implies \top \subseteq V_2$$
$$C_3 := ((V_1 \cap \text{Circle}(\top) \cap \neg\text{Square}(\top)) \not\subseteq \bot) \implies \top \subseteq V_2$$

C_1 is the C_{saf} generated by the AMAT rule, saying that the function can safely accept input from $\text{Square}(\top) \cup \text{Circle}(\top)$. C_2 and C_3 are conjuncts of C_{res}, describing how, if the input overlaps with Square then the output can be anything, and that if the input overlaps with Circle but not Square, then the output can be anything. C_2 and C_3 are trivially satisfiable: $\text{Circle}(\top) \cap \neg\text{Square}(\top)$ is $\text{Circle}(\top)$, so they are essentially saying that V_2 must be $\top$.

When we call simpleArea from area, we are in the branch after the Ngon case has been checked. The scheme for simpleArea is instantiated with the path constraint $V_4 \subseteq \top \cap \neg(\text{Ngon}(\top))$, where V_4 is the annotation for shape, because it is called after we have a failed match with Ngon sides.

Suppose we instantiate V_1, V_2 with fresh V_1', V_2'. The call to simpleArea creates a constraint that $V_4 = V_1'$. Taking this equality into account, the safety constraint is instantiated to $V_4 \subseteq \top \cap \neg(\text{Ngon}(\top)) \implies V_4 \subseteq (\text{Square}(\top) \cup \text{Circle}(\top))$. This is satisfiable for any value of shape, so at every call to area the analysis sees that the safety constraint is satisfied. If we add a Triangle constructor, then the constraint is unsatisfiable any time V_4 is instantiated to a set with Triangle.

Example - Precision on Results of Matching: To illustrate the precision of our analysis for the *results* of pattern matching, we turn to a specialized version of the classic map function:

```
intMap : (Int -> Int) -> List Int -> List Int ->
intMap f l = case l of
  Nil -> Nil
  Cons h t -> Cons (f h) (intMap f t)
```

Suppose we have concrete arguments $\mathtt{f}$: $(\mathtt{Int}^{V_{11}} \rightarrow \mathtt{Int}^{V_{12}})^{V_1}$ and $\mathtt{l}$: $(\mathtt{ListInt})^{V_2}$. The safety constraint for the match is that $V_2 \subseteq \mathtt{Nil} \cup \mathtt{Cons}(\top, \top)$, which is always satisfiable since the match is exhaustive. The result of the case expression is given a fresh variable annotation V_3. From the first branch, we have the constraint that $V_2 \cap \mathtt{Nil} \not\subseteq \bot \implies \mathtt{Nil} \subseteq V_3$.

The analysis is more interesting for the second branch. The bound pattern variables h and t are given annotations $\mathtt{Cons}^{-1}(V_2)$ and $\mathtt{Cons}^{-2}(V_2)$ respectively, since they are the first and second arguments to $\mathtt{Cons}$. Because our recursion is monomorphic, the recursive call $\mathtt{intMap\ f\ t}$ generates the trivial constraint $(V_2 \cap \neg \mathtt{Nil} \cap \mathtt{Cons}(\top, \top)) \not\subseteq \bot \implies V_1 \subseteq V_1$, and the more interesting constraint $(V_2 \cap \neg \mathtt{Nil} \cap \mathtt{Cons}(\top, \top)) \not\subseteq \bot \implies \mathtt{Cons}^{-2}(V_2) \subseteq V_2$. This second constraint may seem odd, but it essentially means that without polymorphic recursion, our program's pattern matches must account for any length of list. This is where having set constraints is extremely useful: if we were to use some sort of symbolic execution to try to determine a single logical value that l could take, then treating the recursive call monomorphically would create an impossible equation. But the set $\{\mathtt{Cons}(\mathtt{a}, \mathtt{Nil}), \mathtt{Cons}(\mathtt{a}, \mathtt{Cons}(\mathtt{b}, \mathtt{Nil})), \ldots\}$ satisfies our set constraints, albeit in an imprecise way.

When checking the body, suppose that V_5 is the fresh variable ascribed to the return type of $\mathtt{intMap}$. For the result of the second branch, we have the constraints $V_2 \cap \neg \mathtt{Nil} \cap \mathtt{Cons}(\top, \top) \not\subseteq \bot \implies \mathtt{Cons}(V_{12}, V_5) \subseteq V_3$. This essentially says that if the input to the function can be $\mathtt{Cons}$, then so can the output, but if the input is always $\mathtt{Nil}$, then this branch contributes nothing to the overall result. Finally, we have a constraint $V_5 = V_3$, generated by the metafunction $\equiv$.

Our result annotation V_3 is constrained by $(V_2 \cap \mathtt{Nil} \not\subseteq \bot \implies \mathtt{Nil} \subseteq V_3) \wedge (V_2 \cap \neg \mathtt{Nil} \cap \mathtt{Cons}(\top, \top) \not\subseteq \bot \implies \mathtt{Cons}(V_{12}, V_3) \subseteq V_3)$, capturing how $\mathtt{intMap}$ returns nil empty result for nil input, and non-nil results for non-nil input.

3   Translating Set Constraints to SMT

While the above analysis provides a fine-grained way to determine which pattern matches may not be safe, it depends on the existence of an external solver to check the satisfiability of the resulting set constraints. We provide a simple, performant solver by translating set constraints into an SMT formula.

3.1   A Primer in Set Constraints

We begin by making precise the definition of the set constraint problem. Consider a set of (possibly 0-ary) functions $\mathcal{F} = \{f_1^{a_1}, \ldots, f_n^{a_n}\}$, where each $a \geq 0$ is the arity of the function f_i^a. The *Herbrand Universe* $\mathcal{H}_{\mathcal{F}}$ is defined inductively: each

$f_i^0 \in \mathcal{F}$ is in $\mathcal{H}_\mathcal{F}$, and if $a > 0$ and $h_1, \ldots, h_a$ are in $\mathcal{H}_\mathcal{F}$, then $f_i^a(h_1, \ldots, h_a)$ is in $\mathcal{H}_\mathcal{F}$. (We write $\mathcal{H}_\mathcal{F}$ as $\mathcal{H}$ when the set $\mathcal{F}$ is clear.) Each f_i^a is injective, but is otherwise uninterpreted, behaving like a constructor in a strict functional language. We assume all terms are finite, although similar analyses can account for laziness and infinite data [28].

This allows us to formalize the semantics of set expressions. The syntax is the same as in Fig. 3, although we use the notation $f_i^a(\overrightarrow{E})$ instead of $K_D(\overrightarrow{E})$ to denote that we are using arbitrary function symbols from some Herbrand universe $\mathcal{H}$, instead of specific constructors for a datatype. Given a substitution $\sigma : \mathcal{V} \to \mathcal{P}(\mathcal{H})$, we can assign a meaning $\mathcal{H}[\![E]\!]_\sigma \subseteq \mathcal{H}$ for an expression E by mapping variables to their substitutions, and applying the corresponding set operations. The full semantics are given in Fig. 6. Note that the expressions on the left are to be interpreted as *syntax*, whereas those on the right are mathematical sets.

$$\mathcal{H}[\![\bot]\!]_\sigma = \emptyset$$
$$\mathcal{H}[\![\top]\!]_\sigma = \mathcal{H}$$
$$\mathcal{H}[\![V]\!]_\sigma = \sigma(V)$$
$$\mathcal{H}[\![\neg E_1]\!]_\sigma = \mathcal{H} \setminus \mathcal{H}[\![E_1]\!]_\sigma$$

$$\mathcal{H}[\![E_1 \cap E_2]\!]_\sigma = \mathcal{H}[\![E_1]\!]_\sigma \cap \mathcal{H}[\![E_2]\!]_\sigma$$
$$\mathcal{H}[\![E_1 \cup E_2]\!]_\sigma = \mathcal{H}[\![E_1]\!]_\sigma \cup \mathcal{H}[\![E_2]\!]_\sigma$$
$$\mathcal{H}[\![f_i^a(E_1, \ldots, E_a)]\!]_\sigma = \{f_i^a(h_1, \ldots, h_a)$$
$$\mid h_1 \in \mathcal{H}[\![E_1]\!]_\sigma, \ldots, h_a \in \mathcal{H}[\![E_a]\!]_\sigma\}$$

Fig. 6. Semantics of set expressions

A *set constraint atom* $\mathcal{A}$ is a constraint of the form $E_1 \subseteq E_2$. These are also referred to as *positive set constraints* in previous work. A *set constraint literal* $\mathcal{L}$ is either an atom or its negation $\neg(E_1 \subseteq E_2)$, which we write as $E_1 \nsubseteq E_2$.

Constraints which contain negative literals are called *negative set constraints*. An unrestricted set constraint, denoted by metavariable $\mathcal{C}$, is a boolean combination (i.e. using $\wedge$, $\vee$ and $\neg$) of set constraint atoms, as we defined in Fig. 3. For example, $(X \subseteq Y \implies Y \subseteq X) \wedge (Y \nsubseteq Z)$ is an unrestricted set constraint.

Given a set constraint C, the satisfiability problem is to determine whether there exists a substitution $\sigma : \mathcal{V} \to \mathcal{P}(\mathcal{H})$ such that, if each atom $E_1 \subseteq E_2$ in C is replaced by the truth value of $\mathcal{H}[\![E_1]\!]_\sigma \subseteq \mathcal{H}[\![E_2]\!]_\sigma$, then the resulting boolean expression is true. Since solving for arbitrary boolean combinations of set constraints is difficult, we focus on a more restricted version of the problem. The *conjunctive* set constraint problem for a sequence of literals $\overrightarrow{L}$ is to find a variable assignment that causes $\bigwedge \overrightarrow{L}$ to be true. We explain how to extend our approach to arbitrary boolean combinations in Sect. 3.7.

One can see that the Herbrand universe $\mathcal{H}$ closely matches the set of terms that can be formed from a collection of algebraic datatypes, and that allowing negative constraints and arbitrary boolean expressions satisfies the desiderata for our pattern match analysis.

3.2 Projection

Many analyses (including ours) on a notion of *projection*. For a set expression E, we denote the jth projection of E for function f_i^a by $f_i^{-j}(E)$. For a substitution σ, we have $\mathcal{H}[\![f_i^{-j}(E)]\!]_\sigma = \{h_j \mid f_i^a(h_1, \ldots, h_j, \ldots h_a) \in E\}$.

While we don't explicitly include projections in our grammar for set expressions, we can easily express them using boolean formulae. Given some constraint $C[f_i^{-j}(E)]$, we can replace this with:

$$C[X_j] \wedge (E \cap f_i^a(\top, \ldots, \top)) = f_i^a(X_1, \ldots, X_j, \ldots X_a) \wedge (E = \bot \iff X_j = \bot)$$

where each X_k is a fresh variable. The first condition specifies that our variable holds the jth component of every $f(\overrightarrow{h})$ in E. The second condition is necessary because $f_i^a(X_1, \ldots, X_j, \ldots X_a) = \bot$ if *any* X_k is empty, so any value of X_j vacuously satisfies $E' = f_i^a(X_1, \ldots, X_j, \ldots X_a)$ if E' and some X_i are empty.

$M \in \mathcal{M}$ (Monadic formulae)

$\boxed{\mathcal{E}[\![E]\!] = M}$ (Predicates for set expressions)

$\mathcal{E}[\![\top]\!] = \forall x.\, P_\top(x) \quad | \quad \mathcal{E}[\![\bot]\!] = \forall x.\, \neg P_\bot(x) \quad | \quad \mathcal{E}[\![X]\!] = \mathbf{T}$

$\mathcal{E}[\![E_1 \cap E_2]\!] \quad = \quad \forall x.\, P_{E_1 \cap E_2}(x) \iff (P_{E_1}(x) \wedge P_{E_2}(x))$

$\mathcal{E}[\![E_1 \cup E_2]\!] \quad = \quad \forall x.\, P_{E_1 \cup E_2}(x) \iff (P_{E_1}(x) \vee P_{E_2}(x))$

$\mathcal{E}[\![\neg E_1]\!] \quad = \quad \forall x.\, P_{\neg E_1}(x) \iff \neg P_{E_1}(x)$

$\mathcal{E}[\![f_i^a(E_1, \ldots, E_a)]\!] \quad = \quad (\forall x_1 \ldots x_a.\, P_{f_i^a(E_1, \ldots, E_a)}(f_i^a(x_1, \ldots, x_a)) \iff P_{E_1}(x_1) \wedge \ldots P_{E_a}(x_a))$

$$\left(\bigwedge_{g_j^{a'} \neq f_i^a} \forall x_1 \ldots x_{a'} P_{f_i^a(E_1, \ldots, E_a)}(g_j^{a'}(x_1, \ldots, x_a')) \iff \mathbf{F} \right)$$

$\boxed{\mathcal{L}[\![L]\!] = M}$ (Literal predicates) $\qquad \boxed{\mathcal{L}[\![\bigwedge \overrightarrow{L}]\!] = M}$ (Conjunction)

$\mathcal{L}[\![E_1 \subseteq E_2]\!] = \forall x.\, P_{E_1}(x) \implies P_{E_2}(x)$ $\quad \mathcal{L}[\![\bigwedge \overrightarrow{L}]\!] = \mathcal{E}[\![E_1]\!] \wedge \ldots \wedge \mathcal{E}[\![E_n]\!] \wedge \bigwedge \overrightarrow{\mathcal{L}[\![L]\!]}$

$\mathcal{L}[\![E_1 \not\subseteq E_2]\!] = \exists y.\, P_{E_1}(y) \wedge \neg P_{E_2}(y)$ $\quad$ where $E_1 \ldots E_n$ all subexpressions of $\overrightarrow{L}$

Fig. 7. Translating set constraints to monadic logic

3.3 Set Constraints and Monadic Logic

The first step in our translation is converting a conjunction of set constraint literals into a formula in first-order monadic logic, for which satisfiability is decidable. We then translate this into a search for a solution to an SMT problem over UF, the theory of booleans, uninterpreted functions and first-order quantification. We gradually build up our translation, first translating set constraints into monadic logic, then translating monadic logic into SMT, then adding optimizations for efficiency. The complete translation is given in Sect. 3.6.

Monadic first order logic, sometimes referred to as the *monadic class*, consists of formulae containing only unary predicates, boolean connectives, and constants. Bachmair et al. [7] found a translation from a conjunction $\bigwedge \overrightarrow{L}$ of positive set constraint atoms to an equisatisfiable monadic formula, which was later extended to negative set constraints with equality [11]. We summarize their procedure here, with a full definition in Fig. 7. For each sub-expression E of $\bigwedge \overrightarrow{L}$, we create a predicate $P_E(x)$, denoting whether an element x is contained in E. Along with this, the formula $\mathcal{E}[\![E]\!]$ gives the statement that must hold for P_E to respect the semantics of set expressions. This is similar to the Tsieten transformations used to efficiently convert arbitrary formulae to a normal form [38]. Given $P_E(x)$ for each E, we can represent the constraint $E_1 \subseteq E_2$ as $\forall x. (P_{E_1}(x) \implies P_{E_2}(x))$. Similarly, $E_1 \not\subseteq E_2$ corresponds to $\exists x. (P_{E_1}(x) \wedge \neg P_{E_2}(x))$.[1]

The key utility of having a monadic formula is the *finite model property* [1,29]:

Theorem 1. *Let $\mathcal{T}$ be a theory in monadic first-order logic with N predicates. Then, for any sentence $\mathcal{S}$ in $\mathcal{T}$, there exists a model satisfying $\mathcal{S}$ if and only if there exists a model satisfying $\mathcal{S}$ with a finite domain of size at most 2^N.*

The intuition behind this is that if there exists a model satisfying $\mathcal{S}$, then we can combine objects that have identical truth values for each predicate. This is enough to naively solve set constraints: we convert them into formulae monadic logic, then search the space of all models of size up to 2^N for one that satisfies the monadic formulae. However, this is terribly inefficient, and disregards much of the information we have from the set constraints.

Example - Translation: Consider C_3 from the safety constraint example in Sect. 2. We see that $\mathcal{L}[\![((V_1 \cap \texttt{Circle}(\top) \cap \neg \texttt{Square}(\top)) \not\subseteq \bot) \implies \top \subseteq V_2]\!]$ is $(\exists y. P_{V_1 \cap \texttt{Circle}(\top) \cap \neg \texttt{Square}(\top)}(y) \wedge \neg \mathbf{F}) \implies (\forall x. \top \implies P_{V_2}(x))$. Applying the $\mathcal{E}[\![]\!]$ equivalences for $\cap, \cup$ and $\neg$ with basic laws of predicate logic gives us:

$$(\exists y. P_{V_1}(y) \wedge P_{\texttt{Circle}(\top)}(y) \wedge \neg P_{\texttt{Square}(\top)}(y)) \implies \forall x. P_{V_2}(x).$$

Finally, adding the $\mathcal{E}[\![]\!]$ conditions for functions gives us:

$$\begin{aligned}
(\forall x. P_{\texttt{Circle}(\top)}(f_{Circle}(x))) \quad &\wedge \quad (\forall x. \neg P_{\texttt{Circle}(\top)}(f_{Square}(x))) \\
\wedge \quad (\forall x. P_{\texttt{Square}(\top)}(f_{Square}(x))) \quad &\wedge \quad (\forall x. \neg P_{\texttt{Square}(\top)}(f_{Circle}(x))) \\
\wedge \quad ((\exists y. P_{V_1}(y) \wedge P_{\texttt{Circle}(\top)}(y) \wedge \neg P_{\texttt{Square}(\top)}(y)) \quad &\implies \quad \forall x. P_{V_2}(x)).
\end{aligned}$$

C_3 is satisfiable iff there is a model defining predicates $P_{V_1}, P_{V_2}, P_{\texttt{Circle}(\top)}$ and $P_{\texttt{Square}(\top)}$, and functions f_{Circle}, f_{Square} in which the above formula is true.

3.4   Monadic Logic in SMT

To understand how to translate monadic logic into SMT, we first look at what exactly a model for a monadic theory is. Suppose $\mathbb{B} = \{\mathbf{T}, \mathbf{F}\}$ is the set of booleans, which we call *bits*, and say a bit is set if it is $\mathbf{T}$. For our purposes,

---

[1] The original translation transformed constants and functions into existential variables. We skip this, since SMT supports uninterpreted functions and constants.

a model consists of a set D, called the *domain*, along with *interpretations* $I_P :$ $D \to \mathbb{B}$ for each predicate P and $f_i^a : D^a \to D$ for each function, which define the value of $P(x)$ and $f(x_1, \ldots, x_a)$ for each $x, x_1, \ldots, x_a \in D$. A naive search for a satisfying model could guess $M \le 2^N$, set $D = \{1 \ldots M\}$, and iterate through all possible truth assignments for each I_P, and all possible mappings for each f_i^a, searching for one that satisfies the formulae in the theory.

However, we can greatly speed up this search if we instead impose structure on D. Specifically, if we have predicates $P_1 \ldots P_N$, we take $D \subseteq \mathbb{B}^N$: each element of our domain is a boolean sequence with a bit for each sub-expression E. The idea is that each element of $\mathbb{B}^N$ models a possible equivalence class of predicate truth values. For $b \in D$, we want b_i to be $\mathbf{T}$ when $P_{E_i}(b)$ holds. This means that our maps I_P are already fixed: $I_{P_{E_i}}(b) = b_i$ i.e. the ith bit of sequence b.

However, with this interpretation, $\mathbb{B}^N$ is too large to be our domain. Suppose we have formulae E_i and E_j where $E_j = \neg E_i$. Then there are sequences in $\mathbb{B}^n$ with both bits i and j set to $\mathbf{T}$. To respect the consistency of our logic, we need D to be a subset of $\mathbb{B}^N$ that eliminates such inconsistent elements.

Suppose that we have a function $\mathcal{D} : \mathbb{B}^N \to \mathbb{B}$, which determines whether a bit-sequence is in the domain of a potential model. If $\mathcal{L}[\![\bigwedge \overrightarrow{L}]\!]$ contains the formula $\forall x_1 \in D \ldots \forall x_n \in D. \Phi[x_1 \ldots x_n]$, for some Φ, we can instead write:

$$\forall b_1 \in \mathbb{B}^N \ldots \forall b_n \in \mathbb{B}^N. \mathcal{D}(b_1) \wedge \ldots \wedge \mathcal{D}(b_n) \implies \Phi[b_1 \ldots b_n].$$

That is, our domain can only contain values that respect the semantics of set expressions. Similarly, if $\mathcal{L}[\![\bigwedge \overrightarrow{L}]\!]$ contains $\exists x. \Phi[x]$, we can write $\exists b \in \mathbb{B}^N. \mathcal{D}(b) \wedge \Phi[b]$. Since all functions in a model are implicitly closed over the domain, we also specify that $\forall \overrightarrow{b} \in (\mathbb{B}^n)^a. \overrightarrow{\mathcal{D}(b)} \implies \mathcal{D}(f_i^a(\overrightarrow{b}))$. This ensures that our formulae over boolean sequences are equivalent to the original formulae.

This is enough to express $\mathcal{L}[\![\bigwedge \overrightarrow{L}]\!]$ as an SMT problem. We assert the existence of $\mathcal{D} : \mathbb{B}^N \to \mathbb{B}$ along with $f_i^a : (\mathbb{B}^N)^a \to \mathbb{B}^N$ for each function in our Herbrand universe. We modify each formula in $\mathcal{L}[\![\bigwedge \overrightarrow{L}]\!]$ to constrain a boolean sequences variable $b_i \in \mathbb{B}^n$ in place of each variable $x_i \in D$ as described above. We add $\mathcal{D}$ qualifiers to existentially and universally quantified formulae, and replace each $P_{E_i}(x_j)$ with the ith bit of b_j. We add a constraint asserting that each f_i^a is closed over the values satisfying $\mathcal{D}$. The SMT solver searches for values for all existential variables, functions, and $\mathcal{D}$ that satisfy this formula.

3.5   Reducing the Search Space

While this translation corresponds nicely to the monadic translation, it has more unknowns than are needed. Specifically, $\mathcal{D}$ will always reject boolean sequences that violate the constraints of each $\mathcal{E}[\![E_i]\!]$. For example, the bit for $P_{E_1 \cap E_2}$ in b must always be exactly $P_{E_1}(b) \wedge P_{E_2}(b)$. In fact, for each form except function applications and set variables, the value of a bit for an expression can be recursively determined by values of bits for its immediate subexpressions (Fig. 8). This means that our boolean sequences need only contain slots for expressions of the form X or $f_i^a(E_1, \ldots E_a)$, shrinking the problem's search space.

$$P_\top(b) \quad := \quad \mathbf{T}$$
$$P_X(b) \quad := \quad \text{bit for } X \text{ in } b$$
$$P_{f_i^a(E_1,\ldots E_a)}(b) \quad := \quad \text{bit for } f_i^a(E_1,\ldots E_a) \text{ in } b$$
$$P_{\neg E_1}(b) \quad := \quad \neg P_{E_1}(b)$$

$$P_\bot(b) \quad := \quad \mathbf{F}$$
$$P_{E_1 \cap E_2}(b) \quad := \quad P_{E_1}(b) \wedge P_{E_2}(b)$$
$$P_{E_1 \cup E_2}(b) \quad := \quad P_{E_1}(b) \vee P_{E_2}(b)$$

Fig. 8. Recursive definition of predicates for the SMT translation

What's more, we now only need to include the constraints from $\mathcal{E}[]$ for expressions of the form X or $f_i^a(E_1,\ldots E_a)$, since the other constraints hold *by definition* given our definitions of each P_E. Similarly, our constraints restrict the freedom we have in choosing f^a. Specifically, we know that $P_{f_i^a(E_1,\ldots,E_a)}(f_i^a(b_1,\ldots,b_a))$ should hold if and only if $P_{E_i}(b_i)$ holds for each $i \le a$. Similarly, we know that $P_{f_i^a(E_1,\ldots,E_a)}(g_j^{a'}(b_1,\ldots,b_{a'}))$ should always be $\mathbf{F}$ when $f \ne g$. So for each f_i^a, it suffices to find a mapping from inputs $b_1,\ldots,b_a$ to the value of $P_X(f_i^a(b_1,\ldots,b_a))$ for each variable X. This reduces the number of unknowns in the SMT problem.

3.6   The Complete Translation

Given a conjunction of literals $\bigwedge \overrightarrow{L}$, let $X_1,\ldots X_k, E_{k+1},\ldots E_N$ be the sequence of variable and function-application sub-expressions of $\overrightarrow{L}$. We define $P_E(b)$ for each sub-expression E of $\overrightarrow{L}$ as in Fig. 8.

As unknowns, we have:

- a function $\mathcal{D} : \mathbb{B}^N \to \mathbb{B}$;
- for each negative literal $E_i \not\subseteq E_i'$, an existential variable $y_i \in \mathbb{B}^N$;
- for each function f_i^a and each variable $X \in \overrightarrow{L}$, a function $f_{iX}^a : (\mathbb{B}^N)^a \to \mathbb{B}$, which takes a sequences of N bits, and computes the value of the bit for P_X in the result.

We define the following known functions:

- $f_{if_i^a(E_1,\ldots,E_a)}^a : (\mathbb{B}^N)^a \to \mathbb{B}$ for each f_i^a and each sub-expression of the form $f_i^a(E_1,\ldots,E_a)$, where $f_{if_i^a(E_1,\ldots,E_a)}^a(b_1,\ldots,b_a) = P_{E_1}(b_1) \wedge \ldots \wedge P_{E_a}(b_a)$;
- $f_{ig_j^{a'}(E_1,\ldots,E_{a'})}^a : (\mathbb{B}^N)^a \to \mathbb{B}$ returning $\mathbf{F}$, for each f_i^a and each sub-expression of the form $g_j^{a'}(E_1,\ldots,E_{a'})$ where $f \ne g$;
- $f_{iSMT}^a : (\mathbb{B}^N)^a \to \mathbb{B}^N$ for each f_i^a, where $f_{iSMT}^a(b_1,\ldots,b_a)$ is the sequence: $f_{iX_1}^a(b_1,\ldots,b_a)\ldots f_{iX_k}^a(b_1,\ldots,b_a)f_{iE_{k+1}}^a(b_1,\ldots,b_a)\ldots f_{iE_N}^a(b_1,\ldots,b_a)$

We assert that the following hold:

- for each negative constraint $E_i \not\subseteq E_i'$ with corresponding existential variable y_i, that $\mathcal{D}(y_i) \wedge P_{E_i}(y_i) \wedge \neg P_{E_i'}(y_i)$ holds;
- $\forall x \in \mathbb{B}^N. (\mathcal{D}(x) \wedge P_{E_i}(x)) \implies P_{E_i'}(x)$ for each positive $E_i \subseteq E_i'$;
- $\forall x_1 \ldots x_a. (\bigwedge_{j=1\ldots a} \mathcal{D}(x_j)) \implies \mathcal{D}(f_{iSMT}^a(x_1,\ldots,x_a))$ for each function f_i^a

A solution to these assertions exists iff the initial set constraint is satisfiable.

3.7 Arbitrary Boolean Combinations

Allowing arbitrary boolean combinations of set constraints enriches our pattern match analysis and to allow us to use projections. To do this, for each atom $E_i \subseteq E_i'$ in a constraint C, we introduce a boolean ℓ_i, which the SMT solver guesses. We modify our translation so that $\mathcal{L}[\![E_i \subseteq E_i']\!] = \ell_i \implies \forall x. (P_{E_i}(x) \implies P_{E_i'}(x))$ and $\mathcal{L}[\![E_i \nsubseteq E_i']\!] = \neg\ell_i \implies (\exists y. P_{E_i}(y) \wedge \neg P_{E_i'}(y))$. So ℓ_i is true iff $E_i \subseteq E_i'$. Finally, we assert the formula that is C where each occurrence of $E_i \subseteq E_i'$ is replaced by ℓ_i and $E_i \nsubseteq E_i'$ is replaced by $\neg\ell_i$. Thus, we force our SMT solver to guess a literal assignment for each atomic set constraint, and then determine if it can solve the conjunction of those literals. When ℓ_i is false, then $\mathcal{L}[\![E_i \subseteq E_i']\!]$ will be vacuously true, with the opposite holding for negative constraints.

4   Evaluation and Discussion

We implemented our translation [18] atop Z3 4.8.5 with `mbqi` and `UFBV`. On an i7-3770 CPU 32 GB RAM machine, we compared the running time of Elm's exhaustiveness check with an implementation of our analysis [17].

Table 1. Compilation time (ms) of exhaustiveness versus pattern match analysis

Library	EX-TN	PMA-TN	EX-FP	PM-FP	EX-TP	PM-TP
elm-graph	50	168	45	178	44	173
elm-intdict	42	115	38	5121*	35	113
elm-interval	40	69	39	1217*	36	1261

In order to make the analysis practical, we implemented several optimizations on top of our analysis. Trivially satisfiable constraints were removed, and obvious simplifications were applied to set expressions. When a match was exhaustive, its safety constraint was omitted, and since non-safety constraints should be satisfiable, calls to Z3 were only made for non-empty safety constraint lists. A union-find algorithm was used to combine variables constrained to be equal, and intermediate variables were merged. Since the constraint of an annotated scheme is copied at each instantiation, these ensured that the size of type annotations did not explode. For simplicity, annotated types were not carried across module boundaries: imported functions were assumed to accept any input and always have return annotation $\top$. Similarly, a conservative approximation was used in place of the full projections when determining pattern variables' annotations.

We ran our tests on the Elm graph [21], intdict [22], and interval [9] libraries. Each of these initially contained safe partial matches, but were modified to return dummy values in unreachable code when Elm 0.19 was released. The results of the evaluation are given in Table 1. Runs with the prefix **EX** used the exhaustiveness check of the original Elm compiler, while those marked **PMA** used our pattern-match analysis. We tested the compilers on three variants of each library, a true-negative (**-TN**) version in which all matches were exhaustive, a false-positive (**-FP**) version in which a match was non-exhaustive but safe, and a true-positive (**-TP**) version in which a required branch was missing and running the program would result in an error. Cases marked with an asterisk (*) are those which were rejected by the Elm compiler, but which our analysis marked as safe. Notably, the elm-graph library relied on the invariant that a connected component's depth-first search forest has exactly one element, which was too complex for our analysis to capture.

Our analysis is slower than exhaustiveness checking in each case. However, the pattern match analysis requires less than one second in the majority of cases, and in the worst case requires only six seconds. The slowdown was most prominent in the false-positive cases that our analysis marks as safe, where Z3 was not able to quickly disprove the satisfiability of the constraints. Conversely, in the **-TN** cases where Z3 was not called, our analysis cause very little slowdown. Partial matches tend to occur rarely in code, so we feel this is acceptable performance for a tool integrated into a compiler.

Future Work: While our translation of set constraints to SMT attempts to minimize the search space, we have not investigated further optimizations of the SMT problem. The SMT solver was given relatively small problems. Few programs contain hundreds of constructors or pattern match cases. Nevertheless, more can be done to reduce the time spent in the SMT solver for larger problems. Solvers like CVC4 [8] are highly configurable with regards to their strategies for solving quantification. Fine tuning the configuration could decrease the times required to solve our problems without requiring a custom solver. Conversely, a solver specialized to quantified boolean arithmetic could yield faster results.

Likewise, type information could be used to speed up analysis. While we have modeled patterns using the entire Herbrand space, values of different data types reside in disjoint universes. Accounting for this could help partition one problem with many variables into several problems with few variables.

Related Work - Set Constraints: The modern formulation of set constraints was established by Heintze and Jaffar [23]. Several independent proofs of decidability for systems with negative constraints were given, using a number-theoretic reduction [2,37], tree automata [20], and monadic logic [11]. Charatonik and Podelski established the decidability of positive and negative constraints with projection [34]. The first tool aimed at a general, practical solver for set constraints was BANE [4], which used a system of rewrite rules to solve a restricted form of set constraints [5]. Banshee improved BANE's performance with code generation and incremental analysis [26]. Neither of these implementations allow for negative constraints or unrestricted projections. Several survey papers give a more in-depth overview of set constraint history and research [3,24,33].

Related Work - Pattern Match Analysis: Several pattern match analyses have been presented in previous work. Koot [27] presents a higher-order pattern match analysis as a type-and-effect system, using a presentation similar to ours.

This work was extended by Koot and Hage [28], who present an analysis based on higher-order polymorphism. This improves the precision of the analysis, but suffers from the same problems as our regarding polymorphic recursion. All of these efforts use restricted versions of set constraints, and do not allow for unrestricted projection, negation, and boolean combinations of constraints.

Previous versions of type inference for pattern matching have utilized *conditional constraints* [6,35,36], similar to our path constraints. Castagna et al. [10] describe a similar system, albeit more focused on type-case than pattern matching. Catch [30] uses a similar system of *entailment*, with a restricted constraint language to ensure finiteness. These systems are similar in expressive power to the constraints that we used in our final implementation, but our underlying constraint logic is more powerful. There are restrictions on where unions and intersections can appear in conditional constraints [6], and there is not full support for projections or negative constraints. In particular, negative constraints allow for analyses to specify that a function's input set must not be empty, so that the type error can point to the function definition rather than the call-site, avoiding the "lazy" inference described by Pottier [36]. While these have not been integrated into our implementation, our constraint logic makes it easy to incorporate these and other future improvements.

Another related line of work is *datasort refinements*. [14–16,19]. As with our work, the goal of datasort refinements is to allow partial pattern matches while eliminating runtime failures. This is achieved by introducing *refinements* of each algebraic data type corresponding to its constructors, possibly with unions or intersections. Datasort refinements are presented as a type system, not as a standalone analysis, so their handling of polymorphism and recursive types is more precise than ours. However, checking programs with refined types requires at least some annotation from the programmer, where our analysis can check programs without requiring additional programmer input.

Conclusion: Unrestricted set constraints previously were used only in theory. With our translation, they can be solved in practice. SMT solvers are a key tool in modern verification, and they can now be used to solve set constraints. We have shown that even NEXPTIME-completeness is not a complete barrier to the use of set constraints in practical verification.

References

1. Ackermann, W.: Solvable Cases of the Decision Problem: Studies in Logic and the Foundations of Mathematics. North-Holland Publishing Company (1954)
2. Aiken, A., Kozen, D., Wimmers, E.: Decidability of systems of set constraints with negative constraints. Inf. Comput. **122**(1), 30–44 (1995). http://www.sciencedirect.com/science/article/pii/S089054018571139X
3. Aiken, A.: Introduction to set constraint-based program analysis. Sci. Comput. Program. **35**(2), 79–111 (1999). http://www.sciencedirect.com/science/article/pii/S0167642399000076

4. Aiken, A., Fähndrich, M., Foster, J.S., Su, Z.: A toolkit for constructing type- and constraint-based program analyses. In: Leroy, X., Ohori, A. (eds.) TIC 1998. LNCS, vol. 1473, pp. 78–96. Springer, Heidelberg (1998). https://doi.org/10.1007/BFb0055513

5. Aiken, A., Wimmers, E.L.: Type inclusion constraints and type inference. In: Proceedings of the Conference on Functional Programming Languages and Computer Architecture, FPCA 1993, pp. 31–41. ACM, New York (1993). http://doi.acm.org/10.1145/165180.165188

6. Aiken, A., Wimmers, E.L., Lakshman, T.K.: Soft typing with conditional types. In: Proceedings of the 21st ACM SIGPLAN-SIGACT Symposium on Principles of Programming Languages, POPL 1994, pp. 163–173. ACM, New York (1994). http://doi.acm.org/10.1145/174675.177847

7. Bachmair, L., Ganzinger, H., Waldmann, U.: Set constraints are the monadic class. In: 1993 Proceedings of the Eighth Annual IEEE Symposium on Logic in Computer Science, pp. 75–83, June 1993

8. Barrett, C., et al.: CVC4. In: Gopalakrishnan, G., Qadeer, S. (eds.) CAV 2011. LNCS, vol. 6806, pp. 171–177. Springer, Heidelberg (2011). https://doi.org/10.1007/978-3-642-22110-1_14.   http://www.cs.stanford.edu/~barrett/pubs/BCD+11.pdf

9. Bell, R.K.: elm-interval (2019). Commit a7f5f8a. https://github.com/r-k-b/elm-interval/

10. Castagna, G., Nguyen, K., Xu, Z., Abate, P.: Polymorphic functions with set-theoretic types: part 2: local type inference and type reconstruction. In: Proceedings of the 42nd Annual ACM SIGPLAN-SIGACT Symposium on Principles of Programming Languages, POPL 2015, pp. 289–302. ACM, New York (2015). http://doi.acm.org/10.1145/2676726.2676991

11. Charatonik, W., Pacholski, L.: Negative set constraints with equality. In: Proceedings of the Ninth Annual IEEE Symposium on Logic in Computer Science, pp. 128–136, July 1994

12. Czaplicki, E.: Introduction to Elm (2019). http://guide.elm-lang.org/

13. Damas, L., Milner, R.: Principal type-schemes for functional programs. In: Proceedings of the 9th ACM SIGPLAN-SIGACT Symposium on Principles of Programming Languages, POPL 1982, pp. 207–212. ACM, New York (1982). http://doi.acm.org/10.1145/582153.582176

14. Dunfield, J.: Refined typechecking with stardust. In: Proceedings of the 2007 Workshop on Programming Languages Meets Program Verification, PLPV 2007, pp. 21–32. ACM, New York (2007). http://doi.acm.org/10.1145/1292597.1292602

15. Dunfield, J., Pfenning, F.: Type assignment for intersections and unions in call-by-value languages. In: Gordon, A.D. (ed.) FoSSaCS 2003. LNCS, vol. 2620, pp. 250–266. Springer, Heidelberg (2003). https://doi.org/10.1007/3-540-36576-1_16. http://dl.acm.org/citation.cfm?id=1754809.1754827

16. Dunfield, J., Pfenning, F.: Tridirectional typechecking. In: Proceedings of the 31st ACM SIGPLAN-SIGACT Symposium on Principles of Programming Languages, POPL 2004, pp. 281–292. ACM, New York (2004). http://doi.acm.org/10.1145/964001.964025

17. Eremondi, J.: Forked elm-compiler (2019). Commit 9581aaf. https://github.com/JoeyEremondi/elm-compiler-patmatch-smt

18. Eremondi, J.: Setconstraintssmt (2019). Commit 03bb754. https://github.com/JoeyEremondi/SetConstraintsSMT

19. Freeman, T., Pfenning, F.: Refinement types for ML. In: Proceedings of the ACM SIGPLAN 1991 Conference on Programming Language Design and Implementation, PLDI 1991, pp. 268–277. ACM, New York (1991). http://doi.acm.org/10.1145/113445.113468

20. Gilleron, R., Tison, S., Tommasi, M.: Solving systems of set constraints with negated subset relationships. In: Proceedings of 1993 IEEE 34th Annual Foundations of Computer Science, pp. 372–380, November 1993

21. Graf, S.: elm-graph (2019). Commit 3672c75. https://github.com/elm-community/graph/

22. Graf, S.: elm-intdict (2019). Commit bf2105d. https://github.com/elm-community/intdict

23. Heintze, N., Jaffar, J.: A decision procedure for a class of set constraints. In: 1990 Proceedings of the Fifth Annual IEEE Symposium on Logic in Computer Science, pp. 42–51, June 1990

24. Heintze, N., Jaffar, J.: Set constraints and set-based analysis. In: Borning, A. (ed.) PPCP 1994. LNCS, vol. 874, pp. 281–298. Springer, Heidelberg (1994). https://doi.org/10.1007/3-540-58601-6_107

25. Klabnik, S., Nichols, C.: The Rust Programming Language. No Starch Press, San Francisco (2018)

26. Kodumal, J., Aiken, A.: Banshee: a scalable constraint-based analysis toolkit. In: Hankin, C., Siveroni, I. (eds.) SAS 2005. LNCS, vol. 3672, pp. 218–234. Springer, Heidelberg (2005). https://doi.org/10.1007/11547662_16

27. Koot, R.: Higher-order pattern match analysis. Master's thesis, Universiteit Utrecht, The Netherlands (2012)

28. Koot, R., Hage, J.: Type-based exception analysis for non-strict higher-order functional languages with imprecise exception semantics. In: Proceedings of the 2015 Workshop on Partial Evaluation and Program Manipulation, PEPM 2015, pp. 127–138. ACM, New York (2015). http://doi.acm.org/10.1145/2678015.2682542

29. Löwenheim, L.: Über möglichkeiten im relativkalkül. Math. Ann. **76**(4), 447–470 (1915). https://doi.org/10.1007/BF01458217

30. Mitchell, N., Runciman, C.: Not all patterns, but enough: an automatic verifier for partial but sufficient pattern matching. SIGPLAN Not. **44**(2), 49–60 (2008). https://doi.org/10.1145/1543134.1411293

31. de Moura, L., Bjørner, N.: Z3: an efficient SMT solver. In: Ramakrishnan, C.R., Rehof, J. (eds.) TACAS 2008. LNCS, vol. 4963, pp. 337–340. Springer, Heidelberg (2008). https://doi.org/10.1007/978-3-540-78800-3_24

32. Nielson, F., Nielson, H.R.: Type and effect systems. In: Olderog, E.-R., Steffen, B. (eds.) Correct System Design. LNCS, vol. 1710, pp. 114–136. Springer, Heidelberg (1999). https://doi.org/10.1007/3-540-48092-7_6. http://dl.acm.org/citation.cfm?id=646005.673740

33. Pacholski, L., Podelski, A.: Set constraints: a pearl in research on constraints. In: Smolka, G. (ed.) CP 1997. LNCS, vol. 1330, pp. 549–561. Springer, Heidelberg (1997). https://doi.org/10.1007/BFb0017466

34. Pacholski, W.C.L.: Set constraints with projections. J. ACM **57**(4), 23:1–23:37 (2010). https://doi.org/10.1145/1734213.1734217

35. Palmer, Z., Menon, P.H., Rozenshteyn, A., Smith, S.: Types for flexible objects. In: Garrigue, J. (ed.) APLAS 2014. LNCS, vol. 8858, pp. 99–119. Springer, Cham (2014). https://doi.org/10.1007/978-3-319-12736-1_6

36. Pottier, F.: A versatile constraint-based type inference system. Nordic J. Comput. **7**(4), 312–347 (2000). http://dl.acm.org/citation.cfm?id=763845.763849
37. Stefansson, K.: Systems of set constraints with negative constraints are NEXPTIME-complete. In: Proceedings of the Ninth Annual IEEE Symposium on Logic in Computer Science, pp. 137–141, July 1994
38. Tseitin, G.S.: On the complexity of derivation in propositional calculus. In: Siekmann, J.H., Wrightson, G. (eds.) Automation of Reasoning. SYMBOLIC, pp. 466–483. Springer, Heidelberg (1983). https://doi.org/10.1007/978-3-642-81955-1_28

Author Index

Printed in the United States
By Bookmasters